HESTER PRYNNE

Major Literary Characters

**THE ANCIENT WORLD THROUGH
THE SEVENTEENTH CENTURY**

ACHILLES
Homer, *Iliad*

CALIBAN
William Shakespeare, *The Tempest*
Robert Browning, *Caliban upon Setebos*

CLEOPATRA
William Shakespeare, *Antony and
    Cleopatra*
John Dryden, *All for Love*
George Bernard Shaw, *Caesar and
    Cleopatra*

DON QUIXOTE
Miguel de Cervantes, *Don Quixote*
Franz Kafka, *Parables*

FALSTAFF
William Shakespeare, *Henry IV, Part I,
    Henry IV, Part II, The Merry Wives
    of Windsor*

FAUST
Christopher Marlowe, *Doctor Faustus*
Johann Wolfgang von Goethe, *Faust*
Thomas Mann, *Doctor Faustus*

HAMLET
William Shakespeare, *Hamlet*

IAGO
William Shakespeare, *Othello*

JULIUS CAESAR
William Shakespeare, *Julius Caesar*
George Bernard Shaw, *Caesar and
    Cleopatra*

KING LEAR
William Shakespeare, *King Lear*

MACBETH
William Shakespeare, *Macbeth*

ODYSSEUS/ULYSSES
Homer, *Odyssey*
James Joyce, *Ulysses*

OEDIPUS
Sophocles, *Oedipus Rex, Oedipus
    at Colonus*

OTHELLO
William Shakespeare, *Othello*

ROSALIND
William Shakespeare, *As You Like It*

SANCHO PANZA
Miguel de Cervantes, *Don Quixote*
Franz Kafka, *Parables*

SATAN
The Book of Job
John Milton, *Paradise Lost*

SHYLOCK
William Shakespeare, *The Merchant
    of Venice*

THE WIFE OF BATH
Geoffrey Chaucer, *The Canterbury
    Tales*

**THE EIGHTEENTH AND
NINETEENTH CENTURIES**

AHAB
Herman Melville, *Moby-Dick*

ISABEL ARCHER
Henry James, *Portrait of a Lady*

EMMA BOVARY
Gustave Flaubert, *Madame Bovary*

DOROTHEA BROOKE
George Eliot, *Middlemarch*

CHELSEA HOUSE PUBLISHERS

Major Literary Characters

DAVID COPPERFIELD
Charles Dickens, *David Copperfield*

ROBINSON CRUSOE
Daniel Defoe, *Robinson Crusoe*

DON JUAN
Molière, *Don Juan*
Lord Byron, *Don Juan*

HUCK FINN
Mark Twain, *The Adventures of Tom Sawyer*, *Adventures of Huckleberry Finn*

CLARISSA HARLOWE
Samuel Richardson, *Clarissa*

HEATHCLIFF
Emily Brontë, *Wuthering Heights*

ANNA KARENINA
Leo Tolstoy, *Anna Karenina*

MR. PICKWICK
Charles Dickens, *The Pickwick Papers*

HESTER PRYNNE
Nathaniel Hawthorne, *The Scarlet Letter*

BECKY SHARP
William Makepeace Thackeray, *Vanity Fair*

LAMBERT STRETHER
Henry James, *The Ambassadors*

EUSTACIA VYE
Thomas Hardy, *The Return of the Native*

TWENTIETH CENTURY

ÁNTONIA
Willa Cather, *My Ántonia*

BRETT ASHLEY
Ernest Hemingway, *The Sun Also Rises*

HANS CASTORP
Thomas Mann, *The Magic Mountain*

HOLDEN CAULFIELD
J. D. Salinger, *The Catcher in the Rye*

CADDY COMPSON
William Faulkner, *The Sound and the Fury*

JANIE CRAWFORD
Zora Neale Hurston, *Their Eyes Were Watching God*

CLARISSA DALLOWAY
Virginia Woolf, *Mrs. Dalloway*

DILSEY
William Faulkner, *The Sound and the Fury*

GATSBY
F. Scott Fitzgerald, *The Great Gatsby*

HERZOG
Saul Bellow, *Herzog*

JOAN OF ARC
William Shakespeare, *Henry VI*
George Bernard Shaw, *Saint Joan*

LOLITA
Vladimir Nabokov, *Lolita*

WILLY LOMAN
Arthur Miller, *Death of a Salesman*

MARLOW
Joseph Conrad, *Lord Jim*, *Heart of Darkness*, *Youth*, *Chance*

PORTNOY
Philip Roth, *Portnoy's Complaint*

BIGGER THOMAS
Richard Wright, *Native Son*

CHELSEA HOUSE PUBLISHERS

Major Literary Characters

HESTER PRYNNE

Edited and with an introduction by
HAROLD BLOOM

CHELSEA HOUSE PUBLISHERS
New York ◇ Philadelphia

Jacket illustration: Painting of Hester Prynne by George H. Boughton from *The Scarlet Letter* (New York: Grolier Club, 1908). Courtesy of Library of Congress Rare Book Reading Room. *Inset:* Title page from the first edition of *The Scarlet Letter* (Boston: Ticknor, Reed, & Fields, 1850). Courtesy of Library of Congress Rare Book Reading Room.

Chelsea House Publishers

Editor-in-Chief Nancy Toff
Executive Editor Remmel T. Nunn
Managing Editor Karyn Gullen Browne
Picture Editor Adrian G. Allen
Art Director Maria Epes
Manufacturing Manager Gerald Levine

Major Literary Characters

Managing Editor S. T. Joshi
Copy Chief Richard Fumosa
Designer Maria Epes

Staff for HESTER PRYNNE

Assistant Editor Neal Dolan
Editorial Assistant Katherine Theodore
Picture Researcher Ed Dixon
Assistant Art Director Loraine Machlin
Production Manager Joseph Romano
Production Assistant Leslie D'Acri

Printed and bound in the United States of America

10   9   8   7   6

Library of Congress Cataloging-in-Publication Data

Hester Prynne / edited and with an introduction by Harold Bloom.
p.   cm.—(Major literary characters)
Includes bibliographical references.
ISBN 0-7910-0945-9.—ISBN 0-7910-1000-7 (pbk.)
1. Hawthorne, Nathaniel, 1804–1864. Scarlet letter.
2. Hawthorne, Nathaniel, 1804–1864—Characters—Hester Prynne.
3. Prynne, Hester (Fictitious character) I. Series
PS1868.H47 1990
813'.3—dc20
89-23855
CIP

CONTENTS

THE ANALYSIS OF CHARACTER

Harold Bloom

"Character," according to our dictionaries, still has as a primary meaning a graphic symbol, such as a letter of the alphabet. This meaning reflects the word's apparent origin in the ancient Greek *charactēr,* a sharp stylus. *Charactēr* also meant the mark of the stylus' incisions. Recent fashions in literary criticism have reduced "character" in literature to a matter of marks upon a page. But our word "character" also has a very different meaning, matching that of the ancient Greek *ēthos,* "habitual way of life." Shall we say then that literary character is an imitation of human character, or is it just a grouping of marks? The issue is between a critic like Dr. Samuel Johnson, for whom words were as much like people as like things, and a critic like the late Roland Barthes, who told us that "the fact can only exist linguistically, as a term of discourse." Who is closer to our experience of reading literature, Johnson or Barthes? What difference does it make, if we side with one critic rather than the other?

Barthes is famous, like Foucault and other recent French theorists, for having added to Nietzsche's proclamation of the death of God a subsidiary demise, that of the literary author. If there are no authors, then there are no fictional personages, presumably because literature does not refer to a world outside language. Words indeed necessarily refer to other words in the first place, but the impact of words ultimately is drawn from a universe of fact. Stories, poems, and plays are recognizable as such because they are human utterances within traditions of utterances, and traditions, by achieving authority, become a kind of fact, or at least the sense of a fact. Our sense that literary characters, within the context of a fictive cosmos, indeed are fictional personages is also a kind of fact. The meaning and value of every character in a successful work of literary representation depend upon our ideas of persons in the factual reality of our lives.

Literary character is always an invention, and inventions generally are indebted to prior inventions. Shakespeare is the inventor of literary character as we know it; he reformed the universal human expectations for the verbal imitation of personality, and the reformation appears now to be permanent and uncannily inevitable. Remarkable as the Bible and Homer are at representing personages, their characters are relatively unchanging. They age within their stories, but their habitual modes of being do not develop. Jacob and Achilles unfold before us, but without metamorphoses. Lear and Macbeth, Hamlet and Othello severely modify themselves not only by their actions, but by their utterances, and most of all through *overhearing themselves,* whether they speak to themselves or to others. Pondering what they themselves have said, they will to change, and actually do change, sometimes extravagantly yet always persuasively. Or else they suffer change, without willing it, but in reaction not so much to their language as to their relation to that language.

I do not think it useful to say that Shakespeare successfully imitated elements in our characters. Rather, it could be argued that he compelled aspects of character to appear that previously were concealed, or not available to representation. This is not to say that Shakespeare is God, but to remind us that language is not God either. The mimesis of character in Shakespeare's dramas now seems to us normative, and indeed became the accepted mode almost immediately, as Ben Jonson shrewdly and somewhat grudgingly implied. And yet, Shakespearean representation has surprisingly little in common with the imitation of reality in Jonson or in Christopher Marlowe. The origins of Shakespeare's originality in the portrayal of men and women are to be found in the *Canterbury Tales* of Geoffrey Chaucer, insofar as they can be located anywhere before Shakespeare himself. Chaucer's savage and superb Pardoner overhears his own tale-telling, as well as his mocking rehearsal of his own spiel, and through this overhearing he is emboldened to forget himself, and enthusiastically urges all his fellow-pilgrims to come forward to be fleeced by him. His self-awareness, and apocalyptically rancid sense of spiritual fall, are preludes to the even grander abysses of the perverted will in Iago and in Edmund. What might be called the character trait of a negative charisma may be Chaucer's invention, but came to its perfection in Shakespearean mimesis.

The analysis of character is as much Shakespeare's invention as the representation of character is, since Iago and Edmund are adepts at analyzing both themselves and their victims. Hamlet, whose overwhelming charisma has many negative components, is certainly the most comprehensive of all literary characters, and so necessarily prophesies the labyrinthine complexities of the will in Iago and Edmund. Charisma, according to Max Weber, its first codifier, is primarily a natural endowment, and implies a primordial and idiosyncratic power over nature, and so finally over death. Hamlet's uncanniness is at its most suggestive in the scene of his long dying, where the audience, through the mediation of Horatio, itself is compelled to meditate upon suicide, if only because outliving the prince of Denmark scarcely seems an option.

Shakespearean representation has usurped not only our sense of literary character, but our sense of ourselves as characters, with Hamlet playing the part of

the largest of these usurpations. Insofar as we have an idea of human disinterestedness, we tend to derive it from the Hamlet of Act V, whose quietism has about
it a ghostly authority. Oscar Wilde, in his profound and profoundly witty dialogue,
"The Decay of Lying," expressed a permanent insight when he insisted that art
shaped every era, far more than any age formed art. Life imitates art, we imitate
Shakespeare, because without Shakespeare we would perish for lack of images.
Wilde's grandest audacity demystifies Shakespearean mimesis with a Shakespearean vivaciousness: "This unfortunate aphorism about art holding the mirror up to
Nature is deliberately said by Hamlet in order to convince the bystanders of his
absolute insanity in all art-matters." Of *Hamlet*'s influence upon the ages Wilde
remarked that: "The world has grown sad because a puppet was once melancholy."
"Puppet" is Wilde's own deconstruction, a brilliant reminder that Shakespeare's
artistry of illusion has so mastered reality as to have changed reality, evidently
forever.

The analysis of character, as a critical pursuit, seems to me as much a
Shakespearean invention as literary character was, since much of what we know
about how to analyze character necessarily follows Shakespearean procedures. His
hero-villains, from Richard III through Iago, Edmund, and Macbeth, are shrewd and
endless questers into their own self-motivations. If we could bear to see Hamlet, in
his unwearied negations, as another hero-villain, then we would judge him the
supreme analyst of the darker recalcitrances in the selfhood. Freud followed the
pre-Socratic Empedocles, in arguing that character is fate, a frightening doctrine that
maintains the fear that there are no accidents, that overdetermination rules us all
of our lives. Hamlet assumes the same, yet adds to this argument the terrible
passivity he manifests in Act V. Throughout Shakespeare's tragedies, the most
interesting personages seem doom-eager, reminding us again that a Shakespearean
reading of Freud would be more illuminating than a Freudian exegesis of Shakespeare. We learn more when we discover Hamlet in the Freudian Death Drive,
than when we read *Beyond the Pleasure Principle* into *Hamlet*.

In Shakespearean comedy, character achieves its true literary apotheosis,
which is the representation of the inner freedom that can be created by great wit
alone. Rosalind and Falstaff, perhaps alone among Shakespeare's personages, match
Hamlet in wit, though hardly in the metaphysics of consciousness. Whether in the
comic or the modern mode, Shakespeare has set the standard of measurement in
the balance between character and passion.

In Shakespeare the self is more dramatized than theatricalized, which is why a
Shakespearean reading of Freud works out so well. Character-formation after the
passing of the Oedipal stage takes the place of fetishistic fragmentings of the self.
Critics who now call literary character into question, and who proclaim also the
death of the author, invariably also regard all notions, literary and human, of a stable
character as being mere reductions of deeper pre-Oedipal desires. It becomes

clear that the fortunes of literary character rise and fall with the prestige of normative conceptions of the ego. Shakespeare's Iago, who wars against being, may be the first deconstructionist of the self, with his proclamation of "I am not what I am." This constitutes the necessary prologue to any view that would regard a fixed ego as a virtual abnormality. But deconstructions of the self are no more modern than Modernism is. Like literary modernism, the decentered ego came out of the Hellenistic culture of ancient Alexandria. The Gnostic heretics believed that the psyche, like the body, was a fallen entity, mechanically fashioned by the Demiurge or false creator. They held however that each of us possessed also a spark or pneuma, which was a fragment of the original Abyss or true, alien God. The soul or psyche within every one of us was thus at war with the self or pneuma, and only that sparklike self could be saved.

Shakespeare, following after Chaucer in this respect, was the first and remains still the greatest master of representing character both as a stable soul and a wavering self. There is a substance that endures in Shakespeare's figures, and there is also a quicksilver rendition of the unsettling sparks. Racine and Tolstoy, Balzac and Dickens, follow in Shakespeare's wake by giving us some sense of pre-Oedipal sparks or drives, and considerably more sense of post-Oedipal character and personality, stabilizations or sublimations of the fetish-seeking drives. Critics like Leo Bersani and Rene Girard argue eloquently against our taking this mimesis as the only proper work of literature. I would suggest that strong fictions of the self, from the Bible through Samuel Beckett, necessarily participate in both modes, the sublimation of desire, and the persistence of a primordial desire. The mystery of Hamlet or of Lear is intimately invested in the tangled mixture of the two modes of representation.

Psychic mobility is proposed by Bersani as the ideal to which deconstructions of the literary self may yet guide us. The ideal has its pathos, but the realities of literary representation seem to me very different, perhaps destructively so. When a novelist like D. H. Lawrence sought to reduce his characters to Eros and the Death Drive, he still had to persuade us of his authority at mimesis by lavishing upon the figures of *The Rainbow* and *Women in Love* all of the vivid stigmata of normative personality. Birkin and Ursula may represent antithetical and uncanny drives, but they develop and change as characters pondering their own pronouncements and reactions to self and others. The cost of a non-Shakespearean representation is enormous. Pynchon, in *The Crying of Lot 49* and *Gravity's Rainbow*, evades the burden of the normative by resorting to something like Christopher Marlowe's art of caricature in *The Jew of Malta*. Marlowe's Barabas is a marvelous rhetorician, yet he is a cartoon alongside the troublingly equivocal Shylock. Pynchon's personages are deliberate cartoons also, as flat as comic strips. Marlowe's achievement, and Pynchon's, are beyond dispute, yet they are like the prelude and the postlude to Shakespearean reality. They do not wish to engage with our hunger for the empirical world and so they enter the problematic cosmos of literary fantasy.

No writer, not even Shakespeare or Proust, alters the available stock that we agree to call reality, but Shakespeare, more than any other, does show us how much of reality we could encounter if only we retained adequate desire. The strong literary representation of character is already an analysis of character, and is part of the healing work of a literary culture, which implicitly seeks to cure violence through a normative mimesis of ego, *as if it were stable,* whether in actuality it is or is not. I do not believe that this is a social quest taken on by literary culture, but rather that we confront here the aesthetic essence of what makes a culture *literary,* rather than metaphysical or ethical or religious. A culture becomes literary when its conceptual modes have failed it, which means when religion, philosophy, and science have begun to lose their authority. If they cannot heal violence, then literature attempts to do so, which may be only a turning inside out of the critical arguments of Girard and Bersani.

I conclude by offering a particular instance or special case as a paradigm for the healing enterprise that is at once the representation and the analysis of literary character. Let us call it the aesthetics of being outraged, or rather of successfully representing the state of being outraged. W. C. Fields was one modern master of such representation, and Nathanael West was another, as was Faulkner before him. Here also the greatest master remains Shakespeare, whose Macbeth, himself a bloody outrage, yet retains our imaginative sympathy precisely because he grows increasingly outraged as he experiences the equivocation of the fiend that lies like truth. The double-natured promises and the prophecies of the weird sisters finally induce in Macbeth an apocalyptic version of the stage actor's anxiety at missing cues, the horror of a phantasmagoric stage fright of missing one's time, of always reacting too late. Macbeth, a veritable monster of solipsistic inwardness but no intellectual, counters his dilemma by fresh murders, that prolong him in time yet provoke him only to a perpetually freshened sense of being outraged, as all his expectations become still worse confounded. We are moved by Macbeth, however estrangedly, because his terrible inwardness is a paradigm for our own solipsism, but also because none of us can resist a strong and successful representation of the human in a state of being outraged.

The ultimate outrage is the necessity of dying, an outrage concealed in a multitude of masks, including the tyrannical ambitions of Macbeth. I suspect that our outrage at being outraged is the most difficult of all our affects for us to represent to ourselves, which is why we are so inclined to imaginative sympathy for a character who strongly conveys that affect to us. The Shrike of West's *Miss Lonely-hearts* or Faulkner's Joe Christmas of *Light in August* are crucial modern instances, but such figures can be located in many other works, since the ability to represent this extreme emotion is one of the tests that strong writers are driven to set for themselves.

However a reader seeks to reduce literary character to a question of marks on a page, she will come at last to the impasse constituted by the thought of death, her death, and before that to all the stations of being outraged that memorialize her own drive towards death. In reading, she quests for evidences that are strong representations, whether of her desire or her despair. Such questings constitute the necessary basis for the analysis of literary character, an enterprise that always will survive every vagary of critical fashion.

EDITOR'S NOTE

This book gathers together a representative selection of the best literary criticism that has been devoted to analyzing the character of Hester Prynne, the heroine of Nathaniel Hawthorne's *The Scarlet Letter*. Twelve critical extracts from longer works begin this volume, and then are followed by eleven essays centering upon Hester as a literary character. Both groupings, extracts and essays, are reprinted here in the chronological order of their original publication. I am grateful to Neal Dolan for his devotion, skill, and judgment in researching this book.

The volume, after my general essay on "The Analysis of Character," opens with my introduction, which emphasizes Hester's centrality as the inaugural heroine of the Protestant will in American prose fiction. In the following critical extracts, we find observations on Hester's ambivalences and ambiguities by critics from Anthony Trollope and W. D. Howells to Harry Levin, and by such distinguished Americanists as Newton Arvin and R. W. B. Lewis, until we come to several leading younger critics, including Richard H. Brodhead, as well as the feminist critics Carolyn G. Heilbrun and Nina Baym.

The fuller-scale essays begin with the English novelist-poet D. H. Lawrence's visionary outrage at *his* Hester, who is a "devil," one of those "leprous-white, seducing, spiritual women" who had driven Lawrence wild, and whom he, in return, had driven quite crazy. Equally zestful and visionary, the American critic Leslie A. Fiedler pursues love and death with Hester, and finds her to be both the first American Faust and "also the wildest Indian of them all."

Austin Warren, who was our finest critic of the New England literary tradition, gives us a rather more tempered view of Hester Prynne, admiring her strength yet seeing how poorly she understands the weakness of her lover Dimmesdale. In Michael Davitt Bell's reading there are hints that Hawthorne himself fears Hester's strength of will and sexuality, while Judith Fryer goes further and sees that Hester's energy is potentially destructive of Hawthorne's sense of reality. Robert Penn Warren asks why Hester should have been drawn to Chillingworth and Dimmesdale among men, and suggests that the very strength of her natural sensuality pushes her to yearn for something "beyond nature."

   Kristin Herzog finds in Hester's "thirst for freedom" the outline of a new American Eve, after which Evan Carton emphasizes how Hawthorne's rhetoric centers upon the difficulties of representing Hester's complex nature in language. In Carol Bensick's interpretation, Hester's adultery demystifies the societal reductive account of adultery, while showing the myths that delimit our understanding of adultery.

   In this book's final essays, James M. Mellard brings a Lacanian perspective, and David S. Reynolds a modified Marxist view, to the study of Hester Prynne. Her continued strength is that she will illuminate all our current fashionable modes of analysis at least as much as they will clarify her continued vitality.

INTRODUCTION

Of all the principal female characters in our national literature, Hester Prynne is clearly the central figure. American male novelists, except for Hawthorne and James, have not been able to represent American women with the force and vivacity that have marked the English tradition that goes from Samuel Richardson's Clarissa Harlowe through E. M. Forster's Schlegel sisters in *Howards End*. In our century, the women portrayed by Faulkner, Hemingway, and Fitzgerald are generally less vivid than the men, with a few significant exceptions. James's heroines, from Isabel Archer on, have a clear family resemblance to aspects of Hawthorne's Hester. If we have a national heroine of our version of the Protestant will in America, then it must be Hester Prynne, and yet Hester, though Hawthorne's triumph, yields only grudgingly to our criticism. She is larger than her book, admirable as *The Scarlet Letter* certainly is, because she incarnates more paradoxes and even contradictions than Dimmesdale does, let alone Chillingworth or the visionary Pearl. Hopelessly old-fashioned critic that I am, I do not regard achieved literary characters as so many marks upon the page, or as metaphors for racial, gender, and class differences. The extraordinary Hawthornian imagination, wandering between mimetic realism and high romance, gave us an overwhelming personality and puzzling moral character in the sensual and tragic Hester, who is at once the ideal object of Hawthorne's desire and a troubled projection of Hawthorne's authorial subjectivity, cast out from him but never definitively. Strong writers of romance are both subject and object of their own quests, and there is a profound sense in which Hester is as much a representation of Hawthorne's deep inwardness as Clarissa is Richardson's vision of his own inmost self.

As many critics tell us, Hester Prynne is primarily a sexual being, a truth about her that scarcely can be overemphasized. As a truth, it possesses terrible pathos, for her heroic sexuality has yielded her two impossible men, her Satanic husband Chillingworth and her inadequate lover Dimmesdale, each of them admirably named. Hester has Pearl, a few poor memories of Dimmesdale, and mostly her own pride to sustain her. Her sexuality has been balked, yet constitutes the core of her resistance to her Puritan persecutors. It constitutes also a considerable part of her strong appeal to Hawthorne and to his readers. What matters most about Hester is the vital intensity of her being, her frustrated promise of more life, which is the Hebraic sense of the Blessing. There are a number of valid ways of explaining Hester's charismatic quality, both in and out of the pages of *The Scarlet Letter,* but the most accurate, I am convinced, is to see her charisma as implicit sexual power.

Critics have found both Puritan and Emersonian strands in Hester, and her uneasy religion indeed is a highly contradictory blend of Calvinism and of Emerson's American religion of Self-reliance. Her daughter Pearl is something wilder, but then Pearl belongs almost wholly to the representational order of high romance. Hester's inconsistencies have exercised critics, but the wonder is that there are not many more of them in someone so tormented by an insanely, even obscenely moralistic society, which is to make a judgment that Hawthorne the novelist certainly would have repudiated. Perhaps it might be fairer to say that the strains in Hester uncover some of the strains in Hawthorne, whose creative drive ensues from a temperament more dialectical even than that of his grudging and involuntary heir, Henry James. Hawthorne has something of the same relationship to Calvinism as his truest precursor, Edmund Spenser, who harmonized antithetical elements with a freedom not available to American romance. It is a kind of aesthetic miracle that *The Scarlet Letter* could be written at all, in a cultural situation as belated as Hawthorne's, one that enables *The Marble Faun* and *The House of the Seven Gables* far more readily than Hawthorne's higher achievement in the best of the tales and *The Scarlet Letter.*

Hester's relation to the personality of Anne Hutchinson has been widely studied, but is bound to remain problematical, because the deepest aspect of the relation is that she does not develop into a second Anne Hutchinson. We sense that the movement of sexual power into an antinomian context is what Hester and Mrs. Hutchinson share, but Hawthorne partly evades such a movement in his Hester. He will not let her prophesy, and will not quite prophesy for her. This makes the book spiritually irritating to some readers, particularly at the present time, but undoubtedly helps create its aesthetic strength, since the reader becomes ever more convinced that there is more to Hester than the storyteller is willing to unfold. We want her to say more, to do more, and yet we understand the appropriateness of the way the book both arouses such desires and refuses to gratify them. Hester does not run away from her story, but she runs off with it. We are left not caring much about Dimmesdale, Chillingworth, and Pearl, because they are not adequate to Hester's greatness, nor are we. Critics who chide Hester for her self-deceptions and her moral inconsistencies always sound as silly to me as the endless heaps of scholars who denounce Shakespeare's Falstaff. Hester does not contain us as Falstaff and Rosalind, Hamlet and Cleopatra contain us, but Hester always precedes us as the most representative fictive portrait of an American woman. She cannot hold together her incompatible impulses, and yet she survives an outrageously dreadful societal and erotic context that ought to have driven her either to madness or to suicide. It is absurd for any critic not to learn from her, while speculating again as to the sources of her extraordinary strength of being.

Hester sends us back to Hawthorne, despite his subtlest efforts to evade an identity with her, efforts that profoundly influenced James's similar evasions in regard to Isabel Archer. Isabel's recoil from Goodwood's aggressive sexuality has no parallel in Hester, who would have enveloped Goodwood had he been available to her, and if he could have been endowed by his author with a few touches of what after all is massively present in poor Dimmesdale, spiritual awareness. There was an overt separation in Hawthorne's consciousness between sexual power and the quest of the Protestant will for its own autonomy and dignity, and that separation is painfully repeated in Hester's mind. But the great artist in Hawthorne knew more, and we receive a sense throughout the novel that Hester is working through, not to an impossible integration, but to a stance prophetic of something evermore about to be, a possible sublimity of a changed relationship between men and women. Since that relationship would require a coherent social sanction, it could not achieve the full autonomy of the American religion of Self-reliance, but then even the theologian of our religion, Emerson himself, refrained from extending his vision into the sexual domain, except in certain poems.

Hester, as critics acknowledge, is herself an artist, and her embroidery has its own affinities to Hawthorne's mixed mode of novel and romance, as well as to the outward show of Puritan Boston in *The Scarlet Letter*. But I think she fails her art, which may be part of the cost of Hawthorne not failing his, and it may be that Hester's compromised condition at the book's close is the consequence of being sacrificed by the author as a substitute for himself. Even as Hester devotes herself to the sufferings of other women, she has yielded to Puritan society's initial judgment upon her. In doing so, she certainly has abandoned much of value in her own passional stance, and we can be tempted into an admiring anger against Hawthorne for having diminished her. And yet the "Conclusion" is not the book, though how else Hawthorne could have concluded one scarcely knows. Hester does not break, and we can believe Hawthorne's affirmation that her own free will prevails, but it becomes a very negative will indeed. The alternative presumably would have been for Hawthorne to have converted the book from romance to tragedy, but that he would not do. Hester was not to be a female version of Melville's Ahab, dying in Promethean and Gnostic defiance of a tyrannical universe, darting a final harpoon into the sanctified flesh of a merely demiurgical creation. Instead Hester submits, but only in part, and with sublime trust in the coming revelation of a woman yet to be.

What if Hawthorne had made of Hester not an embroiderer but a romancer, a writer of narrative, whose "rich, voluptuous, Oriental" nature had ensued in twice-told tales? Since Hawthorne grants Hester extraordinary vitality but inadequate articulation, it might seem as though my question is inappropriate to what is, after all, Hawthorne's Hester. Still, Hester is always telling herself, and Pearl, fictions about her situation, and her refusal to forsake her role, in the "Conclusion," is a stubborn extension of her will-to-power over her own story. Chillingworth and Pearl are well content to be figures of romance, and Dimmesdale finally falls back into the marvelous also, though in the saddest way. Hester forces Hawthorne out of romance and into the psychological novel, which is a mark of her relative freedom and of her author's curious bondage, his inability to make his strongest character conform to his moral expectations. Hester deceives others, and for a time herself, but she does not allow Hawthorne to deceive himself. He might have preferred to see her as a dark woman of romance but in her he did not create either another masochist, as he did with Dimmesdale, or another sadist, as with Chillingworth. We ought never to forget that Dimmesdale fails Hester yet once more, at the novel's conclusion, when she goes up to the scaffold to join him at his insistence, but goes very reluctantly and against her true will. Inadequate as Dimmesdale is to her, she still wants him, and until he dies her impulses remain totally healthy. She does not deny her vitalism; Hawthorne defrauds her, for the sake of his art.

No one who lives in Hawthorne's Puritan Boston could hope to defeat it, and Hawthorne thought better than allowing Hester to try so impossible a project. Yet he lavished upon Hester all his innermost resources of vital apprehension, while denying her the preternatural strength that would have turned his novel into the Promethean mode that he rejected. I begin to doubt that any American novelist, female or male, is going to transcend Hester Prynne as a representation of the irreconcilable demands placed upon an American woman, even in an age supposedly no longer Puritan. Feminism, in its latest phase, struggles with the lasting residuum of Puritan values, while remaining deeply contaminated by them. It may even be that current literary feminism is destined to become our new or newest Puritanism, imposing uniform ideals upon intellectual women, by again refusing any alliance between their sexuality and their potential antinomianism. Hester will then abide as the image condensed into the most powerful single sentence of Hawthorne's book: "The scarlet letter had not done its office." No societal emblem will perform a definitive judgment upon Hester, nor will she be contained by any program, however belatedly it would do justice to her. Richardson's Clarissa achieved her formidable strength, too strong even for the daemonic Lovelace, by her unmediated relationship to the Protestant God, who purified her will until only dying to this life was possible for her. Hawthorne celebrates his version of the Protestant will in Hester, but he has no way open to the Puritan God, and would not wish one, even if it were available to him, or to Hester. Dimmesdale finds the way back to God, but hardly out of strength, as Clarissa did. Hester is very strong, certainly too strong for Dimmesdale, and finally too strong even for Hawthorne. It is a very dialectical moment when Hawthorne condenses into a single sentence both Hester's stance towards life and her grand effect upon his own art: "It was only the darkened house that could contain her."

—H. B.

CRITICAL EXTRACTS

ANTHONY TROLLOPE

With the man, the minister, the lover, the reader finds that he can have nothing in common, though he is compelled to pity his sufferings. The woman has held her peace when she was discovered and reviled and exposed. She will never whisper his name, never call on him for any comfort or support in her misery; but he, though the very shame is eating into his soul, lives through the seven years of the story, a witness of her misery and solitude, while he himself is surrounded by the very glory of sanctity. Of the two, indeed, he is the greater sufferer. While shame only deals with her, conscience is at work with him. But there can be no sympathy, because he looks on and holds his peace. Her child says to him,—her child, not knowing that he is her father, not knowing what she says, but in answer to him when he would fain take her little hand in his during the darkness of night,—"Wilt thou stand here with mother and me to-morrow noontide?" He can not bring himself to do that, though he struggles hard to do it, and therefore we despise him. He can not do it till the hand of death is upon him, and then the time is too late for reparation in the reader's judgment. Could we have sympathized with a pair of lovers, the human element would have prevailed too strongly for the author's purpose.

He seems hardly to have wished that we should sympathize even with her; or, at any rate, he has not bid us in so many words to do so, as is common with authors. Of course, he has wished it. He has intended that the reader's heart should run over with ruth for the undeserved fate of that wretched woman. And it does. She is pure as undriven snow. We know that at some time far back she loved and sinned, but it was done when we did not know her. We are not told so, but come to understand, by the wonderful power of the writer in conveying that which he never tells, that there has been no taint of foulness in her love, though there has been deep sin. He never even tells us why that letter A has been used, though the abominable word is burning in our ears from first to last. We merely see her with

5

her child, bearing her lot with patience, seeking for no comfort, doing what good she can in her humble solitude by the work of her hands, pointed at from all by the finger of scorn, but the purest, the cleanest, the fairest also among women. She never dreams of supposing that she ought not to be regarded as vile, while the reader's heart glows with a longing to take her soft hand and lead her into some pleasant place where the world shall be pleasant and honest and kind to her. I can fancy a reader so loving the image of Hester Prynne as to find himself on the verge of treachery to the real Hester of flesh and blood who may have a claim upon him. Sympathy can not go beyond that; and yet the author deals with her in a spirit of assumed hardness, almost as though he assented to the judgment and the manner in which it was carried out. In this, however, there is a streak of that satire with which Hawthorne always speaks of the peculiar institutions of his own country. The worthy magistrates of Massachusetts are under his lash throughout the story, and so is the virtue of her citizens and the chastity of her matrons, which can take delight in the open shame of a woman whose sin has been discovered. Indeed, there is never a page written by Hawthorne not tinged by satire.

—ANTHONY TROLLOPE, "The Genius of Nathaniel Hawthorne," *North American Review* No. 274 (September 1879): 209–11

FRANCIS HOVEY STODDARD

It is conflict that we have in *Jane Eyre,* an assertion of individual will, a fine capacity of individual emotion, and all this in conflict with the world opposing. But it is struggle, not conflict, the inner, not the outer, warfare, that we have in Hester Prynne. It is the stir and the struggle of the soul afflicted, punished, but growing into larger development, into riper life, through this stress and struggle and affliction. And if I seemed to indicate that the novel was in process of development when I wrote that the vitality of the assertion of life was the essence of individuality, and that because of this vitality *Jane Eyre* was an indication of an advance in the art of fiction beyond the spirit and the method of Jane Austen's day, then I may further claim now that the completed picture of the soul of Hester Prynne is indicative of a step in advance as great as, if less marked than, the step from Jane Austen to Charlotte Brontë. It is a step in advance because the picture of Hester Prynne portrays a human soul not merely as a strong, demanding individuality, but as under stress of such relation to verdict of law and to the rights of fellow-mortals as to compel its development into a completed personality. The novel of the *Scarlet Letter* is one of the links in the development of the novel from a means of portraying single phases of emotion to a vehicle of highest expressional power. It was written by a psychological student of the problems which harass the human soul. There is little need to say much concerning the life of Nathaniel Hawthorne, for it is familiar enough to most of us. And there is little need, in any case, here to present that life, for the *Scarlet Letter* does not reflect the life of Hawthorne in any such sense as does *Villette* or *Jane Eyre* reflect the life of Charlotte Brontë. The *Scarlet Letter* is in no sense an autobiographical novel. It is the study of a development of a human soul under circumstances of stress and conditions of struggle. The scene is in the Puritan colony of Massachusetts in the middle years of the seventeenth century. The conditions of life were hard in the Puritan Colony. The religion the Puritan believed, the religion the Puritan lived, was a hard religion. There was little room for more than justice. There was no poetry in the lives, and little in the hearts, or on the lips, of our stern ancestors in New England two hundred and fifty years ago. Such environment Hawthorne gives to the characters of his story. It is a tragedy—a tragedy sombre, intense, unrelieved. It is almost a fatalistic tragedy; almost as stern as if it had been written by Æschylus. It is not a love story; it is not a story of youth; it is not a story of contemporaneous life; it is not a story of eager hope. Hester Prynne having sinned is doomed for punishment to wear the scarlet letter as the symbol of the seared soul forever on her bosom; made an outcast from social joy forever. And the story is the record of the growth of the thoughtless soul of the girl, Hester Prynne, into the sad, strong soul of a mature woman. As accessories to this record of growth, we have scenery of circumstance and scenery of characters. To get perspective, atmosphere, verisimilitude, Hawthorne goes back to a recognizable era of past history. He paints with steadiness the outward aspects, and makes credible the inner motive, of the Puritan Colony in the Boston of 1658. Yet the book is in no sense an historical novel. To give vividness, concreteness, objectivity, to this story of the inner life, to this record of the growth of the conscience, of the growth of responsibility, of the growth of religion, within the breast of Hester Prynne, Hawthorne uses the symbolism which is the picture language of the infancy of awakening fancy. In the story he carries on the crude symbolism of the Puritan court of justice decreeing a visible A as an objective reminder of the branded heart—carries on this crude symbolism into the most delicate and refined suggestions. The unseen forces, the unseen monitors, the unseen avengers, float before our eyes, are painted on the clouds, are burned upon the flesh, in mystic symbols. These mystic symbols are like the weird sisters in *Macbeth;* they are the objectification of mystery. The revelation of the working of the spirit of regeneration upon the soul of Hester Prynne is embodied for us in the weird child, Pearl. She is a living symbol, at once the incarnation of sin, the personification of the Scarlet Letter, the emblem of hope, and the prophecy of pardon. All this is the poetry of mysticism. Yet the *Scarlet Letter* is no more a mystical romance than it is an historical novel.

But if we have mediæval mysticism in the symbolism of the work, we have something very like Greek simplicity and Greek directness in the development. The novel is a Greek tragedy. Like the Greek, it is synthetic and creative rather than analytic. Like the Greek tragedy, the novel of the *Scarlet Letter* has a single story, few principal characters, largeness, unity of treatment, directness, sternness, relentlessness. As in the Greek tragedy, also, the story begins after the guilt has been incurred, and the motive of the story is the relation of the soul of man to Nemesis and justice. There is Greek suggestion even in the minor detail; Pearl is as a chorus to voice for us the comment of the unseen powers. There is Greek atmosphere. All the characters seem to be being rather than acting. Yet the novel is no more a Greek tragedy than it is an historical tale; it is no more a Greek tragedy than it is a mediæval romance. It is, in one, a Greek tragedy, a mediæval romance, a modern historical tale. It is a master work, limited to no age, belonging to all experiences, to all time.

The *Scarlet Letter* is a study of the working of Nemesis upon three human souls. Hester has sinned, and openly bears that punishment of which the scarlet letter is the visible symbol. Dimmesdale has also sinned, but, not yet overtaken by discovery, is striving by the nobility of his present life to avoid the revenging Fates. Chillingworth, least of the three, has not technically sinned, but has twice violated the sanctity of a human soul, in marrying Hester without love, and in assuming the right to privately punish the guilty. To Chillingworth comes failure and the hopelessness of hate; to Dimmesdale comes salvation through confession and sacrifice; to Hester comes a renewed and sanctified soul perfected through suffering. The message of the novel is that punishment is spiritual, that it avails not to brand the bosom nor to compel penance for the flesh. It is the soul that sins; it is the soul that must atone.

—FRANCIS HOVEY STODDARD, "The Growth of Personality in Fiction,"
The Evolution of the English Novel (New York: Macmillan, 1900),
pp. 75–81

W. D. HOWELLS

In certain things *The Scarlet Letter,* which was the first of Hawthorne's romances, is the modernest and maturest. The remoteness of the time and the strangeness of the Puritan conditions authorize that stateliness of the dialogue which he loved. The characters may imaginably say "methinks" and "peradventure," and the other things dear to the characters of the historical romancer; the narrator himself may use an antiquated or unwonted phrase in which he finds color, and may eschew the short-cuts and informalities of our actual speech, without impeaching himself of literary insincerity. In fact, he may heighten by these means the effect he is seeking; and if he will only keep human nature strongly and truly in mind, as Hawthorne does in *The Scarlet Letter,* we shall gratefully allow him a privilege which may or may not be law. Through the veil of the quaint parlance, and under the seventeenth-century costuming, we see the human heart beating there the same as in our own time and in all times, and the antagonistic motives working which have governed human conduct from the beginning and shall govern it forever, world without end.

Hester Prynne and Arthur Dimmesdale are no mere types of open shame and secret remorse. It is never concealed from us that he was a man whose high and pure soul had its strongest contrast in the nature

Mixt with cunning sparks of hell,

in which it was tabernacled for earth. It is still less hidden that, without one voluntary lure or wicked art, she was of a look and make to win him with the love that was their undoing. "He was a person of a very striking aspect, with a wide, lofty, and impending brow; large, brown, melancholy eyes, and a mouth which, unless he compressed it, was apt to be tremulous.... The young woman was tall, with a figure of perfect elegance on a large scale. She had dark and abundant hair, so glossy that it threw off the sunshine with a gleam, and a face which, besides being beautiful from the regularity of feature and richness of complexion, had the impressiveness belonging to a marked brow and deep black eyes. She was ladylike, too, after the manner of the feminine gentility of those days; characterized by a certain state and dignity, rather than by the delicate, evanescent, and indescribable grace which is now recognized as its indication." They were both of their time and place, materially as well as spiritually; their lives were under the law, but their natures had once been outside it, and might be again. The shock of this simple truth can hardly be less for the witness, when, after its slow and subtle evolution, it is unexpectedly flashed upon him, than it must have been for the guilty actors in this drama, when they recognize that, in spite of all their open and secret misery, they are still lovers, and capable of claiming for the very body of their sin a species of justification.

We all know with what rich but noiseless preparation the consummate artist sets the scene of his most consummate effect; and how, when Hester and Pearl have parted with Roger Chillingworth by the shore, and then parted with each other in the forest, the mother to rest in the shadow of the trees, and the child to follow her fancies in play, he invokes the presence of Arthur Dimmesdale, as it were, silently, with a waft of the hand.

"Slowly as the minister walked, he had almost gone by before Hester Prynne could gather voice enough to attract his observation. At length, she succeeded. 'Arthur Dimmesdale!' she said, faintly at first; then louder, but hoarsely, 'Arthur Dimmesdale!' 'Who speaks?' answered the minister.... He made a step nigher, and discovered the scarlet letter. 'Hester! Hester Prynne!' said he. 'Is it thou? Art thou in life?' 'Even so!' she answered. 'In such life as has been mine these seven years past! And thou, Arthur Dimmesdale, dost thou yet live?' ... So strangely did they meet, in the dim wood, that it was like the first encounter, in the world beyond the grave, of two spirits who had been intimately connected in their former life, but now stood coldly shuddering, in mutual dread; as not yet familiar with their state nor wonted to the companionship of disembodied beings.... It was with fear, and tremulously, and, as it were, by a slow, reluctant necessity, that Arthur Dimmesdale put forth his hand, chill as death, and touched the chill hand of Hester Prynne. The grasp, cold as it was, took away what was dreariest in the interview. They now felt themselves, at least, inhabitants of the same sphere. Without a word more spoken—neither he nor she assuming the guidance, but with an unexpected consent—they glided back into the shadow of the woods, whence Hester had emerged, and sat down on the heap of moss where she and Pearl had before been sitting.... 'Hester,' said he, 'hast thou found peace?' She smiled drearily, looking down upon her bosom. 'Hast thou?' she asked. 'None!—nothing but despair!' he answered. 'What else could I look for, being what I am, and leading such a life as mine?' . . . 'The people reverence thee,' said Hester. 'And surely thou workest good among them. Doth this bring thee no comfort?' 'More misery, Hester!—only the more misery!' answered the clergyman, with a bitter smile. . . . 'Had I one friend— or were it my worst enemy—to whom, when sickened with the praises of all other men, I could daily betake myself, and be known as the vilest of all sinners, methinks my soul might keep itself alive thereby. Even thus much of truth would save me! But, now, it is all falsehood!—all emptiness! all death!' Hester Prynne looked into his face, but hesitated to speak. Yet, uttering his long-restrained emotions so vehe- mently as he did, his words here offered her the very point of circumstance in which to interpose what she came to say. She conquered her fears, and spoke. 'Such a friend as thou hast even now wished for,' said she, 'with whom to weep over thy sin, thou hast in me, the partner of it!'—Again she hesitated, but brought out the words with an effort.—'Thou hast long had such an enemy, and dwellest with him, under the same roof!' The minister started to his feet, gasping for breath, and clutching at his heart, as if he would have torn it out of his bosom. 'Ha! What sayest thou!' cried he. 'An enemy! And under my own roof! What mean you?' . . . 'O Arthur,' cried she, 'forgive me! In all things else I have striven to be true! Truth was the one virtue which I might have held fast and did hold fast, through all extremity; save when thy good—thy life—thy fame—were put in question! Then I consented to a deception. But a lie is never good, even though death threaten on the other side! Dost thou not see what I would say? That old man!—the physician!— he whom they call Roger Chillingworth!—he was my husband!' The minister looked at her for an instant, with all that violence of passion which—intermixed, in more shapes than one, with his higher, purer, softer qualities—was, in fact, the portion of him which the Devil claimed, and through which he sought to win the rest. Never was there a blacker or a fiercer frown than Hester now encountered. For the brief space that it lasted, it was a dark transfiguration. But his character had been so much enfeebled by suffering, that even its lower energies were incapable of more than a temporary struggle. He sank down on the ground, and buried his face in his hands. . . . 'O Hester Prynne, thou little, little knowest all the horror of this thing! And the shame!—the indelicacy!—the horrible ugliness of this exposure of a sick and guilty heart to the very eye that would gloat over it! Woman, woman, thou art accountable for this! I cannot forgive thee!' 'Thou shalt forgive me!' cried Hester, flinging herself on the fallen leaves beside him. 'Let God punish. Thou shalt forgive!' With sudden and desperate tenderness, she threw her arms around him, and pressed his head against her bosom; little caring though his cheek rested on the scarlet letter. He would have released himself, but strove in vain to do so. Hester would not set him free, lest he should look her sternly in the face. All the world had frowned on her—for seven long years had it frowned upon this lonely woman— and still she bore it all, nor even once turned away her firm, sad eyes. Heaven, likewise, had frowned upon her, and she had not died. But the frown of this pale, weak, sinful, and sorrow-stricken man was what Hester could not bear and live! 'Wilt thou yet forgive me?' she repeated, over and over again. 'Wilt thou not frown? Wilt thou forgive?' 'I do forgive you, Hester,' replied the minister, at length, with a deep utterance, out of an abyss of sadness, but no anger. 'I freely forgive you now. May God forgive us both! We are not, Hester, the worst sinners in the world. There is one worse than even the polluted priest! That old man's revenge has been blacker than my sin! He has violated, in cold blood, the sanctity of a human heart. Thou and I, Hester, never did so!' 'Never, never!' whispered she. 'What we did had a consecration of its own. We felt it so! We said so to each other! Hast thou forgotten it?' 'Hush, Hester!' said Arthur Dimmesdale, rising from the ground. 'No; I have not forgotten!' ... 'Thou must dwell no longer with this man,' said Hester, slowly and firmly. 'Thy heart must be no longer under his evil eye!' 'It were far worse than death!' replied the minister. 'But how to avoid it? What choice remains to me? Shall I lie down again on these withered leaves, where I cast myself when thou didst tell me what he was? Must I sink down there, and die at once?' 'Alas, what a ruin has befallen thee!' said Hester, with the tears gushing into her eyes. 'Wilt thou die for very weakness? There is no other cause.' 'The judgment of God is on me,' answered the conscience-stricken priest. 'It is too mighty for me to struggle with!' 'Heaven would show mercy,' rejoined Hester, 'hadst thou but the strength to take advantage of it.' 'Be thou strong for me,' answered he. 'Advise me what to do.' 'Is the world, then, so narrow?' exclaimed Hester Prynne, fixing her deep eyes on the minister's, and instinctively exercising a magnetic power over a spirit so shattered and subdued that it could hardly hold itself erect. 'Whither leads yonder forest track? ... Deeper it goes, and deeper into the wilderness, less plainly to be seen at every step, until, some few miles hence, the yellow leaves will show no vestige of the white man's tread.... Is there not shade enough in all this boundless forest to hide thy heart from the gaze of Roger Chillingworth?' 'Yes, Hester; but only under the fallen leaves,' replied the minister, with a sad smile. 'Then there is the broad pathway of the sea!' continued Hester. 'It brought thee hither. If thou choose, it will bear thee back again.' ... 'O Hester!' cried Arthur Dimmesdale, in whose eyes a fitful light, kindled by her enthusiasm, flashed up and died away, 'thou tellest of running a race to a man whose knees are tottering beneath him! I must die here! There is not the strength or courage left me to venture into the wide, strange, difficult world, alone!' ... 'Thou shalt not go alone!' answered she, in a deep whisper. Then, all was spoken."

There is a greatness in this scene which is unmatched, I think, in the book, and, I was almost ready to say, out of it. At any rate, I believe we can find its parallel only in some of the profoundly impassioned pages of the Russian novelists who, casting aside all the common adjuncts of art, reveal us to ourselves in the appeal from their own naked souls. Hawthorne had another ideal than theirs, and a passing love of style, and the meaning of the music of words. For the most part, he makes us aware of himself, of his melancholy grace and sombre power; we feel his presence in every passage, however deeply, however occultly, dramatic; he overshadows us, so that we touch and see through him. But here he is almost out of it; only a few phrases of comment, so fused in feeling with the dialogue that they are like the voice of a chorus, remind us of him.

It is the most exalted instant of the tragedy, it is the final evolution of Hester Prynne's personality. In this scene she dominates by virtue of whatever is womanly and typical in her, and no less by what is personal and individual. In what follows, she falls like Dimmesdale and Chillingworth under the law of their common doom, and becomes a figure on the board where for once she seemed to direct the game.

In all fiction one could hardly find a character more boldly, more simply, more quietly imagined. She had done that which in the hands of a feeble or falser talent would have been suffered or made to qualify her out of all proportion and keeping with life. But her transgression does not qualify her, as transgression never does unless it becomes habit. She remains exterior and superior to it, a life of other potentialities, which in her narrow sphere she fulfils. What she did has become a question between her and her Maker, who apparently does not deal with it like a Puritan. The obvious lesson of the contrasted fates of Dimmesdale and herself is that to own sin is to disown it, and that it cannot otherwise be expropriated and annulled. Yet, in Hester's strong and obstinate endurance of her punishment there is publicity but not confession; and perhaps there is a lesson of no slighter meaning in the inference that ceasing to do evil is, after all, the most that can be asked of human nature. Even that seems to be a good deal, and in *The Scarlet Letter* it is a stroke of mastery to show that it is not always ours to cease to do evil, but that in extremity we need the help of the mystery "not ourselves, that makes for righteousness," and that we may call Chance or that we may call God, but that does not change in essence or puissance whatever name we give it.

—W. D. HOWELLS, "Hawthorne's Hester Prynne," *Heroines of Fiction*
(New York: Harper & Brothers, 1901), Volume 1, pp. 167–74

NEWTON ARVIN

In nothing that Hawthorne wrote are the tragic possibilities of the theme more richly and intensely realized than in *The Scarlet Letter*. What makes the outcome of its events so pitiful and terrible is not simply that a great sin has had its retribution, but that the harmony of several related lives has been fatally jangled, that they have all been set at odds with the general purposes of the life about them, that all the fair potentialities of personal development have miscarried grievously and come to nothing. When we first hear of the embroidered letter shining on Hester Prynne's bosom, as she stands at the prison door with her child in her arms, it is to be told that the letter "had the effect of a spell, taking her out of the ordinary relations with humanity, and enclosing her in a sphere by herself." It is not for the intrinsic flagrance of the sin she has committed, but for the waywardness and irregularity of all wrongdoing, that she is punished; and the penalty is made to suit the offense, since Hester Prynne can never regain her innocent and normal status among men. In expiation of what she has done, she may adopt the role of a sister of charity, and thus come to have a certain part to perform in the world: "in all her intercourse with society, however, there was nothing that made her feel as if she belonged to it. Every gesture, every word, and even the silence of those with whom she came in contact, implied, and often expressed, that she was banished, and as much alone as if she inhabited another sphere, or communicated with the common nature by other organs and senses than the rest of human kind." In consequence of this alienation, the luxuriance and warmth of her personality undergo a kind of blight, and become austerity, coldness, and a rigid strength. Passion and feeling give way, in the movement of her life, to thought; and her thinking itself becomes bolder and more speculative, expressive not so much of her whole being as of a specialized and "unwomanly" function. At length she loses her clear sense of human realities— loses it so far as to suppose that she and Dimmesdale can achieve happiness by mere escape from the dangers and difficulties that beset them separately. No wonder Roger Chillingworth, in their interview on the edge of the forest, is moved to cry out, "Woman, I could wellnigh pity thee! . . . Thou hadst great elements. Peradventure, hadst thou met earlier with a better love than mine, this evil had not been. *I pity thee, for the good that has been wasted in thy nature!*"

Frustration like that which falls to the lot of Hester Prynne is the punishment of the man who has shared her guilt; and Dimmesdale is made to suffer even more atrociously than she because he has deepened his original wrongdoing by the secrecy with which he has invested it. This cuts him off still more effectually from the redemptive force of normal human relations. "There was an air about this young minister," we are told when he first appears, "as of a being who felt himself quite astray and at a loss in the pathway of human existence, and could only be at ease in some seclusion of his own." His noblest faculties and highest purposes seem engaged in the concealment of what he has done; the reverence in which he is held by his parishioners, and the pure spiritual influence he exercises upon them, are specious voices pleading against confession. But in all this there is too large an element of the unpardonable sin, too abject a surrender to spiritual pride; and the minister gradually discovers how deadly is its effect upon his moral world.

> It is the unspeakable misery of a life so false as his, that it steals the pith and substance out of whatever realities there are around us, and which were meant by Heaven to be the spirit's joy and nutriment. To the untrue man, the whole universe is false,—it is impalpable,—it shrinks to nothing within his grasp.

In such a world, the fruits of personal character cannot ripen; and Dimmesdale's nature, like Hester's, is finally perverted and vitiated by the central falsity of his life. His refined spirituality becomes the instrument for a diseased self-persecution; his spiritual insight turns into a loathsome apprehension of the evil in other men's breasts. As he returns through the town after his interview with Hester in the forest, Dimmesdale is tempted at every step to perpetrate some monstrous impropriety of speech or act—the symbol of a moral sense gone hopelessly awry. Of this disastrous process there can be but one fit culmination, and that is reached and realized by the minister's public self-exposure and death. His own breast has been seared by the scarlet letter!

Neither Hester Prynne nor Dimmesdale, however, is represented as the greatest sinner of the drama, and their punishments are less terrible than that of the third chief personage. The pride of the detached intellect is Roger Chillingworth's error, and it is this, not the wayward passion of the other two, that lies at the very root of the whole tragedy. The initial wrong was committed by the aging man of science who tried to bring warmth into his own benumbed existence by attaching to himself the radiance and vigor of Hester's youth. Her weakness was but the less culpable product of his folly. "I have greatly wronged thee," murmurs Hester in her first interview with her husband. "We have wronged each other," he has the justice to answer. When Hester Prynne tries later to overcome her hatred for the old man by recalling their early life together, she cannot find it in her heart to forgive him: "it seemed a fouler offence committed by Roger Chillingworth, than any which had since been done him, that, in the time when her heart knew no better, he had persuaded her to fancy herself happy by his side." And Chillingworth does not rest content with having brought so much wrong to pass; he applies his great intellectual powers and his vast learning to the task of discovering Hester's partner in guilt, and of then wreaking a subtle revenge upon him. As he does so he ceases to be a man and becomes a moral monster.

> In a word, old Roger Chillingworth was a striking evidence of man's faculty of transforming himself into a devil, if he will only, for a reasonable space of time, undertake a devil's office. This unhappy person had effected such a transformation, by devoting himself, for seven years, to the constant analysis of a heart full of torture, and deriving his enjoyment thence, and adding fuel to those fiery tortures which he analyzed and gloated over.

No trespass committed in passion can vie with this icy and ingenious iniquity. "That old man's revenge," says Dimmesdale to Hester, "has been blacker than my sin. He has violated, in cold blood, the sanctity of a human heart. Thou and I, Hester, never did so!" Of all the spiritual ruin symbolized by the scarlet letter, no part is more awful than the destruction of Roger Chillingworth.

—NEWTON ARVIN, "The House of Pride," *Hawthorne* (Boston: Little, Brown, 1929), pp. 187–91

MARK VAN DOREN

The persons of the tale were long since types to him, as were their souls' predica-ments. The broken law, the hidden guilt, the hunger for confession, the studious, cold heart that watches and does not feel—no one of these was new. There was a new symbol, to be sure, though even that had lain in Hawthorne's memory for years. In "Endicott and the Red Cross," as early as 1837, he had written: "There was likewise a young woman, with no mean share of beauty, whose doom it was to wear the letter A on the breast of her gown, in the eyes of all the world and her own children. And even her own children knew what that initial signified. Sporting with her infamy, the lost and desperate creature had embroidered the fatal token in scarlet cloth, with golden thread and the nicest art of needlework; so that the capital A might have been thought to mean Admirable, or anything rather than Adulteress." In 1844 he had entered in his note-book, evidently as the idea for a story: "The life of a woman, who, by the old colony law, was condemned always to wear the letter A, sewed on her garment, in token of her having committed adultery." And three years later, with or without the husband of such a woman in mind, he had made the entry: "A story of the effects of revenge, diabolizing him who indulges in it." Here was Roger Chillingworth, the familiar devil of the tales, supplied at last with a human motive; as here in Hester Prynne, the wife he had sacrificed to his learning, was a woman into whom Hawthorne could pour every feeling and idea he had about her sex. About sin, too; though in his third person, Arthur Dimmesdale, Hester's lover and Roger's victim, he had a still more perfect vessel for that purpose. It is Dimmesdale whom secrecy tortures; it is he who must confess and die. But Dimmesdale is merely one more ideal scholar in a procession that marches back as far as Fanshawe, merely one more sensitive man rendered helpless before the world. And yet not merely, for his intensity absorbs all of his predecessors and makes them pale by comparison; as Chillingworth surpasses each previous villain; and as Hester becomes a heroine, almost a goddess, into whom the character of every other woman in Hawthorne flows. Hawthorne's witch-lady is here also, in Mistress Hibbins; Hester's elf-daughter, Pearl, is a descendant both of the sweet children who fashioned a play-maiden out of snow and of the fiend's infants who stoned the Gentle Boy; the dignitaries of the book, from Governor Bellingham down, are done in the august style of the provincial tales; and the familiar crowd of citizens, the feeling mob, has all of its old function, its double function of population and chorus.

The difference, at least so far as the three principals are concerned, is in the degree to which Hawthorne feels and honors them as individuals. Formerly his temptation had been to decorate ideas, to produce rhetoric about emotions, at the expense of the persons in whom he placed them. This had caused a certain coldness in the persons, over and above the coldness with which it became conventional for him to charge them. But worse than that, it meant a vagueness, a want of force, consistent with his practice of refusing to define the good or the evil— usually the evil—that was in them. Hawthorne had cultivated in himself a weakness for the abstract. Abstraction is necessary to narrative, but at a deeper level than any which the poet lets us see. It is what makes the people finally important and utterly exciting. But exhibited before our eyes, in the refractory medium of accident and character, of speech and deed, it distracts us so that we can neither believe nor feel. In *The Scarlet Letter* Hawthorne has at last found individuals who can hold all of his thought, and so naturally that even he forgets what his thought is. His thought can be of them, not what they signify.

This in part is because their predicament can state itself. It is simple, it is immemorial. An old scholar in England, already dehumanized by the abstruseness of his studies, makes the mistake of marrying a young wife. He sends her to America, to the Puritan colony of Massachusetts, with instructions to live quietly until he comes. But he does not come until the day when she is being publicly exposed as an adulteress; for she has borne a child, and she will not name its father. She, Hester Prynne, must stand on the scaffold, holding the child, until her shame is thoroughly known; and ever after she must wear the letter A, embroidered in scarlet on her bosom. She recognizes him in the crowd but by a sign is enjoined to secrecy. Announcing himself as a physician, and taking the new name of Roger Chillingworth, he at first cares for her and the child in prison; then, when she is free to live whatever life she may in Boston, he settles down to a vigil not merely over her but over all the town, one of whose men is certainly her lover. Or was for a brief while, for now she is an outcast with only Pearl, her daughter, for company; except that she does embroidery for ladies, and except that more and more she becomes a dark angel of charity, doing good deeds silently among the stern folk who still despise her. Her lover, we slowly learn without being told, is the Reverend Arthur Dimmesdale, a young clergyman of fabulous erudition, piety, and personal beauty—a beauty which matches the still more powerful and splendid beauty of Hester herself. The two seldom meet, and when they do meet they are not alone; they communicate then, but only by looking into each other's eyes, or in words which no listener understands as they understand them. The one thing they do not tell is the truth, namely, that Pearl is Dimmesdale's child. He could prevent Hester's suffering, or he could share it, if words were possible to him. Since they are impossible, he suffers an agony which grows so awful that she, by telling, might somehow save them both. But she continues to protect his name. As we become aware of this, so does Roger Chillingworth. The mysterious illness of Dimmesdale— mysterious to the town—is something he says he can treat, and so he becomes the minister's physician; he even lives with him, to make the cure more certain. The "cure" is both physical and psychological; Dimmesdale must reveal some secret he is keeping in his sick heart, or he will never be well. The secret, painfully revealed, is nevertheless no cure. Only Hester can cure her lover; as at last, meeting him in the forest with Pearl, she does. She tells him who his physician is; she unlocks his heart, so sorely closed these seven years; she even plans an escape for them to the Old World. Chillingworth is to prevent this escape, but in any case it would have been too late for Dimmesdale, who seizes the occasion of Election Day, when all the colony is present, to preach his final sermon and to make public confession of his sin. Doing so he dies, on the very scaffold where Hester had stood, and she is alone again. It is his immortal soul, not his temporal sanity, that has been cured; and even then the crowd, whose adoring members had supposed his long illness to be a sign that he was too good for this world, imperfectly understands his confession.

Such a synopsis leaves out a multitude of important things. *The Scarlet Letter,* brief though it is and barren of incident though it seems, is packed with pictures and events; real at the center, it is rich at every portion of its surface. But any synopsis serves to show that the situation of the principals is indeed concrete. Never before has Hawthorne dealt with stuff so solid; and never again will he be so able or content to let his people determine his plot. His plot in this case is his people.

Above all it is Hester Prynne, whose passion and beauty dominate every other person, and color each event. Hawthorne has conceived her as he has conceived his scene, in the full strength of his feeling for ancient New England. He is the Homer of that New England, as Hester is its most heroic creature. Tall, with dark and abundant hair and deep black eyes, a rich complexion that makes modern women (says Hawthorne) pale and thin by comparison, and a dignity that throws into low relief the "delicate, evanescent, and indescribable grace" by which gentility in girls has since come to be known, from the very first—and we believe it—she is said to cast a spell over those who behold her; and this is not merely because of the scarlet letter, "so fantastically embroidered and illuminated," upon the bosom of her always magnificent dress. It is because of herself, into whom Hawthorne has known how to put a unique importance. Nor is this a remote, a merely stately importance. We are close to her all of the time, and completely convinced of her flesh and blood, of her heart and mind. She is a passionate woman whom Hawthorne does not need to call passionate, for he has the evidence: her state of excitement, bordering on frenzy, in the prison after her first exposure to the crowd—her "moral agony," reflected in the convulsions that have seized the child; her pride, her daring, in after days when she makes more show than she needs to make of the letter on her bosom, the symbol she insists upon adorning with such "wild and picturesque peculiarity"; her alternations of despair and defiance; her continuing love, so unconfessed that we can only assume it to be there, for the man whose weakness seems so little to deserve it; her power of speech, so economical and so tender, when at last she is with this man; her sudden revelation that through years of loneliness she has not consented to let her soul be killed.

"I pity thee," says Chillingworth near the close, "for the good that has been wasted in thy nature." These are terrible words, for they express a fear we have had, the fear that this magnificent woman has lived for nothing; for a few days of love, and then for dreary years of less indeed than nothing. Hawthorne has known how to fasten this fear upon us—it could exist in us only if we loved her too—but he also has known how to make Chillingworth's words untrue. The life of Hester increases, not diminishes, in the bleak world whose best citizen she is. Nor is this done by Hawthorne at the expense of that world. He deplores the "dismal severity" of its moral code, and for all we know he is presenting Hester as the blackest sacrifice it ever offered on its altar. But he is not doctrinaire against the code. His Puritan world is in its own way beautiful. It fully exists, as Hester fully exists. If their existences conflict, then that is the tragedy to be understood. Hester, whose solitary thought takes her far beyond the confines of the code, is nevertheless respectful of the strength in it that could kill her were she not even stronger. She is not the subject of a sermon; she is the heroine of a tragedy, and she understands the tragedy. She understands it because Hawthorne does; because at the same time that he recoils from the Puritan view of sin he honors its capacity to be a view at all. Sin for him, for Hester, and for the people who punish her is equally a solemn fact, a problem for which there is no solution in life. There was no other solution for his story, given Hester's strength, Dimmesdale's weakness, and Chillingworth's perversion, than the one he found. Rather, as we read, it finds itself. And if the conclusion is not depressing, the reason is that nothing before it has been meaningless. This world has not been really bleak. It has been as beautiful as it was terrible; Hester's life has not been hollow, nor has her great nature been wasted.

The weakness of Dimmesdale is personal to him and a part of the story, whose power it magnifies rather than lessens. He is "tremulous," and he holds his hand over his heart—these are two facts about him of which Hawthorne keeps us constantly informed. So constantly, indeed, that we might grow tired of the information were it not so relevant to the agony within. His penances, which extend even to scourging himself until he laughs bitterly at the blood that flows, still do not give him peace. The blood comes, but not his soul, for there is no penitence. He tortures but cannot purify himself. And there is no man for whom purity is more important, no man who more loves the truth and loathes the lie. Yet he maintains the lie, and so diminishes his very existence. "It is the unspeakable misery of a life so false as his," says Hawthorne at one point, "that it steals the pith and substance out of whatever realities there are around us, and which were meant by Heaven to be the spirit's joy and nutriment. To the untrue man the whole universe is false—it is impalpable—it shrinks to nothing within his grasp. And he himself, in so far as he shows himself in a false light, becomes a shadow, or, indeed, ceases to exist. The only truth that continued to give Mr. Dimmesdale a real existence on this earth was the anguish in his inmost soul, and the undissembled expression of it in his aspect. Had he once found power to smile, and wear a face of gayety, there would have been no such man!"

He is redeemed for us only because his suffering makes him beautiful and because Hester continues to love him. He would be fantastic, he would be one of Hawthorne's figments, had she not loved him in the first place. We believe this because we believe everything about her, and understand how much distinction she gives the objects of her love. The explanation for her superior strength, which never shows itself more clearly than when "with sudden and desperate tenderness" she throws her arms around him in the forest, is not merely that she has had the comparative luck to live in public shame. We are convinced that she would have been strong in any case, with the wisdom not to pervert either herself or him. As always with Hawthorne's women, she has more courage than the man with whom her lot is joined. This was true of Dorcas Bourne, of Faith Brown, of Dorothy

Pearson, of Martha Pierson, of Beatrice Rappaccini; it was even true, in *Fanshawe,* of Mrs. Melmoth and Ellen Langton; it will be true of Phoebe, Zenobia, and Miriam. Somewhere, if not in the New England of his time, Hawthorne unearthed the image of a goddess supreme in beauty and power; and this included, whether he planned it or not, erotic power. "Those words 'genteel' and 'lady-like,' " he said, "are terrible ones, and do us infinite mischief, but it is because (at least, I hope so) we are in a transition state, and shall emerge into a higher mode of simplicity than has ever been known to past ages." One of the reasons he set so many of his tales in the past must have been that there, and there only, he could find the women he wanted for his art. As early as 1829, in his sketch "The Canal Boat," he had written: "Here was the pure, modest, sensitive, and shrinking woman of America—shrinking when no evil is intended, and sensitive like diseased flesh, that thrills if you but point at it; and strangely modest, without confidence in the modesty of other people; and admirably pure, with such a quick apprehension of all impurity." And as late as 1863, in *Our Old Home,* he was to assess his "dear countrywomen" as having "a certain meagreness, . . . a deficiency of physical development, a scantiness, so to speak, in the pattern of their material make, a paleness of complexion, a thinness of voice." Sir Peter Lely's Nell Gwyn, he decided, was "one of the few beautiful women" he had seen on canvas. Nor was the woman of his imagination's choice deficient in the mysterious powers belonging to her sex. D. H. Lawrence found these powers terrible in Hester, and supposed them so destructive of Dimmesdale that he died hating her. Hawthorne, a profounder psychologist, did not so protest against the might he recognized. He recorded it as true, and let it work. It seldom worked for him with such intensity as here, but it is present in all of his interesting tales—more mild, more submerged, in "The Wives of the Dead" and "The Great Carbuncle," but certainly present. It is why he can suggest in so few words that love exists between two persons, and can interest us so deeply in this fact; it is why, for instance, *The Scarlet Letter* is one of the great love stories of the world although it gives us no details of love. Hawthorne went to the center of woman's secret, her sexual power, and stayed there. For him it was not intellectual power. The women he considered, from Mrs. Hutchinson on, he never could praise if their minds had got the better of them. Hester threatens to become a feminist in the injustice of her solitude, but he saves her from that fate. "We may be sure," says Henry James, "that in women his taste was conservative." It was more than that. It was classic.

—MARK VAN DOREN, *"The Scarlet Letter," Nathaniel Hawthorne* (New York:
William Sloane Associates, 1949), pp. 146–56

R. W. B. LEWIS

The opening scene of *The Scarlet Letter* is the paradigm dramatic image in American literature. With that scene and that novel, New World fiction arrived at its first fulfilment, and Hawthorne at his. And with that scene, all that was dark and treacherous in the American situation became exposed. Hawthorne said later that the writing of *The Scarlet Letter* had been oddly simple, since all he had to do was to get his "pitch" and then to let it carry him along. He found his pitch in an opening tableau fairly humming with tension—with coiled and covert relationships that contained a force perfectly calculated to propel the action thereafter in a direct line to its tragic climax.

It was the tableau of the solitary figure set over against the inimical society, in a village which hovers on the edge of the inviting and perilous wilderness; a handsome young woman standing on a raised platform, confronting in silence and pride a hostile crowd whose menace is deepened by its order and dignity; a young woman who has come alone to the New World, where circumstances have divided her from the community now gathered to oppose her; standing alone, but vitally aware of the private enemy and the private lover—one on the far verges of the crowd, one at the place of honor within it, and neither conscious of the other—who must affect her destiny and who will assist at each other's destruction. Here the situation inherent in the American scene was seized entire and without damage to it by an imagination both moral and visual of the highest quality: seized and located, not any longer on the margins of the plot, but at its very center.

The conflict is central because it is total; because Hawthorne makes us respect each element in it. Hawthorne felt, as Brown and Cooper and Bird had felt, that the stuff of narrative (in so far as it was drawn from local experience) consisted in the imaginable brushes between the deracinated and solitary individual and the society or world awaiting him. But Hawthorne had learned the lesson only fitfully apprehended by Cooper. In *The Scarlet Letter* not only do the individual and the world, the conduct and the institutions, measure each other: the measurement and its consequences are precisely and centrally what the novel is about. Hester Prynne has been wounded by an unfriendly world; but the society facing her is invested by Hawthorne with assurance and authority, its opposition is defensible and even valid. Hester's misdeed appears as a disturbance of the moral structure of the universe; and the society continues to insist in its joyless way that certain acts deserve the honor of punishment. But if Hester has sinned, she has done so as an affirmation of life, and her sin is the source of life; she incarnates those rights of personality that society is inclined to trample upon. The action of the novel springs from the enormous but improbable suggestion that the society's estimate of the moral structure of the universe may be tested and found inaccurate.

The Scarlet Letter, like all very great fiction, is the product of a controlled division of sympathies; and we must avoid the temptation to read it heretically. It has always been possible to remark, about Hawthorne, his fondness for the dusky places, his images of the slow movement of sad, shut-in souls in the half-light. But it has also been possible to read *The Scarlet Letter* (not to mention "The New Adam and Eve" and "Earth's Holocaust") as an indorsement of hopefulness: to read it as a hopeful critic named Loring read it (writing for Theodore Parker's forward-looking *Massachusetts Quarterly Review*) as a party plea for self-reliance and an attack upon the sterile conventions of institutionalized society. One version of him would align Hawthorne with the secular residue of Jonathan Edwards; the other would bring him closer to Emerson. But Hawthorne was neither Emersonian nor Edwardsean; or rather he was both. The characteristic situation in his fiction is that of the Emersonian figure, the man of hope, who by some frightful mischance has stumbled into the time-burdened world of Jonathan Edwards. And this grim picture is given us by a writer who was skeptically cordial toward Emerson, but for whom the vision of Edwards, filtered through a haze of hope, remained a wonderfully useful metaphor. The situation, in the form which Hawthorne's ambivalence gave it, regularly led in his fiction to a moment of crucial choice: an invitation to the lost Emersonian, the thunder-struck Adam, to make up his mind—whether to accept the world he had fallen into, or whether to flee it, taking his chances in the allegedly free wilderness to the west. It is a decision about ethical reality, and most of Hawthorne's heroes and heroines eventually have to confront it.

That is why we have the frantic shuttling, in novel after novel, between the village and the forest, the city and the country; for these are the symbols between which the choice must be made and the means by which moral inference is converted into dramatic action. Unlike Thoreau or Cooper, Hawthorne never suggested that the choice was an easy one. Even Arthur Mervyn had been made to reflect on "the contrariety that exists between the city and the country"; in the age of hope the contrariety was taken more or less simply to lie between the restraints of custom and the fresh expansiveness of freedom. Hawthorne perceived greater complexities. He acknowledged the dependence of the individual, for nourishment, upon organized society (the city), and he believed that it was imperative "to open an intercourse with the world." But he knew that the city could destroy as well as nourish and was apt to destroy the person most in need of nourishment. And while he was responsive to the attractions of the open air and to the appeal of the forest, he also understood the grounds for the Puritan distrust of the forest. He retained that distrust as a part of the symbol. In the forest, possibility was unbounded; but just because of that, evil inclination was unchecked, and witches could flourish there.

For Hawthorne, the forest was neither the proper home of the admirable Adam, as with Cooper; nor was it the hideout of the malevolent adversary, as with Bird. It was the ambiguous setting of moral choice, the scene of reversal and discovery in his characteristic tragic drama. The forest was the pivot in Hawthorne's grand recurring pattern of escape and return.

It is in the forest, for example, that The Scarlet Letter version of the pattern begins to disclose itself: in the forest meeting between Hester and Dimmesdale, their first private meeting in seven years. During those years, Hester has been living "on the outskirts of the town," attempting to cling to the community by performing small services for it, though there had been nothing "in all her intercourse with society . . . that made her feel as if she belonged to it." And the minister has been contemplating the death of his innocence in a house fronting the village graveyard. The two meet now to join in an exertion of the will and the passion for freedom.

They very nearly persuade themselves that they can escape along the forest track, which, though in one direction it goes "backward to the settlement," in another goes onward—"deeper it goes, and deeper into the wilderness, until . . . the yellow leaves will show no vestiges of the white man's tread." But the energy aroused by their encounter drives them back instead, at the end, to the heart of the society, to the penitential platform which is also the heart of the book's structure.

—R. W. B. LEWIS, "The Return into Time: Hawthorne," *The American Adam: Innocence, Tragedy and Tradition in the Nineteenth Century* (Chicago: University of Chicago Press, 1955), pp. 111–14

HARRY LEVIN

The dark-haired Hester Prynne, emerging to mount the pillory, babe in arms, is presented as a virtual madonna, despite the token of self-denunciation which she has embroidered into her attire. When the Reverend Mr. Dimmesdale is invited to expostulate with her, "as touching the vileness and blackness of your sin," the irony is precarious; for we are not yet in a position to recognize him as her guilty partner; nor is it until the next chapter that we witness her recognition-scene with her long estranged and elderly husband, who conceals his identity under the name of Chillingworth. The interrelationship between open shame and secret guilt is dramatized by a tense alternation of public tableaux and private interviews. All men are potentially sinners, though they profess themselves saints. Here in old Boston, as in the Salem of "Young Goodman Brown," the Black Man does a thriving traffic in witchcraft. If the letter is his mark, as Hester tells her daughter, it must also be accepted as the universal birthmark of mankind. Once, when she tries to fling it away, it is borne back to her upon a stream; thereafter she accepts it as her doom; she learns to live with it.

Therein she becomes innately superior to those fellow citizens who despise her, and whose trespasses are compounded by their hypocrisies. Their social ostracism may turn her into a "type of . . . moral solitude"; but it endows her with "a sympathetic knowledge of the hidden sin in other hearts," which ultimately leads to a kind of redemption, as it does with the virtuous prostitutes of Victor Hugo and Dostoevsky. The letter proves to be a talisman which establishes bonds of sympathy; whereas the proud mantle of Lady Eleanor cut her off from sympathetic involvements. Though Hester lives a life of saintly penance, she does not repent her unhallowed love. On the contrary, she shields her repentant lover, and tells him: "What we did has a consecration of its own." Since their lapse was natural, it is pardonable; it has a validity which her marriage with Chillingworth seems to have lacked. What is unnatural is the pharisaical role into which Dimmesdale is consequently forced. He cannot ease his conscience by wearing a black veil, like the minister of Hawthorne's parable; for he is not mourning the hidden sin of others; he is hiding his own, which is palpable enough. The pulpit and the pillory are the contrasting scenes of his triumph and his self-abasement. His internal anguish, projected against the sky in a gigantic A, is finally relieved when he bares his breast to reveal the counterpart of Hester's letter. Hawthorne is purposefully vague in reporting these phenomena and whether they happen by miracle, hallucination, or expressionistic device. His Dostoevskian point is that every happening must be an accusation to the sinner, who must end by testifying against himself.

Hawthorne rejects an alternative he ironically suggests, whereby the supposedly blameless pastor dies in the arms of the fallen woman in order to typify Christian humility. Nor is her rehabilitation achieved at the expense of the cleric's integrity, as it would be for Anatole France's *Thaïs*. Nor is he thoroughly corrupted, like an evangelical beachcomber out of Somerset Maugham. Arthur Dimmesdale is an unwilling hypocrite, who purges himself by means of open confession. Among the possible morals, the one that Hawthorne selects is: "Be true! Be true! Be true! Show freely to the world, if not your worst, yet some trait whereby the worst may be inferred." Hester is true; and so is Dimmesdale at last; but the third injunction rings hollow. These two have been a sinful pair, and he—by Hawthorne's standard—has been more sinful than she. But the most sinful member of the triangle is, most unnaturally, the injured party. Dimmesdale atones for his trespass by his death; Hester for hers by her life; but for Chillingworth, avenging their violation of his existence, there can be no atonement. "That old man's revenge has been blacker than my sin," exclaims Dimmesdale. "He has violated, in cold blood, the sanctity of a human heart. Thou and I, Hester, never did so." While their trespass has been sensual passion, Chillingworth's is intellectual pride. In short, it is the unpardonable sin of Ethan Brand, of Hawthorne's dehumanized experimentalists, and of that spiritualized Paul Pry whose vantage-point comes so uncomfortably close to the author's. Chillingworth, whose assumed name betrays his frigid nature, plays the role of the secret sharer, prying into his wife's illicit affair, spying upon her lover unawares, and pulling the strings of the psychological romance.

—HARRY LEVIN, "The Skeleton in the Closet," *The Power of Blackness: Hawthorne, Poe, Melville* (New York: Knopf, 1958), pp. 74–77

FREDERICK C. CREWS

I would insist . . . that Henry James was originally right in saying that Hawthorne "cared for the deeper psychology," and that his works offer glimpses of "the whole deep mystery of man's soul and conscience." The majority view, I feel, rests on both a misapprehension of "deep psychology" and an inattentive habit of reading Hawthorne. We must, in the first place, question the popular notion that *individuality* and *detail* are the key virtues of psychological portraiture. A richly particular character, such as James's Isabel Archer, may be represented as living almost entirely in the realm of conscious moral choice, while her instinctual nature and her conflicts of feeling are hidden under an abundance of surface strokes. Hawthorne's Hester

Prynne, in contrast, is rendered in terms of struggle between feelings that she neither controls nor perfectly understands. Her remorse toward her husband versus her sympathy for her lover, her desire to flee versus her compulsion to remain, her maternal instinct versus her shame at what Pearl represents, her voluptuousness versus her effort to repent and conform—these tensions are the very essence of our idea of Hester. If she is a more schematic figure than Isabel, her motives are deeper and are better known to us. It is precisely because Hawthorne is not afraid to schematize, to stress underlying patterns of compulsion rather than superficial eccentricities, that he is able to explore "the depths of our *common* nature."

The power of Hawthorne's best fiction comes largely from a sense that nothing in human behavior is as free or fortuitous as it appears. Even with characters much less fully observed than Hester, the emphasis falls on buried motives which are absolutely binding because they are unavailable to conscious criticism. Furthermore, even the most wooden heroes bear witness to a psychological preoccupation. Whatever is subtracted from overt psychology tends to reappear in imagery, even in the physical setting itself. It is as if there were a law of the conservation of psychic energy in Hawthorne's world; as the characters approach sentimental stereotypes, the author's language becomes correspondingly more suggestive of unconscious obsession. And, in fact, one of the abiding themes of Hawthorne's work is the fruitless effort of people to deny the existence of their "lower" motives. The form of his plots often constitutes a return of the repressed— a vengeance of the denied element against an impossible ideal of purity or spirituality. Thus it is not enough, in order to speak of Hawthorne's power as a psychologist, merely to look at his characters' stated motives. We must take into account the total, always intricate dialogue between statement and implication, observing how Hawthorne—whether or not he consciously means to—invariably measures the displacements and sublimations that have left his characters two-dimensional. ⟨. . .⟩

We are now prepared to understand the choice that the poor minister faces when Hester holds out the idea of escape. It is not a choice between a totally unattractive life and a happy one (not even Dimmesdale could feel hesitation in that case), but rather a choice of satisfactions, of avenues into the citadel. The seemingly worthless alternative of continuing to admit the morally condemned impulse by the way of remorse has the advantage, appreciated by all neurotics, of preserving the status quo. Still, the other course naturally seems more attractive. If only repression can be weakened—and this is just the task of Hester's rhetoric about freedom— Dimmesdale can hope to return to the previous "breach" of adultery.

In reality, however, these alternatives offer no chance for happiness or even survival. The masochistic course leads straight to death, while the other, which Dimmesdale allows Hester to choose for him, is by now so foreign to his withered, guilt-ridden nature that it can never be put into effect. The resolution to sin will, instead, necessarily redouble the opposing force of conscience, which will be stronger in proportion to the overtness of the libidinal threat. As the concluding chapters of *The Scarlet Letter* prove, the only possible result of Dimmesdale's attempt to impose, in Hawthorne's phrase, "a total change of dynasty and moral code, in that interior kingdom," will be a counter-revolution so violent that it will slay Dimmesdale himself along with his upstart libido. We thus see that in the forest, while Hester is prating of escape, renewal, and success, Arthur Dimmesdale unknowingly faces a choice of two paths to suicide.

Now, this psychological impasse is sufficient in itself to refute the most "liberal" critics of *The Scarlet Letter*—those who take Hester's proposal of escape as Hawthorne's own advice. However much we may admire Hester and prefer her boldness to Dimmesdale's self-pity, we cannot agree that she understands human nature very deeply. Her shame, despair, and solitude "had made her strong," says Hawthorne, "but taught her much amiss." What she principally ignores is the truth embodied in the metaphor of the ruined wall, that men are altered irreparably by their violations of conscience. Hester herself is only an apparent exception to this rule. She handles her guilt more successfully than Dimmesdale because, in the first place, her conscience is less highly developed than his; and secondly because, as he tells her, "Heaven hath granted thee an open ignominy, that thereby thou mayest work out an open triumph over the evil within thee, and the sorrow without." Those who believe that Hawthorne is an advocate of free love, that adultery has no ill effects on a "normal" nature like Hester's, have failed to observe that Hester, too, undergoes self-inflicted punishment. Though permitted to leave, she has remained in Boston not simply because she wants to be near Arthur Dimmesdale, but because this has been the scene of her humiliation. "Her sin, her ignominy, were the roots which she had struck into the soil," says Hawthorne. "The chain that bound her here was of iron links, and galling to her inmost soul, but never could be broken." ⟨. . .⟩

However much we may admire Dimmesdale's final asceticism, there are no grounds for taking it as Hawthorne's moral ideal. The last developments of plot in *The Scarlet Letter* approach the "mythic level" which redemption-minded critics love to discover, but the myth is wholly secular and worldly. Pearl, who has hitherto been a "messenger of anguish" to her mother, is emotionally transformed as she kisses Dimmesdale on the scaffold. "A spell was broken. The great scene of grief, in which the wild infant bore a part, had developed all her sympathies; and as her tears fell upon her father's cheek, they were the pledge that she would grow up amid human joy and sorrow, nor for ever do battle with the world, but be a woman in it." Thanks to Chillingworth's bequest—for Chillingworth, too, finds that a spell is broken when Dimmesdale confesses, and he is capable of at least one generous act before he dies—Pearl is made "the richest heiress of her day, in the New World." At last report she has become the wife of a European nobleman and is living very happily across the sea. This grandiose and perhaps slightly whimsical epilogue has one undeniable effect on the reader: it takes him as far as possible from the scene and spirit of Dimmesdale's farewell. Pearl's immense wealth, her noble title, her lavish and impractical gifts to Hester, and of course her successful escape from Boston all serve to disparage the Puritan sense of reality. From this distance we look back to Dimmesdale's egocentric confession, not as a moral example which Hawthorne would like us to follow, but as the last link in a chain of compulsion that has now been relaxed.

To counterbalance this impression we have the case of Hester, for whom the drama on the scaffold can never be completely over. After raising Pearl in a more generous atmosphere she voluntarily returns to Boston to resume, or rather to begin, her state of penitence. We must note, however, that this penitence seems to be devoid of theological content; Hester has returned because Boston and the scarlet letter offer her "a more real life" than she could find elsewhere, even with Pearl. This simply confirms Hawthorne's emphasis on the irrevocability of guilty acts. And though Hester is now selfless and humble, it is not because she believes in Christian submissiveness but because all passion has been spent. To the women who seek her help "in the continually recurring trials of wounded, wasted, wronged, misplaced, or erring and sinful passion," Hester does not disguise her conviction that women are pathetically misunderstood in her society. She assures her wretched friends that at some later period "a new truth would be revealed, in order to establish the whole relation between man and woman on a surer ground of mutual happiness." Hawthorne may or may not believe the prediction, but it has a retrospective importance in *The Scarlet Letter*. Hawthorne's characters originally acted in ignorance of passion's strength and persistence, and so they became its slaves.

"It is a curious subject of observation and inquiry," says Hawthorne at the end, "whether hatred and love be not the same thing at bottom. Each, in its utmost development, supposes a high degree of intimacy and heart-knowledge; each renders one individual dependent for the food of his affections and spiritual life upon another; each leaves the passionate lover, or the no less passionate hater, forlorn and desolate by the withdrawal of his object." These penetrating words remind us that the tragedy of *The Scarlet Letter* has chiefly sprung, not from Puritan society's imposition of false social ideals on the three main characters, but from their own inner world of frustrated desires. Hester, Dimmesdale, and Chillingworth have been ruled by feelings only half perceived, much less understood and regulated by consciousness; and these feelings, as Hawthorne's bold equation of love and hatred implies, successfully resist translation into terms of good and evil. Hawthorne does not leave us simply with the Sunday-school lesson that we should "be true," but with a tale of passion through which we glimpse the ruined wall—the terrible certainty that, as Freud put it, the ego is not master in its own house. It is this intuition that enables Hawthorne to reach a tragic vision worthy of the name: to see to the bottom of his created characters, to understand the inner necessity of everything they do, and thus to pity and forgive them in the very act of laying bare their weaknesses.

—FREDERICK C. CREWS, *The Sins of the Fathers: Hawthorne's Psychological Themes* (New York: Oxford University Press, 1966), pp. 16–17, 142–44, 151–53

CAROLYN G. HEILBRUN

It is tempting to call the eighteen forties the decade of the Victorian androgynous novel, particularly if we expand the range of discussion to include the great American novel *The Scarlet Letter*. The greatest androgynous novel of them all, *Wuthering Heights,* did not attract immediate attention; if it speaks clearly to our generation, it hardly spoke at all to its own. But *Vanity Fair* and *The Scarlet Letter,* not to mention *Jane Eyre,* immediately gained large and enthusiastic audiences. Henry James, in his study of Hawthorne, mentions that the publication of *The Scarlet Letter* was "a literary event of the first importance. The book was the finest piece of imaginative writing yet put forth in this country. There was a consciousness of this in the welcome that was given it—a satisfaction in the idea of America having produced a novel that belonged to literature and to the forefront of it." Almost a century and a quarter after the novel's publication, we can see with what extraordinary pertinacity *The Scarlet Letter* was to remain in the forefront of American literature. From that day to this, America has not produced a novel whose androgynous implications match those of *The Scarlet Letter,* nor a novel with as great a central female character. American literature, like American society, has so far turned its back on the "feminine" impulse.

The Scarlet Letter, like the other great androgynous novels before the twentieth century, *Clarissa, Vanity Fair, Wuthering Heights,* is unique in its author's career. For Richardson alone, the greatest novel was not the first; *Pamela* was no doubt necessary as preparation for *Clarissa.* When a writer creates a masterpiece in a wholly new genre he has largely founded, *some* preparation is necessary: Richardson had little enough.

The points of similarity between *The Scarlet Letter* and *Clarissa* are noteworthy. The chief difference, of course, is between the characters Dimmesdale and Lovelace: the phrase used in connection with Dimmesdale, "dewy purity of thought," places him in another sphere of being from Lovelace. The rake was no part of Hawthorne's world. For Richardson, we may fairly guess, the creation of Lovelace required the great artistic imaginative leap. For Hawthorne, the miracle lay in the creation of Hester Prynne. An American Clarissa, in a Puritan and as yet unmonied and unclassed society, Hester Prynne chose her sin. The sexual act was not forced upon her. On the contrary, our sight of Dimmesdale and Hester together in the forest confirms our judgment that it is she who has the greater energy; when they meet in the forest she must "buoy him up with her own energy." Moreover, not only is Hester's sexuality palpable, though represented only through the magnificent gesture of allowing her luxuriant hair to escape from its confining cap, it is she who has had previous sexual experience. Dimmesdale was virginal before the act, and, like Clarissa in this, fit only for death afterward.

It is in Hester's sense of herself that she resembles Clarissa, and in her choice of living with and through the fact of the sexual event, the act for Clarissa, the condemnation of the act for Hester. Hester's "roots were the sin which she had struck into the soil." If she did not wholly believe herself to have sinned, as Clarissa might be said, in some sense, not to have sinned at all, both of them understood that from that moment forward their destiny was in the soil of the sin, and nowhere else. For Clarissa, the outcome was bodily death and heavenly redemption; for Hester, social death and social redemption. Both are alike in their quality of martyrdom and sainthood. Hester knows, like Clarissa, that "the torture of her daily shame would at length purge her soul, and work out another purity than that which she had lost; more saintlike, because the result of martyrdom." Hester's greatness, like Clarissa's, is allowed to assume its almost mythic proportions; it is never chiseled down to fit a conventional view of woman's limitations. In *The Scarlet Letter,* as in *Clarissa,* this is made evident: had she not had Pearl to care for, Hawthorne says of Hester, "she might have come down to us in history, hand in hand with Anne Hutchinson, as the foundress of a religious sect. She might, in one of her phases, have been a prophetess. She might, and not improbably would, have suffered death from the stern tribunals of the period, for attempting to undermine the foundations of the Puritan establishment." Like Clarissa, who insists upon her fated death, Hester will not release the mark of her experience, the scarlet letter itself. Roger Chillingworth tells her that the magistrates might be persuaded to permit her to leave it off. "It lies not with the pleasure of the magistrates," she answers, "to take off this badge. Were I worthy to be quit of it, it would fall away of its own nature, or be transformed into something that should speak a different purport." It is, of course, so transformed, as is Clarissa herself.

Both Clarissa and Hester, great and stunted powers, seem to suggest a great sense of waste. "Thou hadst great elements," Chillingworth says to Hester. "Peradventure, hadst thou met earlier with a better love than mine, this evil had not been. I pity thee, for the good that has been wasted in thy nature." Yet both Hester and Clarissa turn the apparent waste of their lives, by recognition of what is called their sin, into tremendous sources of androgynous energy. For Hester, "the scarlet letter was her passport into regions where other women dared not tread."

That both the "sin" and the rape in the two novels are acts of distorted sexuality is significant. The difference is one of the marks, of which Henry James was to point out so many others, between the old and the new world. In the old country, the sexes have been so radically distinguished and segregated that rape is the only act left which can, by shocking us, bring us into sight of the lost androgynous ideal. In the new world, the branding of the sexual union as sinful plunges the society into the same morass of sexually segregated life. Only in the primeval forest where Pearl, "the unpremeditated offshoot of a passionate moment," is wholly at home can Dimmesdale and Hester meet, other than on the scaffold that condemns their sin. The greatest miracle of *The Scarlet Letter* is the extent to which the book allows the magnificence of that one act of love to shine as the single living moment in a hard and sterile world. "What we did had a consecration of its own," Hester says to Dimmesdale in the forest. "We felt it so! We said so to each other! Hast thou forgotten it?"

"Thou shalt not go alone!" Hester says to Dimmesdale, when she offers to flee to the old world with him. But he was to die alone with the words "the sin here so awfully revealed" on his lips. His was a prophetic death, for none of his literary progeny, none of the principal male characters who followed him in American literature, was to wish to be anything but "alone" in the sense of preferring male company. Hester and Dimmesdale are buried beside one another, finally, and "one tombstone served for both." There is, as there has not yet been again in American literature, an echo of the final speech by Caesar in *Antony and Cleopatra:* "No grave upon the earth shall clip in it a pair so famous."

No more than Dimmesdale was Hester Prynne to have any literary descendants. When Hester returned to the Puritan town that had pilloried her, she became a source of comfort. Women especially "came to Hester's cottage demanding why they were so wretched, and what the remedy! Hester comforted them, too, of her firm belief, that, at some brighter period, when the world should have grown ripe for it, in Heaven's own time, a new truth would be revealed, in order to establish the whole relation between man and woman on a surer ground of mutual happiness. Earlier in life, Hester had vainly imagined that she herself might be the destined prophetess. . . . The angel and apostle of the coming revelation must be a woman, indeed, but lofty, pure, and beautiful; and wise, moreover, not through dusky grief, but through the ethereal medium of joy."

The angel and apostle of the expected revelation has not come. From the day of Hester's creation to this day, no American literary character (if we exclude characters of Henry James, who did not remain in America) has so much as touched the hem of her gown, or drawn any inspiration from her. That she was created at all is the more extraordinary in that Hawthorne was strongly anti-feminist in his opinions, and ultraconventional in his view of the proper destiny of the sexes. In *The Scarlet Letter* itself, he refers to "man-like Elizabeth" (the Queen) and is capable of so conventional a view as that which refers to "the delicate toil of the needle," the art from which "women derive a pleasure, incomprehensible to the other sex." The pleasures of needlework, we now know, are incomprehensible to many women and attractive to many men, if they may undertake them without the ridicule of society. Yet never is Hawthorne's novel limited by his conventional views. He knows, of the governor and the men surrounding him, that "out of the whole human family, it would not have been easy to select the same number of wise and virtuous persons, who should be less capable of sitting in judgment on an erring woman's heart." He knows of John Wilson, the eldest clergyman of Boston, who preaches to Hester, that "he looked like the darkly engraved portraits which we see prefixed to old volumes of sermons; and had no more right than one of those portraits would have, to step forth, as he now did, and meddle with a question of human guilt, passion, and anguish." Hawthorne created Hester Prynne and Dimmesdale, and Roger Chillingworth, with the truth of imagination, a truth which only Henry James of all writers born in America after Hawthorne was to understand.

—CAROLYN G. HEILBRUN, "The Woman as Hero," *Toward a Recognition of Androgyny* (New York: Knopf, 1973), pp. 62–67

RICHARD H. BRODHEAD

Leslie Fiedler notes that "one of the major problems involved in reading *The Scarlet Letter* is determining the ontological status of the characters, the sense in which we are being asked to believe in them." The characterization of Chillingworth shows why this is so: ontology is a problem because the characters in the novel are endowed with radically different sorts of reality. Hester's mode of existence is at the furthest extreme from Chillingworth's. We have already seen some examples of her ability to attenuate or complicate the implications of the forms the Puritans seek to impose on her. When she does accept Puritan designations she does so out of a process of mind that belies their meaning. Thus in the beautiful chapter "Hester at Her Needle" Hawthorne observes with fine tact the process by which she comes to reject the pleasures of her art as sinful. She senses that her art might be a way of expressing, and thus of soothing, her repressed passion, and in order to protect her love she rejects—and labels as sin—whatever might help her to sublimate it. Here she employs Puritan terminology in a most un-Puritan strategy of consciousness, using it to perpetuate an inner need which she is unable to act out and unwilling to relinquish. Her effort to retain her passion intact leads her, in the chapter "Hester and Pearl," to commit a conscious deception. In the face of Pearl's earnest questionings Hester senses that Pearl might be capable of becoming a confidante, a friend, and thus of helping her to "overcome the passion, once so wild, and even yet neither dead nor asleep." In telling Pearl that she wears the scarlet letter for the sake of its gold thread she is not true, to Pearl, to her badge, or to herself. But her falseness here is another strategy by which she attempts to maintain all the elements of her true self in suspension. She cannot achieve in her life the full expression of her complex self that she has wrought into her symbol, but she instinctively and covertly moves to keep this alive as a possibility.

Hawthorne writes that "the tendency of her fate and fortunes had been to set her free." Her freedom is a mixed state of lucidity and self-deception, integrity and falsehood, love and hate: she experiences herself as being, like her letter, a "mesh of good and evil." What is most exciting about Hester is her openness to all the varieties of experience—intellectual, imaginative, emotional—that the continuing emergency of her life brings to her. When she meets Chillingworth at the seaside she has a clear vision of what he has become; she perceives her own share of the responsibility for his transformation; she desperately insists on the possibility of a free act of forgiveness; and she recoils with bitterness from his grim refusal. No other character in the book is capable of this range of feeling. When she decides to go to Dimmesdale's aid she is prompted by her love, by her perception of his weakness, and by her recognition of the responsibility she has incurred for his destruction by promising to keep Chillingworth's identity secret. In defining a duty for herself she generates an ethical imperative out of a clear insight into the whole range of contradictory desires and obligations that confront her. Again, no other character in the book is capable of the adventure of free ethical choice that Hester undertakes here.

Hawthorne lavishes on Hester all of the psychological analysis that he deliberately withholds from Chillingworth. He endows her with the complex reality of a whole self as he becomes increasingly content simply to present Chillingworth's diabolical face. This is what creates the discrepancy between their ontological statuses, and it should be obvious by now that this discrepancy is neither careless nor purposeless. The way in which we are asked to believe in them as characters is a function of the way in which they believe in themselves. Chillingworth relinquishes his own freedom and adopts, in a perverted because atheistic way, the deterministic outlook of the Puritans. A dark necessity, he tells Hester, rules their fates: "Let the black flower blossom as it may!" As he does so he gives up his complexity of being and becomes a rigidified figure of diabolical evil, a character in the sort of providential romance that the Puritans imagine. Hester is allowed the freedom and variegated selfhood of a character in a more realistic mode because she first opens herself to the full complexity of her existence. It is as if in deciding how they will understand themselves and their world the characters also get to decide what sort of literary reality their author will let them acquire; the different fictional modes in which they are realized become explicit reflections of their own imaginative outlooks.

Charles Feidelson notes that Hawthorne carefully sets *The Scarlet Letter* at the historical watershed between the medieval and the modern, and that the novel presents the interaction of these ages as a conflict between two ways of creating and perceiving meaning. One of these sees experience as having meaning within a context of divine truth; within this context its symbolism tends toward fixity of significance, and its moral perception similarly moves to fix the value of characters and acts within rigidly separated categories of good and evil. The other is more secular and indeterminate. It sees meaning and value as generated from within human experience itself, so that its symbolic expressions and moral discriminations are valid to the extent that they emerge from a recognition of the whole complexity of life, including its inseparable mixture of good and evil. The contrast between Chillingworth's determinism and Hester's openness is only one version of this conflict; we see it again in the contrast between the A the Puritans impose on Hester and the A she creates, and between the sense of duty implicit in the Puritan's legal and religious forms and the sense of duty that leads Hester to go to Dimmesdale's rescue.

—RICHARD H. BRODHEAD, *"The Scarlet Letter," Hawthorne, Meville, and the Novel* (Chicago: University of Chicago Press, 1976), pp. 62–64

SACVAN BERCOVITCH

Perhaps the most misleading commonplace of recent criticism is that our major literature through Emerson is Antinomian. The Puritans banished Anne Hutchinson, we recall, because she set her private revelation above the public errand. The controversy foreshadows the fundamentally opposed concepts of greatness in Emerson and Carlyle. Emerson's hero, like Mather's Winthrop, derives his greatness from the enterprise he represents. Despite his distaste for, and fear of, the mass of actual Americans, he did not need to dissociate himself from America because he had already dissociated the mass from the American idea. Carlyle's hero gathers strength precisely in proportion to his alienation. He stands sufficient in himself, a titan born to master the multitude. As the Frankenstein's monster of left-wing Protestantism, he finds his place in a latter-day Antinomian brotherhood that includes Shaw's Superman and Ibsen's Master Builder; Nietzsche's Zarathustra, that "terrible teacher of the great contempt"; Byron's banished saint, whose immortal mind "makes itself/Requital for its good or evil thoughts."

In contrast to all of these, Emerson posed the severely ethical code of the true American. European geniuses like Goethe and Carlyle, he complained, "have an undisguised dislike or contempt for common virtue standing on common principles." Accordingly, he reminded himself in his journals to "beware of Antinomianism," and declared in public that his rejection of popular standards was a battle *against* "mere Antinomianism," in the interests of turning society towards the higher laws of chastity, simplicity, spiritual and intellectual awareness. "There was never a country in the world which could so easily exhibit this heroism as ours." Of course, Emerson never denounced Antinomianism with the vehemence of Winthrop, Mather, and Edwards. Once or twice he spoke of it with a condescending admiration, as a "vein of folly" that helps the enthusiast reach "the people," and often enough we feel a powerful Antinomian impulse in the absolutism of his claims. Nonetheless, his concept of representative heroism denies the tenets of Antinomianism, in any meaningful sense of the term. More accurately, his teleology redefines his Antinomian impulse, somewhat in the manner of Edwards (who was similarly accused of Antinomianism), as the revelation of the New World spirit. If Emerson differs from the chauvinist by his Romantic self-reliance, he differs equally from the Romantic Antinomian by his reliance on a national mission. The natural habitat of the *Übermensch* is the sublime, anywhere; Emerson's is America. "Greatness appeals to future," he explains in "Self-Reliance" (1839), and other essays.

> It is [therefore] for want of self-culture that the superstition of Travelling, whose idols are Italy, England, Egypt, retains its fascination for all educated Americans.... The force of character is cumulative. All the foregone days of virtue work their health into this. What makes the majesty of the heroes of the senate and the field, which so fills the imagination? The consciousness of a train of great days and victories behind. They shed a united light on the advancing actor.... That is it which throws thunder into Chatham's voice, and dignity into Washington's port, and America into Adam's eye.... Accept the place the divine providence has found for you, the society of your contemporaries, the connection of events, ... transcendent destiny; and ... [become] guides, redeemers, and benefactors, obeying the Almighty effort.

Emerson's exhortation to greatness speaks directly to the paradox of a litera-ture devoted at once to the exaltation of the individual and the search for a perfect community. Self-reliance builds upon both these extremes. It is the con-summate expression of a culture which places an immense premium on indepen-dence while denouncing all forms of eccentricity and elitism. The denunciation, as Emerson indicates, is less a demand for conformity than a gesture against Antino-mianism. Anne Hutchinson's self-reliance, like Wordsworth's, Byron's, Carlyle's, and Nietzsche's, may hold out grand prospects for mankind, but it locates the divine center in the individual. The self-reliant American may declare his whim superior to the entire legal code, but he remains by definition the hero as guide and national benefactor.

Or heroine: as Michael Bell has shown, a commonplace of the American historical romance is the representative American woman—Judd's Margaret, for example, and Hope Leslie, the spirit incarnate of democracy, liberty, progress, and the divine " 'principle' behind the events of seventeenth-century New England." The supreme instance, of course, is Hester Prynne, Hawthorne's "living sermon" against the "haughty" and "carnal" Mrs. Hutchinson, who "could find no peace in this chosen land." To some extent, his argument builds upon the tradition of the biblical Esther—homiletic *exemplum* of sorrow, duty, and love, and *figura* of the Virgin Mary: "Hester meke / Who did the serpents hede of[f] streke"; "Hester la tres amé / Ke sauve la genz jugé." But primarily Hawthorne's "sermon" traces the edu-cation of an *American* Esther. As her name implies, she is "the hidden one" who emerges as the "star" of the new age. Christologically, the "A" she wears expands from "Adulteress" to "Angelic." Historically, as "the 'A' for America," it leads for-ward from the Puritan "Utopia" to that "brighter period" when the country will fulfill its "high and glorious destiny." More than any other aspect of the novel, this fusion of personal and federal eschatology makes *The Scarlet Letter* an American romance. Like Hester, Anna Karenina is a moral *exemplum* ("Vengeance is mine; I will repay, saith the Lord") as well as the victim of particular social and psychological forces. But for all of Tolstoy's didacticism the two levels of meaning conflict, and for all his nationalism he never asks us to think of Anna, or even Levin, as an emblem of Russia. Despite Hawthorne's celebrated irony, and despite his unresolved am-bivalence toward the Puritan past and the democratic present, his novel yields an emphatically national design. His heroine is an intermediary prophetess, neither merely a doomed Romantic Dark Lady at her worst nor wholly a world-redeeming Romantic savior at her best, but a *figura medietatis,* like the Grey Champion "the pledge that New England's sons [and daughters] will vindicate their ancestry."

The representative quality of American Romantic heroism expresses the fur-thest reach of Mather's daring auto-American-biographical strategy in the *Magnalia.* By comparison, the European great man, for all his superiority to the mass, is sadly restricted. His very self-reliance implies an adversary Other, not only the great precursor poet but everyone to whom he is superior, everything from which he is alienated—history, the common laws, the representative men and women that constitute social normality. American intermediate selfhood has no such limits. Indeed, the very concept of "Americanus," from Mather through Emerson, advances a mode of personal identity designed as a compensatory *replacement* for (rather than an alternative to) the ugly course of actual events. By definition the flight of the "true American" to the imagination embraces individual and society alike, without allowing either for Romantic hero-worship or for the claims of social pluralism. Hester herself is an inadequate example of this kind of heroism. Because she is part of a larger, complex design, the problems of history assume a weight equal to, if not greater than, the prophetic solace she offers; it may be that an imperfect society actually usurps her representative stature. This, at any rate, is the implicit view of those who admire her as an Antinomian, and insofar as Hawthorne shared their admiration (in spite of his repeated, severe strictures to the contrary), he upheld the immemorial Old World convention, through *Antigone* to *Anna Karenina,* that the great soul reveals itself by confronting social realities and recognizing its limitations.

—SACVAN BERCOVITCH, "The Myth of America," *The Puritan Origins of the American Self* (New Haven: Yale University Press, 1975), pp. 174–78

NINA BAYM

In Hester Prynne, Hawthorne created the first true heroine of American fiction, as well as one of its enduring heroes. Hester is a heroine because she is deeply implicated in, and responsive to, the gender structure of her society, and because her story, turning on "love," is "appropriate" for a woman. She is a hero because she has qualities and actions that transcend this gender reference and lead to heroism as it can be understood for anyone.

"Such helpfulness was found in her,—so much power to do, and power to sympathize,—that many people refused to interpret the scarlet A by its original signification. They said that it meant Able; so strong was Hester Prynne, with a woman's strength." "Neither can I any longer live without her companionship; so powerful is she to sustain,—so tender to soothe!" It is impossible to miss, in these and many other passages, the stress on Hester's remarkable strength as well as the fundamentally humane uses to which she puts it. Without going beyond the license that Hawthorne allows, one might allegorize Hester as Good Power, which is, after all, precisely what, in the basic structural scheme of all narrative, one looks for in a hero. The power is remarkable in that its existence seems so improbable in an outcast woman. If the Puritan state draws its power from the consensual community and the laws that uphold it, then clearly Hester has access to a completely different source of power—or is, perhaps, herself an alternative source of power. And it is a power that even the Puritan world cannot deny, for "with her native energy of character, and rare capacity, it could not entirely cast her off."

Perhaps, however, it is precisely her essential alienation from the community that explains this power. Although Hester can hardly doubt the power of the Puritan community to punish her and define the circumstances of her life, she knows—as we do—that they have this power only because she has granted it to them. She is free to leave Boston whenever she chooses. Her decision to stay entails a submission to Puritan power, but since she can withdraw her consent at any time this submission is always provisional. Her reasons for staying may be misguided, but they are her own. In schematic terms, if the Puritans symbolize the law, then Hester symbolizes the individual person—with this important proviso: she also symbolizes good. It would be easy to deduce from this polarity that Hawthorne wants us to think that law is bad and the individual good—but that would be too easy. Matters in Hawthorne are never so clear-cut. But he certainly gives us a situation wherein two kinds of power confront each other in conflict, and strongly suggests that any society that regards the power of the individual only as an adversary to be overcome, is profoundly defective and deeply inhuman.

Hester's situation, even before the commission of her "sin," is that of an outsider. She was sent to Massachusetts in advance of her husband; he had decided to emigrate, not she. The native strength of her character is certainly abetted by the fact that, as a young woman in a society dominated by aging men, she has no public importance. Even when she becomes a public figure through her punishment, her psyche is largely left alone. The magistrates condemn her to wear the letter but thereafter seem to have only a very superficial interest in her. A minister who sees her on the street may take the opportunity to preach an extempore sermon; people stare at the letter; children jeer; but none of this behavior represents an attempt to change Hester's mind. It is hoped that the external letter will work its way down into Hester's heart and cause repentance, but nobody really cares and this indifference is Hester's freedom. In fact, the effect of the letter so far as Hester's character is concerned is the opposite of what was intended: turning her into a public symbol, it conceals her individuality and thus protects it.

As the representative of individuality, Hester, rather than subjecting herself to the law, subjects it to her own scrutiny; as I have said, she takes herself as a law. She is not, by nature, rebellious; and during the seven-year period of *The Scarlet Letter*'s action, she certainly attempts to accept the judgment implicit in the letter. If she could accept that judgment she would be able to see purpose and meaning in her suffering. But ultimately she is unable to transcend her heartfelt conviction that she has not sinned. She loves Dimmesdale, with whom she sinned; she loves the child that her sin brought forth. How, then, can she agree that her deed was wrong?

She goes so far in her thinking as to attribute her own law to God, thus denying the entire rationale of the Puritan community, their certainty that their laws conform to divine intention. "Man had marked this woman's sin by a scarlet letter, which had such potent and disastrous efficacy that no human sympathy could reach her, save it were sinful like herself. God, as a direct consequence of the sin which man thus punished, had given her a lovely child, whose place was on that same dishonored bosom, to connect her parent for ever with the race and descent of mortals, and to be finally a blessed soul in heaven!"

In fact, while the outward Hester performs deeds of mercy and kindness throughout the seven years, the inward Hester grows ever more alienated and over time becomes—what she was not at first—a genuine revolutionary and social radical.

> The world's law was no law for her mind. It was an age in which the human intellect, newly emancipated, had taken a more active and a wider range than for many centuries before. Men of the sword had overthrown nobles and kings. Men bolder than these had overthrown and rearranged—not actually, but within the sphere of theory, which was their most real abode—the whole system of ancient prejudice, wherewith was linked much of ancient principle. Hester Prynne imbibed this spirit. She assumed a freedom of speculation, then common enough on the other side of the Atlantic, but which our forefathers, had they known of it, would have held to be a deadlier crime than that stigmatized by the scarlet letter.

Had she spoken her thoughts, she probably would "have suffered death from the stern tribunals of the period, for attempting to undermine the foundations of the Puritan establishment." If it were not for the existence of Pearl, for whose sake she lives quietly in Boston, she would have become, like Anne Hutchinson, a religious reformer.

But just as Hester refuses to take the road to witchcraft on account of Pearl, she rejects Hutchinson's radical path for the same reason. She feels particular obligations to human beings far more than she feels general social responsibilities. She behaves as a sister of mercy in the community because this is the way to live unmolested, not because she believes in doing good. And she wants to live un-molested so that she can bring up Pearl. Staying in Boston on account of Dimmes-dale, and living there as she does on account of Pearl, Hester's behavior is appropriate to her role as representative of individual and personal, rather than social, power. A reformer is dedicated to social power and has abandoned an individual center. No doubt this makes the whole issue of social reform on behalf of individualism highly problematic; so far as Hester is concerned—and this is our concern at present—the very consistency of her individualism keeps her within the sphere of the personal. At the end of the story, with her group of women clustered about her, she invokes the memory of Hutchinson only to contrast with it. The subject of talk among the women is entirely personal, centered on secular love; Hester counsels patience. Thus, the narrator's suggestion that her radicalism stems from an unquiet heart is partly validated by her behavior. If in Hawthorne's world a true radical, motivated by the impersonal, is somehow anti-individual, and if a true individual, motivated by the personal, is ultimately not radical, then our current popular understanding of these terms is quite different from Hawthorne's. His distinction is between ideologues and individuals rather than between varieties of ideology: an "individual-ist" is an ideologue. The individual as a reality rather than a concept is always extremely vulnerable.

Among Hester's key defining traits we cannot overlook her "skill at her needle." If her nature includes the characters of outcast, rebel, lover, mother, and sister of mercy, it also includes the character of artist. Her gift for needlework is the expression of an artist's nature; the embroideries that she produces are genuine works of art.

We meet her skill first, of course, in the letter, which, "surrounded with an elaborate embroidery and fantastic flourishes of gold thread," is "so artistically done, and with so much fertility and gorgeous luxuriance of fancy, that it had all the effect of a last and fitting decoration" to her splendid apparel. Hester's grand costuming for the scaffold scene, far more elegant than what the dress code of the colony normally would allow her, is not seen again. She wears nothing but drab gray gowns. Her dreary dress, however, becomes a frame for the letter, and the letter remains, as it is clearly meant to be, an ornament. Beautifying the letter through art is another way in which Hester breaks the Puritan law (although the Puritan rulers— unlike the women in the crowd—are too literal-minded to notice it). The letter becomes the chief ground for the struggle between Hester and the Puritans, and it is able to play this role because of Hester's gift as an artist.

It is tempting here to associate artistic skill with social rebellion, but the equation does not hold. For Hester supports herself in Puritan Boston chiefly by making the elaborate decorative garments that the magistrates wear for public occasions and that are allowed to the better-off in the colony. "Deep ruffs, painfully wrought bands, and gorgeously embroidered gloves, were all deemed necessary to the official state of men assuming the reins of power; and were readily allowed to individuals dignified by rank or wealth." Art does not have an inherently political nature, although—as the instance of the letter shows—it can become highly po- liticized. Rather, it is the expression of an original and creative energy, of fertility, of imagination, and of the love for the beautiful, even the gorgeous. This energy and creativity have no reference to society at all. Artists and their products can be appropriated by society or condemned by it; but society cannot make art, only individuals can. Indeed, only individuals who retain, or contain, a profound nonsocial element in their makeup (as Hester does) can make art. Although the social struc- ture of the age denies virtually all forms of artistic expression to women, it does allow this one, and Hester makes use of it as an outlet for this side of her nature. For its part, society makes use of *her*. The Puritans may be incapable of producing art, but they certainly want to possess it. Therefore, despite everything, they want Hester in their community; and they want her *as she is*. But this is something they have to learn about themselves; and if they do not learn in time, there will be a society with no more Hesters.

—NINA BAYM, "Who? The Characters," The Scarlet Letter: *A Reading*
(Boston: Twayne, 1986), pp. 62–67

CRITICAL ESSAYS

D. H. Lawrence

NATHANIEL HAWTHORNE AND *THE SCARLET LETTER*

Nathaniel Hawthorne writes romance.

And what's romance? Usually, a nice little tale where you have everything As You Like It, where rain never wets your jacket and gnats never bite your nose and it's always daisy-time. *As You Like It* and *Forest Lovers,* etc. *Morte D'Arthur.*

Hawthorne obviously isn't this kind of romanticist: though nobody has muddy boots in *The Scarlet Letter,* either.

But there is more to it. *The Scarlet Letter* isn't a pleasant, pretty romance. It is a sort of parable, an earthly story with a hellish meaning.

All the time there is this split in the American art and art-consciousness. On the top it is as nice as pie, goody-goody and lovey-dovey. Like Hawthorne being such a blue-eyed darling, in life, and Longfellow and the rest such sucking-doves. Hawthorne's wife said she "never saw him in time," which doesn't mean she saw him too late. But always in the "frail effulgence of eternity."

Serpents they were. Look at the inner meaning of their art and see what demons they were.

You *must* look through the surface of American art, and see the inner diabolism of the symbolic meaning. Otherwise it is all mere childishness.

That blue-eyed darling Nathaniel knew disagreeable things in his inner soul. He was careful to send them out in disguise.

Always the same. The deliberate consciousness of Americans so fair and smooth-spoken, and the under-consciousness so devilish. *Destroy! destroy! destroy!* hums the under-consciousness. *Love and produce! Love and produce!* cackles the upper consciousness. And the world hears only the Love-and-produce cackle. Refuses to hear the hum of destruction underneath. Until such time as it will *have* to hear.

The American has got to destroy. It is his destiny. It is his destiny to destroy

---

From *Studies in Classic American Literature* (New York: Thomas Seltzer, 1923; rpt. New York: Viking Press, 1964), pp. 83–99.

the whole corpus of the white psyche, and white consciousness. And he's got to do it secretly. As the growing of a dragon-fly inside a chrysalis or cocoon destroys the larva grub, secretly.

Though many a dragon-fly never gets out of the chrysalis case: dies inside. As America might.

So the secret chrysalis of *The Scarlet Letter,* diabolically destroying the old psyche inside.

Be good! Be good! warbles Nathaniel. *Be good, and never sin! Be sure your sins will find you out.*

So convincingly that his wife never saw him "as in time."

Then listen to the diabolic undertone of *The Scarlet Letter.*

Man ate of the tree of knowledge, and became ashamed of himself.

Do you imagine Adam had never lived with Eve before that apple episode? Yes, he had. As a wild animal with his mate.

It didn't become "sin" till the knowledge-poison entered. That apple of Sodom.

We are divided in ourselves, against ourselves. And that is the meaning of the cross symbol.

In the first place, Adam knew Eve as a wild animal knows its mate, momentaneously, but vitally, in blood-knowledge. Blood-knowledge, not mind-knowledge. Blood-knowledge, that seems utterly to forget, but doesn't. Blood-knowledge, instinct, intuition, all the vast vital flux of knowing that goes on in the dark, antecedent to the mind.

Then came that beastly apple, and the other sort of knowledge started.

Adam began to look at himself. "My hat!" he said. "What's this? My Lord! What the deuce!—And Eve! I wonder about Eve."

Thus starts KNOWING. Which shortly runs to UNDERSTANDING, when the devil gets his own.

When Adam went and took Eve, *after* the apple, he didn't do any more than he had done many a time before, in act. But in consciousness he did something very different. So did Eve. Each of them kept an eye on what they were doing, they watched what was happening to them. The wanted to KNOW. And that was the birth of sin. Not *doing* it, but KNOWING about it. Before the apple, they had shut their eyes and their minds had gone dark. Now, they peeped and pried and imagined. They watched themselves. And they felt uncomfortable after. They felt self-conscious. So they said, "The *act* is sin. Let's hide. We've sinned."

No wonder the Lord kicked them out of the Garden. Dirty hypocrites.

The sin was the self-watching, self-consciousness. The sin, and the doom. Dirty understanding.

Nowadays men do hate the idea of dualism. It's no good, dual we are. The cross. If we accept the symbol, then, virtually, we accept the fact. We are divided against ourselves.

For instance, the blood *hates* being KNOWN by the mind. It feels itself destroyed when it is KNOWN. Hence the profound instinct of privacy.

And on the other hand, the mind and the spiritual consciousness of man simply *hates* the dark potency of blood-acts: hates the genuine dark sensual orgasms, which do, for the time being, actually obliterate the mind and the spiritual consciousness, plunge them in a suffocating flood of darkness.

You can't get away from this.

Blood-consciousness overwhelms, obliterates, and annuls mind-consciousness.

Mind-consciousness extinguishes blood-consciousness, and consumes the blood.

We are all of us conscious in both ways. And the two ways are antagonistic in us.

They will always remain so.

That is our cross.

The antagonism is so obvious, and so far-reaching, that it extends to the smallest thing. The cultured, highly-conscious person of to-day *loathes* any form of physical, "menial" work: such as washing dishes or sweeping a floor or chopping wood. This menial work is an insult to the spirit. "When I see men carrying heavy loads, doing brutal work, it always makes me want to cry," said a beautiful, cultured woman to me.

"When you say that, it makes me want to beat you," said I, in reply. "When I see you with your beautiful head pondering heavy thoughts, I just want to hit you. It outrages me."

My father hated books, hated the sight of anyone reading or writing.

My mother hated the thought that any of her sons should be condemned to manual labour. Her sons must have something higher than that.

She won. But she died first.

He laughs longest who laughs last.

There is a basic hostility in all of us between the physical and the mental, the blood and the spirit. The mind is "ashamed" of the blood. And the blood is destroyed by the mind, actually. Hence pale-faces.

At present the mind-consciousness and the so-called spirit triumphs. In America supremely. In America, nobody does anything from the blood. Always from the nerves, if not from the mind. The blood is chemically reduced by the nerves, in American activity.

When an Italian labourer labours, his mind and nerves sleep, his blood acts ponderously.

Americans, when they are *doing* things, never seem really to be doing them. They are "busy about" it. They are always busy "about" something. But truly *immersed* in *doing* something, with the deep blood-consciousness active, that they never are.

They *admire* the blood-conscious spontaneity. And they want to get it in their heads. "Live from the body," they shriek. It is their last mental shriek. *Co-ordinate.*

It is a further attempt still to rationalize the body and blood. "Think about such and such a muscle," they say, "and relax there."

And every time you "conquer" the body with the mind (you can say "heal" it, if you like) you cause a deeper, more dangerous complex or tension somewhere else.

Ghastly Americans, with their blood no longer blood. A yellow spiritual fluid. The Fall.

There have been lots of Falls.

We *fell* into *knowledge* when Eve bit the apple. Self-conscious knowledge. For the first time the mind put up a fight against the blood. Wanting to UNDERSTAND. That is to intellectualize the blood.

The blood must be *shed,* says Jesus.

Shed on the cross of our own divided psyche.

Shed the blood, and you become mind-conscious. Eat the body and drink the blood, self-cannibalizing, and you become extremely conscious, like Americans and some Hindus. Devour yourself, and God knows what a lot you'll know, what a lot you'll be conscious of.

Mind you don't choke yourself.

For a long time men *believed* that they could be perfected through the mind, through the spirit. They believed, passionately. They had their ecstasy in pure consciousness. They *believed* in purity, chastity, and the wings of the spirit.

America soon plucked the bird of the spirit. America soon killed the *belief* in the spirit. But not the practice. The practice continued with a sarcastic vehemence. America, with a perfect inner contempt for the spirit and the consciousness of man, practises the same spirituality and universal love and KNOWING all the time, incessantly, like a drug habit. And inwardly gives not a fig for it. Only for the *sensation.* The pretty-pretty *sensation* of love, loving all the world. And the nice fluttering aeroplane *sensation* of knowing, knowing, knowing. Then the prettiest of all sensations, the sensation of UNDERSTANDING. Oh, what a lot they understand, the darlings! *So* good at the trick, they are. Just a trick of self-conceit.

The Scarlet Letter gives the show away.

You have your pure-pure young parson Dimmesdale.

You have the beautiful Puritan Hester at his feet.

And the first thing she does is to seduce him.

And the first thing he does is to be seduced.

And the second thing they do is to hug their sin in secret, and gloat over it, and try to understand.

Which is the myth of New England.

Deerslayer refused to be seduced by Judith Hutter. At least the Sodom apple of sin didn't fetch him.

But Dimmesdale was seduced gloatingly. Oh, luscious Sin!

He was such a pure young man.

That he had to make a fool of purity.

The American psyche.

Of course, the best part of the game lay in keeping up pure appearances.

The greatest triumph a woman can have, especially an American woman, is the triumph of seducing a man: especially if he is pure.

And he gets the greatest thrill of all, in falling.—"Seduce me, Mrs. Hercules."

And the pair of them share the sublest delight in keeping up pure appearances, when everybody knows all the while. But the power of pure appearances is something to exult in. All America gives in to it. *Look* pure!

To seduce a man. To have everybody know. To keep up appearances of purity. Pure!

This is the great triumph of woman.

A. The Scarlet Letter. Adulteress! The great Alpha. Alpha! Adulteress! The new Adam and Adama! American!

A. Adulteress! Stitched with gold thread, glittering upon the bosom. The proudest insignia.

Put her upon the scaffold and worship her there. Worship her there. The Woman, the Magna Mater. A. Adulteress! Abel!

Abel! Abel! Abel! Admirable!

It becomes a farce.

The fiery heart. A. Mary of the Bleeding Heart. Mater Adolerata! A. Capital A. Adulteress. Glittering with gold thread. Abel! Adultery. Admirable!

It is, perhaps, the most colossal satire ever penned. *The Scarlet Letter*. And by a blue-eyed darling of a Nathaniel.

Not Bumppo, however.

The human spirit, fixed in a lie, adhering to a lie, giving itself perpetually the lie.

All begins with A.

Adulteress. Alpha. Abel, Adam. A. America.

The Scarlet Letter.

"Had there been a Papist among the crowd of Puritans, he might have seen in this beautiful woman, so picturesque in her attire and mien, and with the infant at her bosom, an object to remind him of the image of Divine Maternity, which so many illustrious painters have vied with one another to represent; something which should remind him, indeed, but only by contrast, of that sacred image of sinless Motherhood, whose infant was to redeem the world."

Whose infant was to redeem the world indeed! It will be a startling redemption the world will get from the American infant.

"Here was a taint of deepest sin in the most sacred quality of human life, working such effect that the world was only the darker for this woman's beauty, and more lost for the infant she had borne."

Just listen to the darling. Isn't he a master of apology?

Of symbols, too.

His pious blame is a chuckle of praise all the while.

Oh, Hester, you are a demon. A man *must* be pure, just so that you can seduce him to a fall. Because the greatest thrill in life is to bring down the Sacred Saint with a flop into the mud. Then when you've brought him down, humbly wipe off the mud with your hair, another Magdalen. And then go home and dance a witch's jig of triumph, and stitch yourself a Scarlet Letter with gold thread, as duchesses used to stitch themselves coronets. And then stand meek on the scaffold and fool the world. Who will all be envying you your sin, and beating you because you've stolen an advantage over them.

Hester Prynne is the great nemesis of woman. She is the KNOWING Ligeia risen diabolic from the grave. Having her own back. UNDERSTANDING.

This time it is Mr. Dimmesdale who dies. She lives on and is Abel.

His spiritual love was a lie. And prostituting the woman to his spiritual love, as popular clergymen do, in his preachings and loftiness, was a tall white lie. Which came flop.

We are so pure in spirit. Hi-tiddly-i-ty!

Till she tickled him in the right place, and he fell.

Flop.

Flop goes spiritual love.

But keep up the game. Keep up appearances. Pure are the pure. To the pure all things, etc.

Look out, Mister, for the Female Devotee. Whatever you do, don't let her start tickling you. She knows your weak spot. Mind your Purity.

When Hester Prynne seduced Arthur Dimmesdale it was the beginning of the end. But from the beginning of the end to the end of the end is a hundred years or two.

Mr. Dimmesdale also wasn't at the end of his resources. Previously, he had lived by governing his body, ruling it, in the interests of his spirit. Now he has a good time all by himself torturing his body, whipping it, piercing it with thorns, macerating himself. It's a form of masturbation. He wants to get a mental grip on his body. And since he can't quite manage it with the mind, witness his fall—he will give it what for, with whips. His will shall *lash* his body. And he enjoys his pains. Wallows in them. To the pure all things are pure.

It is the old self-mutilation process, gone rotten. The mind wanting to get its teeth in the blood and flesh. The ego exulting in the tortures of the mutinous flesh. I, the ego, I *will* triumph over my own flesh. Lash! Lash! I am a grand free spirit. *Lash!* I am the master of my soul! *Lash! Lash!* I am the captain of my soul. *Lash!* Hurray! "In the fell clutch of circumstance," etc., etc.

Good-bye Arthur. He depended on women for his Spiritual Devotees, spiritual bribes. So, the woman just touched him in his weak spot, his Achilles Heel of the flesh. Look out for the spiritual bride. She's after the weak spot.

It is the battle of wills.

"For the will therein lieth, which dieth not—"

The Scarlet Woman becomes a Sister of Mercy. Didn't she just, in the late war. Oh, Prophet Nathaniel!

Hester urges Dimmesdale to go away with her, to a new country, to a new life. He isn't having any.

He knows there is no new country, no new life on the globe to-day. It is the same old thing, in different degrees, everywhere. *Plus ça change, plus c'est la même chose.*

Hester thinks, with Dimmesdale for her husband, and Pearl for her child, in Australia, maybe, she'd have been perfect.

But she wouldn't. Dimmesdale had already fallen from his integrity as a minister of the Gospel of the Spirit. He had lost his manliness. He didn't see the point of just leaving himself between the hands of a woman and going away to a "new country," to be her thing entirely. She'd only have despised him more, as every woman despises a man who has "fallen" to her; despises him with her tenderest lust.

He stood for nothing any more. So let him stay where he was and dree out his weird.

She had dished him and his spirituality, so he hated her. As Angel Clare was dished, and hated Tess. As Jude in the end hated Sue: or should have done. The women make fools of them, the spiritual men. And when, as men, they've gone flop in their spirituality, they can't pick themselves up whole any more. So they just crawl, and die detesting the female, or the females, who made them fall.

The saintly minister gets a bit of his own back, at the last minute, by making public confession from the very scaffold where she was exposed. Then he dodges into death. But he's had a bit of his own back, on everybody.

" 'Shall we not meet again?' whispered she, bending her face down close to him. 'Shall we not spend our immortal life together? Surely, surely we have ransomed one another with all this woe! Thou lookest far into eternity with those bright dying eyes. Tell me what thou seest!' "

" 'Hush, Hester—hush,' said he, with tremulous solemnity. 'The law we broke!—the sin here so awfully revealed! Let these alone be in thy thoughts. I fear! I fear!' "

So he dies, throwing the "sin" in her teeth, and escaping into death.

The law we broke, indeed. You bet!

Whose law!

But it is truly a law, that man must either stick to the belief he has grounded himself on, and obey the laws of that belief, or he must admit the belief itself to be inadequate, and prepare himself for a new thing.

There was no change in belief, either in Hester or in Dimmesdale or in Hawthorne or in America. The same old treacherous belief, which was really cunning disbelief, in the Spirit, in Purity, in Selfless Love, and in Pure Consciousness. They would go on following this belief, for the sake of the sensationalism of it. But they would make a fool of it all the time. Like Woodrow Wilson, and the rest of modern Believers. The rest of modern Saviours.

If you meet a Saviour, to-day, be sure he is trying to make an innermost fool of you. Especially if the saviour be an UNDERSTANDING WOMAN, offering her love.

Hester lives on, pious as pie, being a public nurse. She becomes at last an acknowledged saint, Abel of the Scarlet Letter.

She would, being a woman. She has had her triumph over the individual man, so she quite loves subscribing to the whole spiritual life of society. She will make herself as false as hell, for society's sake, once she's had her real triumph over Saint Arthur.

Blossoms out into a Sister-of-Mercy Saint.

But it's a long time before she really takes anybody in. People kept on thinking her a witch, which she was.

As a matter of fact, unless a woman is held, by man, safe within the bounds of belief, she becomes inevitably a destructive force. She can't help herself. A woman is almost always vulnerable to pity. She can't bear to see anything *physically* hurt. But let a woman loose from the bounds and restraints of man's fierce belief, in his gods and in himself, and she becomes a gentle devil. She becomes subtly diabolic. The colossal evil of the united spirit of Woman. WOMAN, German woman or American woman, or every other sort of woman, in the last war, was something frightening. As every *man* knows.

Woman becomes a helpless, would-be-loving demon. She is helpless. Her very love is a subtle poison.

Unless a man believes in himself and his gods, *genuinely:* unless he fiercely obeys his own Holy Ghost; his woman will destroy him. Woman is the nemesis of doubting man. She can't help it.

And with Hester, after Ligeia, woman becomes a nemesis to man. She bolsters him up from the outside, she destroys him from the inside. And he dies hating her, as Dimmesdale did.

Dimmesdale's spirituality had gone on too long, too far. It had become a false thing. He found his nemesis in woman. And he was done for.

Woman is a strange and rather terrible phenomenon, to man. When the subconscious soul of woman recoils from its creative union with man, it becomes a destructive force. It exerts, willy-nilly, an invisible destructive influence. The woman herself may be as nice as milk, to all appearance, like Ligeia. But she is sending out waves of silent destruction of the faltering spirit in men, all the same. She doesn't know it. She can't even help it. But she does it. The devil is in her.

The very women who are most busy saving the bodies of men, and saving the children: these women-doctors, these nurses, these educationalists, these public-spirited women, these female saviours: they are all, from the inside, sending out waves of destructive malevolence which eat out the inner life of a man, like a cancer. It is so, it will be so, till men realize it and react to save themselves.

God won't save us. The women are so devilish godly. Men must save themselves in this strait, and by no sugary means either.

A woman can use her sex in sheer malevolence and poison, while she is *behaving* as meek and good as gold. Dear darling, she is really snow-white in her blamelessness. And all the while she is using her sex as a she-devil, for the endless hurt of her man. She doesn't know it. She will never believe it if you tell her. And if you give her a slap in the face for her fiendishness, she will rush to the first magistrate, in indignation. She is so *absolutely* blameless, the she-devil, the dear, dutiful creature.

Give her the great slap, just the same, just when she is being most angelic. Just when she is bearing her cross most meekly.

Oh, woman out of bounds is a devil. But it is man's fault. Woman never *asked,* in the first place, to be cast out of her bit of an Eden of belief and trust. It is man's business to bear the responsibility of belief. If he becomes a spiritual fornicator and liar, like Ligeia's husband and Arthur Dimmesdale, how *can* a woman believe in him? Belief doesn't go by choice. And if a woman doesn't believe in a *man,* she believes, essentially, in nothing. She becomes, willy-nilly, a devil.

A devil she is, and a devil she will be. And most men will succumb to her devilishness.

Hester Prynne was a devil. Even when she was so meekly going round as a sick-nurse. Poor Hester. Part of her wanted to be saved from her own devilishness. And another part wanted to go on and on in devilishness, for revenge. Revenge! REVENGE! It is this that fills the unconscious spirit of woman to-day. Revenge against man, and against the spirit of man, which has betrayed her into unbelief. Even when she is most sweet and a salvationist, she is her most devilish, is woman. She gives her man the sugar-plum of her own submissive sweetness. And when he's taken this sugar-plum in his mouth, a scorpion comes out of it. After he's taken this Eve to his bosom, oh, so loving, she destroys him inch by inch. Woman and her revenge! She will have it, and go on having it, for decades and decades, unless she's stopped. And to stop her you've got to believe in yourself and your gods, your own Holy Ghost, Sir Man; and then you've got to fight her, and never give in. She's a devil. But in the long run she is conquerable. And just a tiny bit of her wants to be conquered. You've got to fight three-quarters of her, in absolute hell, to get at the final quarter of her that wants a release, at last, from the hell of her own revenge. But it's a long last. And not yet.

"She had in her nature a rich, voluptuous, Oriental characteristic—a taste for the gorgeously beautiful." This is Hester. This is American. But she repressed her nature in the above direction. She would not even allow herself the luxury of labouring at fine, delicate stitching. Only she dressed her little sin-child Pearl vividly, and the scarlet letter was gorgeously embroidered. Her Hecate and Astarte insignia.

"A voluptuous, oriental characteristic—" That lies waiting in American women. It is probable that the Mormons are the forerunners of the coming real America. It is probable that men will have more than one wife, in the coming America. That you will have again a half-oriental womanhood, and a polygamy.

The grey nurse, Hester. The Hecate, the hell-cat. The slowly-evolving voluptuous female of the new era, with a whole new submissiveness to the dark, phallic principle.

But it takes time. Generation after generation of nurses and political women and salvationists. And in the end, the dark erection of the images of sex-worship once more, and the newly submissive women. That kind of depth. Deep women in that respect. When we have at last broken this insanity of mental-spiritual consciousness. And the women *choose* to experience again the great submission.

"The poor, whom she sought out to be the objects of her bounty, often reviled the hand that was stretched to succour them."

Naturally. The poor hate a salvationist. They smell the devil underneath.

"She was patient—a martyr indeed—but she forbore to pray for her enemies, lest, in spite of her forgiving aspirations, the words of the blessing should stubbornly twist themselves into a curse."

So much honesty, at least. No wonder the old witch-lady Mistress Hibbins claimed her for another witch.

"She grew to have a dread of children; for they had imbibed from their parents a vague idea of something horrible in this dreary woman gliding silently through the town, with never any companion but only one child."

"A vague idea!" Can't you see her "gliding silently?" It's not a question of a vague idea imbibed, but a definite feeling directly received.

"But sometimes, once in many days, or perchance in many months, she felt an eye—a human eye—upon the ignominious brand, that seemed to give a momentary relief, as if half her agony were shared. The next instant, back it all rushed again, with a still deeper throb of pain; for in that brief interval she had sinned again. Had Hester sinned alone?"

Of course not. As for sinning again, she would go on all her life silently, changelessly "sinning." She never repented. Not she. Why should she? She had brought down Arthur Dimmesdale, that too-too snow-white bird, and that was her life-work.

As for sinning again when she met two dark eyes in a crowd, why, of course. Somebody who understood as she understood.

I always remember meeting the eyes of a gipsy woman, for one moment, in a crowd, in England. She knew, and I knew. What did we know? I was not able to make out. But we knew.

Probably the same fathomless hate of this spiritual-conscious society in which the outcast woman and I both roamed like meek-looking wolves. Tame wolves waiting to shake off their tameness. Never able to.

And again, that "voluptuous, Oriental" characteristic that knows the mystery of the ithyphallic gods. She would not betray the ithyphallic gods to this white, leprous-white society of "lovers." Neither will I, if I can help it. These leprous-white, seducing, spiritual women, who "understand" so much. One has been too often seduced, and "understood." "I can read him like a book," said my first lover of me. The book is in several volumes, dear. And more and more comes back to me the gulf of dark hate and *other* understanding, in the eyes of the gipsy woman. So different from the hateful white light of understanding which floats like scum on the eyes of white, oh, so white English and American women, with their understanding voices and their deep, sad words, and their profound, *good* spirits. Pfui!

Hester was scared only of one result of her sin: Pearl. Pearl, the scarlet letter incarnate. The little girl. When women bear children, they produce either devils or sons with gods in them. And it is an evolutionary process. The devil in Hester produced a purer devil in Pearl. And the devil in Pearl will produce—she married an Italian Count—a piece of purer devilishness still.

And so from hour to hour we ripe and ripe.

And then from hour to hour we rot and rot.

There was that in the child "which often impelled Hester to ask in bitterness of heart, whether it were for good or ill that the poor little creature had been born at all."

For ill, Hester. But don't worry. Ill is as necessary as good. Malevolence is as necessary as benevolence. If you have brought forth, spawned, a young malevolence, be sure there is a rampant falseness in the world against which this malevolence must be turned. Falseness has to be bitten and bitten, till it is bitten to death. Hence Pearl.

Pearl. Her own mother compares her to the demon of plague, or scarlet fever, in her red dress. But then, plague is necessary to destroy a rotten, false humanity.

Pearl, the devilish girl-child, who can be so tender and loving and *understanding,* and then, when she has understood, will give you a hit across the mouth, and turn on you with a grin of sheer diabolic jeering.

Serves you right, you shouldn't be *understood.* That is your vice. You shouldn't want to be loved, and then you'd not get hit across the mouth. Pearl will love you: marvelously. And she'll hit you across the mouth: oh, so neatly. And serves you right.

Pearl is perhaps the most modern child in all literature.

Old-fashioned Nathaniel, with his little-boy charm, he'll tell you what's what. But he'll cover it with smarm.

Hester simply *hates* her child, from one part of herself. And from another, she cherishes her child as her one precious treasure. For Pearl is the continuing of her female revenge on life. But female revenge hits both ways. Hits back at its own mother. The female revenge in Pearl hits back at Hester, the mother, and Hester is simply livid with fury and "sadness," which is rather amusing.

"The child could not be made amenable to rules. In giving her existence a great law had been broken; and the result was a being whose elements were perhaps beautiful and brilliant, but all in disorder, or with an order peculiar to themselves, amidst which the point of variety and arrangement was difficult or impossible to discover."

Of course, the order is peculiar to themselves. But the point of variety is this: "Draw out the loving, sweet soul, draw it out with marvellous understanding; and then spit in its eye."

Hester, of course, didn't at all like it when her sweet child drew out her motherly soul, with yearning and deep understanding: and then spit in the motherly eye, with a grin. But it was a process the mother had started.

Pearl had a peculiar look in her eyes: "a look so intelligent, yet so inexplicable, so perverse, sometimes so malicious, but generally accompanied by a wild flow of spirits, that Hester could not help questioning at such moments whether Pearl was a human child."

A little demon! But her mother, and the saintly Dimmesdale, had borne her. And Pearl, by the very openness of her perversity, was more straightforward than her parents. She flatly refuses any Heavenly Father, seeing the earthly one such a fraud. And she has the pietistic Dimmesdale on toast, spits right in his eye: in both his eyes.

Poor, brave, tormented little soul, always in a state of recoil, she'll be a devil to men when she grows up. But the men deserve it. If they'll let themselves be "drawn," by her loving understanding, they deserve that she shall slap them across the mouth the moment they *are* drawn. The chickens! Drawn and trussed.

Poor little phenomenon of a modern child, she'll grow up into the devil of a modern woman. The nemesis of weak-kneed modern men, craving to be love-drawn.

The third person in the diabolic trinity, or triangle, of the Scarlet Letter, is Hester's first husband, Roger Chillingworth. He is an old Elizabethan physician, with a grey beard and a long-furred coat and a twisted shoulder. Another healer. But something of an alchemist, a magician. He is a magician on the verge of modern science, like Francis Bacon.

Roger Chillingworth is of the old order of intellect, in direct line from the mediæval Roger Bacon alchemists. He has an old, intellectual belief in the dark sciences, the Hermetic philosophies. He is no Christian, no selfless aspirer. He is not an aspirer. He is the old authoritarian in man. The old male authority. But without passional belief. Only intellectual belief in himself and his male authority.

Shakespeare's whole tragic wail is because of the downfall of the true male authority, the ithyphallic authority and masterhood. It fell with Elizabeth. It was trodden underfoot with Victoria.

But Chillingworth keeps on the *intellectual* tradition. He hates the new spiritual aspirers, like Dimmesdale, with a black, crippled hate. He is the old male authority, in intellectual tradition.

You can't keep a wife by force of an intellectual tradition. So Hester took to seducing Dimmesdale.

Yet her only marriage, and her last oath, is with the old Roger. He and she are accomplices in pulling down the spiritual saint.

"Why dost thou smile so at me——" she says to her old, vengeful husband. "Art thou not like the Black Man that haunts the forest around us? Hast thou not enticed me into a bond which will prove the ruin of my soul?"

"Not thy soul!" he answered with another smile. "No, not thy soul!"

It is the soul of the pure preacher, that false thing, which they are after. And the crippled physician—this other healer—blackly vengeful in his old, distorted male authority, and the "loving" woman, they bring down the saint between them.

A black and complementary hatred, akin to love, is what Chillingworth feels for the young, saintly parson. And Dimmesdale responds, in a hideous kind of love.

Slowly the saint's life is poisoned. But the black old physician smiles, and tries to keep him alive. Dimmesdale goes in for self-torture, self-lashing, lashing his own white, thin, spiritual saviour's body. The dark old Chillingworth listens outside the door and laughs, and prepares another medicine, so that the game can go on longer. And the saint's very soul goes rotten. Which is the supreme triumph. Yet he keeps up appearances still.

The black, vengeful soul of the crippled, masterful male, still dark in his authority: and the white ghastliness of the fallen saint! The two halves of manhood mutually destroying one another.

Dimmesdale has a "coup" in the very end. He gives the whole show away by confessing publicly on the scaffold, and dodging into death, leaving Hester dished, and Roger as it were, doubly cuckolded. It is a neat last revenge.

Down comes the curtain, as in Ligeia's poem.

But the child Pearl will be on in the next act, with her Italian Count and a new brood of vipers. And Hester greyly Abelling, in the shadows, after her rebelling.

It is a marvellous allegory. It is to me one of the greatest allegories in all literature, *The Scarlet Letter*. Its marvellous under-meaning! And its perfect duplicity.

The absolute duplicity of that blue-eyed *Wunderkind* of a Nathaniel. The American wonder-child, with his magical allegorical insight.

But even wonder-children have to grow up in a generation or two.

And even SIN becomes stale.

Leslie A. Fiedler
ACCOMMODATION
AND TRANSCENDENCE

II

Hawthorne's sense of having produced a "hell-fired" book may have been aggravated by the fact that he was dealing, however obliquely, with the ticklish subject of adultery. Certainly, *The Scarlet Letter,* is the only eminent American book before the modern period to have made—or to have seemed to make—passionate love its center, and it was this which moved the scandalized critics to talk about the beginnings of "a French era" in our chaste literature. Actually, Hawthorne's short novel is not as much against the American grain as it superficially appears to be. Master of duplicity, he is especially duplicitous in this regard, refusing, for instance, even to mention in his text the word "adultery," though the "A" which symbolizes it glows at the center of almost every scene. The little Puritan children of the seventeenth century, franker than adults of the nineteenth, are permitted "the utterance of the word that had no distinct purport to their own minds, but was more than terrible to her [Hester] . . ."; but the reader is not permitted to overhear it. As a matter of fact, little children in more recent generations, taking the book off the shelves in the children's library, where it has been permitted to stay by the most high-minded librarians, have doubtless been puzzled over what the mysterious letter does stand for, since no word for Hester's crime that is familiar to them begins with that chaste letter.

Though sex is centrally present in *The Scarlet Letter* as it is not in our other great novels, it is there rendered reticently, incomprehensibly enough to seem, though not innocent, perhaps, as good as innocent. Hawthorne's book seems finally not one of those disturbing "French" books at all! To understand just how shadowy and sterilized its treatment of passion really is, it is only necessary to compare Hawthorne's novella with a real example of the continental novel, with Rousseau's *Nouvelle Héloïse,* for instance. Vernon Loggins has argued quite convincingly that

From *Love and Death in the American Novel* (New York: Criterion Books, 1960), pp. 495–519.

this anti-bourgeois sentimental novel was one of the prototypes in Hawthorne's mind when he began his own work. We know that he regarded it highly all his life, first reading it because it was forbidden, and describing it as "admirable" in a list of books which he prepared for himself at the age of sixteen. More importantly, he returned to it just when he was ready to produce *The Scarlet Letter,* bogging down this time, but reviving in himself a sense of that forbidden and secretly relished work. In the course of a pilgrimage to the Rousseau country in 1859, he wrote:

> In Switzerland, I found myself more affected by Clarens, the scene of the love of St. Preux and Julia, than I have often been by the scenes of romance and poetry. I read Rousseau's romance with great sympathy when I was hardly more than a boy; ten years ago or more I tried it again, without success; but from my feeling of yesterday I think it still retains its hold on my imagination.

It is possible to exaggerate the parallels between the book that moved Hawthorne in his youth and the one he wrote in his middle age, yet certain general similarities are really there. The three characters of Julie, Saint-Preux, and Wolmar correspond illuminatingly with Hester, Dimmesdale, and Chillingworth; and the basic pattern of the *Nouvelle Héloïse* is repeated in *The Scarlet Letter:* a second temptation after a first fall, ending in an unnatural triangle perpetuated under strange circumstances. The differences, however, are more striking and more significant, especially the expurgation in Hawthorne's book of all direct reference to the physical aspects of passion. From Hawthorne's imagination, fired in adolescence, Rousseau's fable must pass through his conscience, created in solitude and confirmed in his marriage to a good woman; and it emerges finally much transformed. The dangerous doctrines that passion justifies all and that adulterous love renounced on earth will be recognized in heaven survive in Hawthorne not as articles of faith, but as problematical convictions, temptations to Faustian pride. Moreover, passion is rendered in *The Scarlet Letter* not as lived, but as remembered or proposed. The reality of the flesh, which in Rousseau provides a counterbalance to his excessive sentimentality, tends to disappear in Hawthorne. For the latter, sex is sex-in-the-head; and the nearest thing to a passionate moment in *The Scarlet Letter* comes, as we have noted, when Hester unbinds her luxurious hair.

The anti-rhetoric of Hawthorne, which defends him against sentimentality, also prevents him from rendering sensuality, dissolves all ecstacies in ironies. Everywhere in his work a peculiar tension is created between the passionate analogues he evokes and the dispassionate quality of his actual text. Behind Dimmesdale and Hester, we are aware not only of Saint-Preux and Julie, but of the original Abelard and Héloïse, castrated priest and his beloved, and of David and Bathsheba, whose love is portrayed in the tapestries of Dimmesdale's house. Again and again in the text, references are made to the infamous Overbury case, Chillingworth being identified with the Dr. Forman who was its chief villain. But the filth involved in that case: the suggestions of homosexuality, the aphrodisiacs, the poison enemas, the wax mommets with a "thorn thrust through the privity"—all these are transmuted into abstract evocations of evil and concupiscence.

In the end, we are left with the sense that surely something more terrible than mere adultery is at stake behind all the reticences and taboos, that Hawthorne may be dealing, half-consciously at least, with the sin of incest, for which his mother's family, the Mannings, had once been publicly disgraced. So at least one commentator (Vernon Loggins in *The Hawthornes*) has suggested, and this Hawthorne's life-long preoccupation with the theme, as well as the moment at which he composed his greatest novel, would seem to confirm. *Felt's Annals,* referred to in the "Custom-House Introduction," records the unsavory case of the Mannings; and the pictures it evokes jibe with the key images of *The Scarlet Letter:* two girls in the market-place, each with an "I" in her cap; and their beloved brother fleeing through the lawless wilderness! Brother-sister incest: it is the kind of love, as we have seen, proper to the gothic tale, of which *The Scarlet Letter* is the supreme example in our fiction; but in that book, it has been translated down to a less terrible crime, which itself has been reduced to its own mere initial. Historically, a woman found guilty of adultery would have been condemned to wear the two letters "AD"; but this seems to Hawthorne not abstract enough, and he substitutes the single "A," that represents the beginning of all things, and that, in the primers of New England, stood for *Adam's Fall*—in which we (quite unspecifically) sinned all!

The carnal act upon which adultery depends is not merely unnamed in *The Scarlet Letter;* it is further deprived of reality by being displaced in time, postulated rather than described. So displaced, that act becomes, in the psychologist's sense, prehistoric; affects us much as the spied-upon primal scene (mother and father intertwined in bed), blurred by the amnesia of guilt. It is an original sin, more an "emblem" or a "type," in Hawthorne's terms, than a deed. "Ye that wronged me are not sinful," Chillingworth says to his wife and her lover, "save in a kind of typical illusion." In one sense, the postulated original sin seems merely a convenient explanatory device. Certainly, it accounts naturalistically for the existence of Pearl, the illegitimate daughter of Hester. But Pearl seems less a real child than an allegorical representation of the fruits of sin; and we are offered, as if jestingly, the alternative explanation that she is a by-blow of the Devil. In addition, Hester must be from the very beginning a mother (it is, as if, while presumably expurgating *Geschwisterinzest* from his novel, Hawthorne is pushing it back toward its pure Oedipal form), though she appears among men who are, within the time of the story itself, rendered as impotent. The impotence of Dimmesdale, however, must be felt as a punishment, the typical self-castration of the seducer, celebrated in the American novel from the time of *Charlotte Temple;* and we are, therefore, asked to believe that at some point before the action begins he traduced Hester's innocence, thus unmanning himself. Actually, he is portrayed as one for whom sex is a remembered nightmare or a futilely longed-for hope; and he does not even kiss Hester at his moment of Satanic exhilaration in the forest.

If it is finally hard for us to believe *on a literal level* in the original adultery of

Hester and Dimmesdale, this is because their whole pre-history remains shadowy and vague. Hawthorne's gestures at indicating the social backgrounds and historical contexts of his characters are half-hearted and unconvincing, a bow toward realism. And his book is finally dream-like rather than documentary, not at all the historical novel it has been often called—evoking the past as nightmare rather than fact. But a nightmare of the past calls up a past without a past of its own. It is, therefore, easier to believe in the diabolical transportation of Chillingworth from Germany than in any more rational theory of his arrival on the scene; just as it is easier to imagine Pearl plucked from a rosebush than carried for nine months within her mother. All the characters come into existence when the book begins and do not survive it. Hester is simply not there until the prison doors open; and at that moment Chillingworth drops from the air. So born they must die with the action's close—contrary to the traditions of the Victorian novel. For all his desire to end his book like his contemporaries, Hawthorne finds it difficult to say simply that Pearl left the country and married well. He is much more comfortable with the end of Chillingworth, who withered away, as is quite proper for a protagonist regarded by his author as a "shadowy figure," one of a "tribe of unrealities," who cease to exist when he stops thinking of them.

Actors in a dark hallucination, Hawthorne's protagonists are aptly moved by a guilt as hallucinatory as themselves: a crime as vaguely defined, though as inescapable in its consequences, as the unknowable transgression in Kafka's *The Trial.* It is enough for Hawthorne to suggest the Oedipus situation: an equivocal mother, an evil father—and between them, Dimmesdale, who is described at first as "childlike" and at last as "childish." The whole action moves toward the climactic moment, when, after years of cowardly silence and a momentary temptation to flee, that child-figure totters into the noonday public square to confess his fault before the whole community. At that point, Oedipus-Dimmesdale blends with the image of Doctor Johnson standing in the Uttotexter market-place to make public amends for an offense against his father. It is a story which obsessed Hawthorne all his life, which he wrote out as an exemplary tale for children and told himself in his diary, a story obviously representing to him some buried guilt of his own.

That guilt the prehistoric fall of *The Scarlet Letter* explains, too, in encoded form. It is incarnate in Hester, most "gorgeous" of his Dark Ladies; for "gorgeous" is to Hawthorne a dirty word—a token of pollution. But why is gorgeousness a trap and love a crime, why beauty forbidden and joy banned to the nineteenth-century American? There was, *The Scarlet Letter* suggests, another fall in the Eden of the New World at precisely the moment at which the book unfolds, a communal fall to match Hester's private one. The very first page tells us that "whatever Utopia of human virtue and happiness" men may imagine in whatever land, they find it necessary "to allot a portion of the virgin soil as a cemetery, and another portion as the site of a prison." Before such a prison, Hawthorne's tale begins, and in such a cemetery, it comes to a close; and between, he attempts to explain how sin and death, for whose sake they exist, have come into the Puritan Commonwealth. Yet it is, finally, his own crisis of conscience that Hawthorne translates into a mythical history of America, his own experience of womanhood that he projects in Hester.

Sitting day after day beside the bed of his dying mother, confronted by his wife of whom she did not approve, and watching through the window his daughter Una playing the death scene to which she must eventually come—Hawthorne must have become aware with special poignancy of the web of femaleness in which we are involved from cradle to grave. But what this glimpse into the maternal mysteries did to him we do not know, except for the fact that he wept once when his mother died, again when he had finished the "hell-fired" book which is her memorial; and that somewhere between these two public betrayals of emotion, he suffered from what his family called "brain fever." The book itself betrays the recrudescence in his imagination of the incest theme which had prompted "Alice Doane's Appeal," and of the Oedipal guilt which that unmanageable story projects.

The incest theme, however, even in its disguise of adultery, belongs primarily to the pre-plot of *The Scarlet Letter;* its plot is concerned with a second, quite different fall. Like the *Nouvelle Héloïse,* Hawthorne's book is in two parts: the first a little scandalous, the second quite moral; but unlike his French counterpart, Hawthorne, the good American, has not written the first part at all! It is there only by implication; and the kind of reader who skips the more virtuous half of Rousseau's novel, must give up reading Hawthorne entirely. His book is concerned only with a second temptation, in the face of which his characters, postulated as having been powerless before the "dark necessity" of their original fall, are portrayed as capable of free choice. Yet their freedom is ironic, for what they must learn freely to accept is the notion that freedom is the recognition of necessity. *The Scarlet Letter* is the most anti-utopian of American books: not the Paradise Regained it seems at first, but only an Eden Revisited.

In the seeming Eden of the New World, a man and woman, who are still essentially the old Adam and Eve, deceive themselves for a moment into believing that they can escape the consequences of sin. The woman has served a prison term and bears on her breast the sign of her shame, and the man, who was the occasion of that shame, has lived secretly with his guilt and powerless remorse; yet in their deluded hope, they meet in the forest, plot a flight from the world of law and religion. For an instant, that hope seems to transfigure not only them but the dark wood into which they have strayed. When Hester flings aside the scarlet letter and lets down her hair, the forest glows to life: "Such was the sympathy of ... wild, heathen Nature ... never subjugated by law, nor illumined by higher truth with the bliss of these two spirits. Love ... must always create a sunshine that overflows upon the natural world."

Yet Hawthorne cannot grant these lovers even the mitigated bliss he earlier permitted the May King and Queen in "The Maypole of Merry Mount"; for between them lies the taboo of adultery, as real to him as to his ancestors. And even the forest, symbol to Hawthorne of the unredeemed primitive, can hold its glow no longer than can Hester's face. The forest brook, which has all along played a chorus to their scene, leaves off its illusory song of joy, and begins again its melancholy murmuring "with not a whit more cheerfulness than for ages heretofore." The promise of Eden Redeemed has turned out to be illusory for Hester and Dimmesdale, who have tried to persuade themselves that passion has a sanctity of its own, capable of transfiguring the natural world; but have ended up on the verge of a second sin more terrible than their first. This time they are about to sin not in the blindness of passion but in full consciousness, to fall not in prehistory but in time. This second fall, whose essence is a denial of the first, Hawthorne describes in terms of inscribing oneself in the Black Man's Book, selling one's soul to the Devil.

Hawthorne does not accept without qualification the judgment of his ancestors, though he condemns Hester's proposal of flight even as they would have, uses to describe it the Faustian metaphor. He is, after all, a modern, secular thinker, for whom nothing is self-evident, everything problematical; and he is being tempted as he writes to make a retreat from his own community very like Hester's. Yet, for all his quarrel with Puritanism and its persecuting zeal, he knows that no American can really leave behind the America which the Puritans have once and for all defined. An implicit theme of *The Scarlet Letter* suggests that there is no way, short of self-destruction, to escape from the "settlement": the middle ground between the abandoned terror of Europe (feudalism and Catholicism, turned into meaningless tyranny) and the still unpenetrated terror of the heathen wilderness. Hester and Dimmesdale meditate both avenues of escape that have, ever since, teased the imaginations of discontented Americans: Europe and the West, a living past and an eternally receding future. They learn, however, that they must accept the American present, though it means death or life-long penance; for all else is "damnation," a capitulation to the diabolical Chillingworth. European conjurer and Indian medicine man in one, he represents the evil spell of both impossible worlds which lure the American from his true identity and true center; and he is quite properly defeated in the market-place of Boston.

America represents for Hawthorne not only the marginal settlement, set between corrupt civilization and unredeemed nature, but also the rule of moral law in the place of self-justifying passion or cynical gallantry. In *The Scarlet Letter,* passion justifies nothing, while its denial redeems all. The fallen Eden of this world remains fallen; but the sinful priest purges himself by public confession, becomes worthy of his sole remaining way to salvation, death. Even Hester, though sin and suffering have made her an almost magical figure, a polluted but still terrible goddess, must finally accept loneliness and self-restraint instead of the love and freedom she dreamed. She cannot become the greater Ann Hutchinson she might have been had she remained unfallen, cannot redeem her sex from the indignities against which she once raged and plotted in secret. Passion has opened up for her no new possibilities, only closed off older ones.

The relationship of Hester and Dimmesdale is not, however, the only passionate connection in the novel. Through the five years covered by the book's action (the unwritten pre-plot takes up two more, from the marriage with Chillingworth to the birth of Pearl, thus adding up to the mystic seven), one relationship grows in intimacy, depth, and terror. In it, Dimmesdale plays a key role once more, though this time a passive, feminine one, his tremulous hand laid to his heart. Between him and Chillingworth, grows an intense, destructive emotion (a "dark passion," Hawthorne calls it), compounded of the intolerable intimacy of doctor and patient, analyst and analysand, husband and wife, father and son, cuckold and cuckolder. It is a bond like that which elsewhere in American literature joins together Simon Legree and Uncle Tom, Claggart and Billy Budd, Babo and Benito Cereno.

Both earlier and later in Hawthorne's own work, such connections exist between the sexes: father and daughter, as in "Rappaccini's Daughter"; husband and wife, as in "The Birthmark"; mesmerist and female subject, as in *The Blithedale Romance;* or lover and beloved, as in "Ethan Brand." Esther in the latter work, Hawthorne describes as "the girl whom, with such cold and remorseless purpose, Ethan Brand had made the subject of a psychological experiment, and wasted, absorbed and perhaps annihilated her soul in the process." It is a pattern as old in our fiction as Brockden Brown's *Wieland;* and the prototype of the destructive lover is Carwin, in whom the seducer is merged (following Goethe's example) with the scientist, Don Juan with Faust. In Brown, however, as in Hawthorne everywhere else, the dark passion exists between a man and a woman. Chillingworth, however, is as much a devil as a man; while Dimmesdale is, of course, male: a one-time seducer reduced by unconfessed guilt to feminine passivity. And their relationship seems an odd combination of the tie between Faust and Gretchen, on the one hand, with that between Faust and Mephistopheles on the other.

The terms used to define the nature of their union are significant: "a kind of intimacy," a "paternal and reverential love," described by Dimmesdale's parishioners as the "best possible measure . . . unless he had selected some one of the many blooming damsels to become his devoted wife." Hester, who has been the wife of one and the mistress of the other, yet never as close to either as they are to each other, says reproachfully to Chillingworth: "no man is so near to him as you. . . . You are beside him, sleeping and waking. . . . You burrow and rankle in his heart. Your clutch is on his life." "Burrow" is the key word for Chillingworth's penetration of Dimmesdale's heart: "burrow into his intimacy . . . deep into the patient's bosom . . . delving . . . probing . . . in a dark cavern." The climax comes with the exposure of the secret of Dimmesdale's bosom, his own scarlet letter, embossed (perhaps!) in the very flesh. "He laid his hand on his bosom, and thrust aside the vestment," Hawthorne says at the moment of revelation, portraying Chillingworth in an ecstasy, leaping into the air. He knows at last the ultimate secret of his dearest enemy; and knowing it, has possessed him, accomplished a rape of the spirit beyond any penetration of the flesh. "He has violated," Hester comments, echoing Hawthorne's description of Ethan Brand, "the sanctity of the human heart."

Hawthorne is not content, however, to leave the last word with Hester, answering her in his own voice, his own typically hypothetical manner:

> It is a curious subject of observation and inquiry, whether hatred and love be not the same thing at bottom. Each, in its utmost development, supposes a high degree of intimacy and heart knowledge; each renders one individual dependent for the food . . . of his spiritual life upon another. . . . In the spiritual world, the old physician and the minister—may, unawares, have found their earthly stock of hatred and antipathy transmuted into golden love.

Out of the ambivalence of love and hatred, the constitutionally double-dealing Hawthorne has distilled an equivocation which undercuts, at the last moment, the whole suggested meaning of his book. He has not, to be sure, committed himself finally; but his last qualification for the passion of Chillingworth and Dimmesdale is favorable, while his last word on that of Hester and Dimmesdale is quite the opposite. Though earlier Hester has boasted, "What we did had a consecration of its own," the only proof of her assertion she could offer was, "We felt it so! We said so to each other!" Dimmesdale does not demur in the forest, where he is temporarily mad; but he answers Hester in the market-place, at his moment of greatest insight: "It may be that we forgot our God—when we violated our reverence for each other's soul. . . ."

As one bucket goes up, the other goes down; and we are left with the disturbing paradox (mitigated, to be sure, by Hawthorne's customary, pussyfooting subjunctives: "may have found," "may be that we forgot") that love may conceal a destructive impulse and work for ill, while hatred may be only a disguised form of love and eventuate in good. If on the one hand, *The Scarlet Letter* leads toward a Goethe-like justification of diabolism as an instrument of salvation, on the other hand, it insists, in a very American way, upon the dangers of passion. It is certainly true, in terms of the plot, that Chillingworth drives the minister toward confession and penance, while Hester would have lured him to evasion and flight. But this means, for all of Hawthorne's equivocations, that the eternal feminine does not draw us on toward grace, rather that the woman promises only madness and damnation. It is the eternal demonic—personified in the wronged husband—which leads Dimmesdale on; and saved by his personal Serpent, he can in turn save his Eve—his apparent weakness deliver her apparent strength.

There is, however, a turn of the screw even beyond this; for though Hester works, perhaps unwittingly, to destroy Dimmesdale, saps his courage and brings him to the verge of selling his soul, it is to her that he must turn for support. Morally, he is finally stronger than she, but physically he depends upon her as a child upon its mother. It is on her arm that he ascends the scaffold, on her breast that he rests his trembling head. "Is she angel or devil?" Hawthorne's wife had asked him of Beatrice Rappaccini, when he was in the process of creating that prototype of Hester; and his answer was that he did not know! With Hester herself, he is still equivocal; she is the female temptress of Puritan mythology, but also, though sullied, the secular madonna of sentimental Protestantism, a true descendant, via Julie, of Clarissa.

Similarly, Dimmesdale is a descendant of Lovelace via Saint-Preux; though he is further transformed, as we have noted, following the example of Mrs. Rowson's Montraville. There is, in Hawthorne, a certain irony in the treatment of the un-manned seducer who represents, if not himself, an important aspect of that self; yet not even Montraville staggers to his end as feebly as Dimmesdale. His final reduc-tion makes explicit the relationship in which the man and woman, who in the book's pre-history played Lovelace and Clarissa, now stand: "It was hardly a man with life in him that tottered on his path so nervelessly. . . . He still walked onward, if that movement could be so described, which rather resembled the wavering effort of an infant with its mother's arms in view. . . ." Such motherly arms do, indeed, wait to receive him, the arms of Hester, of whom earlier Hawthorne has written: "Had there been a Papist among the crowd of Puritans . . . he might have seen in this beautiful woman . . . the image of Divine Maternity. . . ." The guilty lovers' consum-mation plotted in the forest between the minister and the outcast does not take place; but that minister, become a child, embraces innocently that outcast, sanctified by motherhood. "They beheld the minister, leaning on Hester's shoulder and supported by her arm around him. . . . Hester partly raised him, and supported his head against her bosom. . . ." At the last moment of his life, Dimmesdale, the eternal son, has found his way back to the breast, no longer barred to him by law or taboo. The qualified happy ending comes this time not from *Paradise Lost* but *Paradise Regained:* "Home to his Mothers house private return'd." It is the most suitable of endings for a book produced out of the anguish of personal failure and the death of a mother.

The Scarlet Letter is, then, our only classic book which makes passion a central theme. Born into an age and a class pledged to gentility, Hawthorne was denied a vocabulary adequate to his subject, driven back on duplicity and cunning; and in the end, he seems to adorn that subject rather than present it, conceal it with fancy needlework, "so that the Capital A might have been thought to mean . . . anything other than Adulteress." Indeed, the phrase from "Endicott and the Red Cross," written some thirteen years before *The Scarlet Letter,* suggests that from the first the cryptic "A" may have represented to Hawthorne not only "Adultery" but "Art." Certainly, he regarded his own art as involving precisely that adornment of guilt by craft which he attributes to Hester's prototype: "sporting with her infamy, the lost and desperate creature had embroidered the fatal token with golden thread and the nicest art of needlework. . . ."

Unable to break through the limitations of his era or to repress the shame he felt at trifling with them, Hawthorne ended by writing in the form of a love story an elegiac treatise on the death of love. *The Scarlet Letter* is, in one of its major aspects, a portrayal of the attenuation of sex in America, the shrinking on our shores from Brobdingnagian parents to Lilliputian children. In a note in his journal,

Hawthorne reminds himself that Brobdingnag, where Gulliver once sat astride the nipples of gross, lusty girls, was located on the coast of North America, home of the mid-nineteenth-century fleshless bluestocking! *The Scarlet Letter* is concerned not only with passion but also with America (another possible signification of Hester's letter), that is to say, it attempts to find in the story of Hester and Dimmesdale a paradigm of the fall of love in the New World. The Puritans who move through Hawthorne's pages belong to a first-generation community, which, despite its revolt against the paternal figures of kings and bishops, has not itself lost "the quality of reverence" or contracted "the disease of sadness, which almost all children in these latter days inherit along with the scrofula...." The inhabitants of Hawthorne's seventeenth-century world still live in the Elizabethan afterglow; "for they were the offspring of sires ... who had known how to be merry...." It is the generation which succeeds them that made gaiety a "forgotten art" by darkening American life with "the blackest shade of Puritanism."

Hawthorne recreates these first ancestors not merely as merry rebels, but as mythical progenitors. Twice over he describes them as they pass ceremonially, a "procession of majestic and venerable fathers," among them his own ultimate "dim and dusky grandsire ... grave, bearded, sable-cloaked and steeple-crowned ..." And the mothers who inhabit Hawthorne's dream are scarcely less overwhelming. "The women ... stood within less than half a century of the period when Elizabeth had been the not altogether unsuitable representative of her sex ... The bright morning sun, therefore, shone on broad shoulders and well developed busts, and on round and ruddy cheeks, that ... had hardly grown paler and thinner in the atmosphere of New England." Hawthorne is, to be sure, somewhat ambivalent about the abundant fleshliness of these mothers of his race, suggesting that their "moral diet was not a bit more refined" than the beef and ale with which they satisfied their bellies. Yet there is something nostalgic, even rueful about his acknowledgement that since those early days "every successive mother has transmitted to her child a fainter bloom, a more delicate and briefer beauty, and a slighter physical frame...."

To the world of such lush and substantial women, Hester unquestionably belongs. She is not an "ethereal" latter-day invalid like Sophia Hawthorne, but "lady-like ... after the manner ... of those days; characterized by a certain state and dignity, rather than by the delicate, evanescent and indescribable grace, which is now recognized as its indication." Dimmesdale, however, is no father, no mythic progenitor at all; after his love affair, at least (in which surely he was more seduced than seducing), he has been shrunken to Lilliputian size—seems a modern, alienated, anguished artist, transported into a more heroic age. He is not a Puritan, but a child of the Puritans, their diminished offspring, inheritor of melancholy, and the prototype of Hawthorne's own fallen generation. His fall from potency and his return to the maternal embrace just before death constitute an "emblem" of the fate of the American male. After Hawthorne's account of the conversion of the "majestic and venerable fathers" into American boys the way is clear for the de-sexed evasions of

Melville and Mark Twain: the story of an orphaned Ishmael, picked up by the cruising *Rachel;* or the tale of the "motherless boy," Huck Finn, in his struggle with the world of mothers.

I I I

The Scarlet Letter is finally not essentially a love story at all; and though it is possible to gain some insights into its theme and tone by considering it an American, which is to say, a denatured and defleshed, *Nouvelle Héloïse,* it is more valuable to approach it as an American, which is to say, a less violent and hopeless, version of *The Monk.* Like Lewis' horror novel, Hawthorne's little book deals with a man of God led by the desire for a woman to betray his religious commitment, and finally almost (Hawthorne repents at the last moment, as Lewis does not) to sell his soul to the Devil. Certainly, it makes more sense to compare the figure of Hester with that of the active Matilda, and Dimmesdale with the passive Ambrosio, who is seduced by her, than to try to find analogues for the American pair in Goethe's Gretchen and Faust. If Hawthorne's novella is, indeed, as has often been suggested, an American *Faust,* it is a *Faust* without a traduced maiden. Much less sentimental and Richardsonian than Goethe, Hawthorne is not concerned with the fall of innocence at the seducer's hand or with that seducer's salvation by the prayers of his victim.

The Faustianism of Hawthorne is the melodramatic Faustianism of the gothic romancers: of Lewis, whom he read avidly, and of Maturin, from whose *Melmoth the Wanderer* he borrowed the name of a minor character in *Fanshawe.* Not only Lewis and Maturin, but Mrs. Radcliffe and Brockden Brown were favorite authors of the young Hawthorne; and from them he learned how to cast on events the lurid light, the air of equivocal terror which gives *The Scarlet Letter* its "hell-fired" atmosphere. The very color scheme of the book, the black-and-whiteness of its world illuminated only by the baleful glow of the scarlet letter, come from the traditional gothic palette; but in Hawthorne's imagination, those colors are endowed with a moral significance. Black and white are not only the natural colors of the wintry forest settlement in which the events unfold, but stand, too, for that settlement's rigidly distinguished versions of virtue and vice; while red is the color of sexuality itself, the fear of which haunts the Puritan world like a bloody specter. The book opens with a description of "the black flower of civilized society, a prison" and closes on a gravestone, a "simple slab of slate," whose escutcheon is "sombre . . . and relieved only by one ever-glowing point of light gloomier than a shadow:—ON A FIELD SABLE, THE LETTER A, GULES."

It is the scarlet letter itself which is finally the chief gothic property of Hawthorne's tale, more significant than the portents and signs, the meteors in the midnight sky, or even "the noise of witches; whose voices, at that period, were often heard . . . as they rode with Satan through the air. . . ." Into that letter are compressed the meanings of all the demonic fires, scarlet blossoms, and red jewels which symbolize passion and danger in his earlier tales. It glows with a heat genital and Satanic at once—burning his fingers even centuries later, Hawthorne tells us in his introduction, like "red-hot iron"; and its "lurid gleam," the text declares, is derived "from the flames of the infernal pit." Its "bale-fire," at any rate, lights up the book with a flickering glare representing at once Hester's awareness of guilt and Hawthorne's: his doubts over his plunge into the unconscious, and hers over her fall through passion into the lawless world of Nature.

The wearer of such a sign is transformed into a gothic villainess-heroine: a taboo figure, utterly alienated from the world of the unfallen, yet capable of bestowing on that world, in its moments of pain and death, a signal kind of relief. Worn openly, the genital brand, "red-hot with internal fire," becomes a sacred charm, like the cross on a nun's bosom; grants powers of healing, immunity to Indians, a strange and terrible insight into the sinfulness of others. What Hester inwardly perceives the book makes explicit: that the scarlet letter belongs not to her alone but to the whole community which has sought to exclude her. It is repeated everywhere: in the child she bears, who is the scarlet letter made flesh; in the heavens of secret midnight; on the tombstone which takes up her monitory role after she is dead; and especially in the secret sign on the breast of the minister, whom the community considers its special saint. In his dumb flesh is confessed what his articulate mouth cannot avow, not his transgression alone but that of all men who have cast the first stone. At the heart of the American past, in the parchment scroll which is our history, Hawthorne has discovered not an original innocence but a primal guilt—and he seeks to evoke that past not in nostalgia but terror.

It is on the frontier, the margin where law meets lawlessness, the community nature, that Hawthorne imagines his exemplary drama played out; but his primitive world is much more like Brockden Brown's than Cooper's. To him, the "dark inscrutable forest" seems rather the allegorical *selva oscura* of Dante than Natty Bumppo's living bride: the symbol of that moral wilderness into which man wanders along the byways of sin, and in which he loses himself forever. In its darkness, Hawthorne says of Hester at one point, "the wildness of her nature might assimilate itself with a people alien to the law. . . ." He projects no idyllic dream of finding in the forest the Noble Savage, only a nightmare of confronting the barbaric warrior and the Devil whom he serves; and the occasional Indian who emerges from his wilderness takes up a place not beside the pariah-artist but the black magician.

The virgin sea seems to him as unredeemed as the land, a second realm of gloomy lawlessness. "But the sea, in those old times," he writes, "heaved swelled and foamed, very much at its own will . . . with hardly any attempts at regulation by human law." And its denizens he considers, therefore, as lost as those of the forest, can imagine a Queequeg no more easily than he can a Chingachgook. For him sailors are ignoble savages, too: "the swarthy-cheeked wild men of the ocean, as the Indians were of the land. . . ." Neither Hawthorne's Indians nor seamen, however, play a critical part in the development of the action; they merely stand symbolically by, in their appropriate garb, speaking no word but watching "with countenances of inflexible gravity, beyond what even the Puritan aspect could attain." In the two important scenes at the foot of the scaffold, which so symmetrically open and close the book, there are red men in attendance, on the second occasion flanked by their even wilder confreres, the mariners "rough-looking desperadoes, with sun-blackened faces, and an immensity of beard." Yet neither the black desperadoes of the deep nor the swarthy and stolid Indians play the role in *The Scarlet Letter* entrusted to Cooper's Mingoes or the gothic savages of Brockden Brown.

The Magua of Hawthorne's novella is Chillingworth, the white doctor and man of science, so oddly at home in the alien world of the primitive. "By the Indian's side, and evidently sustaining a companionship with him, stood a white man, clad in a strange disarray of civilized and savage costume"; "old Roger Chillingworth, the physician, was seen to enter the market-place, in close and familiar talk with the commander of the questionable vessel." From his Indian captors and friends, Chillingworth has learned a darker "medicine" to complement his European science; but he has not ceased to be still "the misshapen scholar . . . eyes dim and bleared by lamplight," whose "scientific achievements were esteemed hardly less than super-natural." If on the one hand, Chillingworth is portrayed as the heir to the lore of the "savage priests," on the other, he is presented as a student of the black magic of "Doctor Forman, the famous old conjurer." He blends into a single figure, that is to say, the gothic bugaboo of *The Monk* and that of *Edgar Huntly.* To represent the horror of Europe, however, Chillingworth must be white, while to stand for that of America he must be colored; he is, in fact, a white man who grows black. Even the other protagonists notice his gradual metamorphosis ("his dark complexion seemed to have grown duskier . . .") into the very image of the Black Man, which is to say, Satan himself: "a striking evidence of man's faculty of transforming himself into a devil . . . if he only will . . . undertake a devil's office."

Of course, Hawthorne does not accept the language of gothicism as literal truth; and only *metaphorically* can Chillingworth be understood as having been changed into a demon. His metaphorical role, however, constantly threatens his integrity as a realistic character; and it is, perhaps, best to take him as more "projection" than protagonist, an aspect of Dimmesdale's mind, given only a token semblance of actuality. In general, one of the major problems involved in reading *The Scarlet Letter* is determining the ontological status of the characters, the sense in which we are being asked to believe in them. Caught between the analytic mode of the sentimental novel and the projective mode of the gothic, Hawthorne ends by rendering two of his five main characters (Hester and Dimmesdale) analytically, two ambiguously (Chillingworth and Pearl), and one projectively (Mistress Hibbins). Hester and Dimmesdale are exploited from time to time as "emblems" of psychological or moral states; but they remain rooted always in the world of reality. Chillingworth, on the other hand, makes so magical an entrance and exit that we find it hard to believe in him as merely an aging scholar, who has nearly destroyed himself by attempting to hold together a loveless marriage with a younger woman; while Pearl, though she is presented as the fruit of her mother's sin, seems hardly flesh and blood at all, and Mistress Hibbins is quite inexplicable in naturalistic terms, despite Hawthorne's perfunctory suggestion that she is simply insane.

The latter three are, perhaps, best understood as the "daemons" or "shadows" of the more actual protagonists. Chillingworth is clearly enough the shadow of Dimmesdale, an *animus* figure, who projects the minister's sense of guilt and desire for self-punishment, which end by producing in his flesh a terrible analogue of Hester's letter. In one aspect, Chillingworth is a paternal image, the Bad Father who speaks with the voice of Dimmesdale's Calvinist heritage; and in another, he is a tormenting alter ego, capable of slipping past the barriers of cowardice and self-pity to touch the hidden truth. When Dimmesdale, hounded to penitence by his shadow, mounts the scaffold to expose his own long-hidden scarlet letter, Hawthorne offers us what seem alternative explanations of its genesis. It may be, he suggests, the result of some hideous self-inflicted torture, the psychosomatic effect of remorse, or the work, scientific or magical, of Chillingworth; but these we can see are only apparent alternatives, which properly translated reduce to a single statement: Dimmesdale and Chillingworth are one, as body and soul are one.

Certainly, Chillingworth cannot survive the minister's death, after which "he positively withered up, shrivelled away, almost vanished from sight." And when the process is complete, the old physician gone, leaving to the bastard child of his wife enough money to make her "the richest heiress of her day"—both that child and her mother disappear, too. From their refuge in the Old World, Hester returns alone to her place of shame and assumes again the burden of her guilt; for there is no longer any function for the "demon child" who was her shadow. From the first, Pearl has been projected as "a forcible type . . . of the moral agony which Hester Prynne had borne. . . ." Redeemed, however, by her father's last penance, and endowed with the wealth of his shadow, she vanishes, too, not out of the world but *into* it: "A spell was broken . . . and as her tears fell upon her father's cheek, they were the pledge that she would grow up amid human joy and sorrow, nor forever do battle with the world, but be a woman in it. Towards her mother, too, Pearl's errand . . . was all fulfilled." Once she has ceased to be an *anima* figure and has become merely human, Boston cannot hold Pearl; and she is dispatched to the shadowy world of Europe.

Taken as a character constructed in psychological depth, Pearl is intolerable. Though she is the first child in American fiction whose characterization is based on painstaking observation of a real little girl (an astonishing number of details in her portrayal come from the notes Hawthorne took on his little daughter, Una), she is so distorted in the interests of her symbolic role that she seems by turns incredible and absurd. It is partly a question of the *tone* in which her actions are described, a tone sometimes sentimental and condescending (Hawthorne's son, Julian, interpreted the book as essentially a defense of bastards!), sometimes mystifying and heavily gothic. The only character in our literature who even remotely resembles her is Mrs. Stowe's Topsy, another scarcely endurable example of a cute "daemon"! Daemonic Pearl certainly is, in her immunity to man-made law, her babbling in strange tongues, her uncanny insight into her mother's heart. But she is disconcertingly benign—as often compared to a blossom from a rosebush as to a witch! Her name is the clue to her essential nature, as surely as is Chillingworth's icy appellation; for she is "the gem of her mother's bosom," the Pearl of great price: not only Hester's torment, but also her salvation. "Thus early had this child saved her from Satan's snare. . . ."

Unaware of exactly what he is doing with his shadow characters: incapable of committing himself unreservedly to the gothic modes, but unable either to translate them into terms of psychological inwardness—Hawthorne tempers the daemonic in Chillingworth's case with melodrama, in Pearl's with sentimentality, and in Mistress Hibbins' with a kind of skeptical irony. The wizard Hawthorne can regard with horror, the elf-child with condescension; but to the full-blown witch, he responds with uneasy evasions, unwilling perhaps to grant reality to the nightmare which had aroused the persecuting zeal of his ancestors. Mistress Hibbins is, nonetheless, the third daemon of the book, the shadow of a sixth protagonist that we have not yet named: the Puritan community itself, which Hawthorne portrays as haunted by "the noise of witches; whose voices at that period, were often heard to pass over the settlements or lonely cottages, as they rode with Satan through the air."

The name of Mistress Hibbins is mentioned in Hawthorne's text before that of any of the other major characters of the book; and at four critical moments she appears on the scene. On her first appearance, she pleads with Hester to come with her to the forest and sign her name in the Black Man's book; on her second, she peers from her window into the darkness where the minister stands alone on the scaffold and cries out in anguish; on her third, she hails the minister as a fellow-communicant of Satan after he has met Hester in the forest and agreed to run off. The fourth scene is the longest, involving an interchange with Hester in which Mistress Hibbins claims fellowship not only with her and her lover, but impugns the whole community, for whose undermind of filth and fear she speaks: "Many a church-member saw I, walking behind the music, that has danced in the same measure with me when Somebody was fiddler, and, it might be, an Indian powwow or a Lapland wizard changing hands with us!" Yet despite her critical role in the book, the dour-faced witch lady is rendered more as hallucination than fact. Her first entrance is hedged about with such phrases as: "it is averred" and "if we suppose this interview . . . to be authentic and not a parable . . ."; her second ends: "the old lady . . . vanished. Possibly, she went up among the clouds"; the third introduces the disturbing phrase, "and his encounter, if it were a real incident . . ." Only the fourth does not qualify its assertion of what happened with doubt, merely attributes Mistress Hibbins' diatribe to her "insanity, as we would term it."

Yet hedged about with doubts and characterized as mad, Magistrate Bellingham's sister is the mouthpiece through which the Faustian theme is introduced into the book. The Faustian theme, however, constitutes the very center of *The Scarlet Letter:* a profound crisis of the soul, for which Hawthorne was able to find no other image than one appropriate to the crazy dreams of a self-styled witch, or the blood-curdling story told to a child. Chapters XVI to XX, which make up the center of Hawthorne's tale, describe the encounter of Dimmesdale and Hester, the evocation of their old love, their momentary illusion of freedom, and the minister's moral collapse; but what begins as romance ends in gothic horror. It is Pearl who gives us the clue, asking her mother to tell the very story that she and her lover have been acting out: "a story about the Black Man. . . . How he haunts this forest, and carries a book with him,—a big, heavy book, with iron clasps, and how this ugly Black Man offers his book and an iron pen to everybody that meets him here among the trees; and they are to write their names with their own blood. And then he sets his mark on their bosoms!" This is, indeed, the tale which Hawthorne tells in *The Scarlet Letter,* though for his characters the problem is not, as in the older versions of the story, whether they *shall* make such a pact, but whether they *have made* it; for in his new Faustian legend, one may enter into such an agreement unawares. According to Mistress Hibbins, all the major protagonists, as well as the community as a whole, have long since inscribed themselves in the Black Man's book; but for Hester and Dimmesdale, even for Chillingworth, all remains ambiguous to the last.

Over and over the essential question is asked. Pearl herself puts it to her mother just after her request for a gothic story, "Didst thou ever meet the Black Man, mother?" and Hester answers, "Once in my life I met the Black man! . . . This scarlet letter is his mark!" Even earlier, Hester has inquired of Chillingworth, "Art thou like the Black Man that haunts the forest round about us? Hast thou enticed me into a bond that will prove the ruin of my soul?" But Chillingworth, smiling, has only evaded her query, "Not thy soul. . . . No, not thine!" It is Dimmesdale whom he implies he has lured into the infernal pact; and it is Dimmesdale who questions himself finally, though impelled by Hester's temptation rather than Chillingworth's torment, "Am I mad? or am I given over utterly to the fiend? Did I make a contract with him in the forest, and sign it with my blood?" This time it is Hawthorne himself who answers: "The wretched minister! He had made a bargain very like it! Tempted by a dream of happiness he had yielded himself with deliberate choice, as he had never done before, to what he knew was deadly sin."

For Hawthorne, the Faustian man is one who, unable to deny the definitions of right and wrong by which his community lives, chooses nonetheless to defy them. He is the individual, who, in pursuit of "knowledge" or "experience" or just "happiness" (though this sounds more like Emma Bovary than Faust!), places himself outside the sanctions and protection of society. He chooses, that is to say, to listen to his own instinct or whim (the Devil) rather than to abide by law or the codes of religion. His loneliness and alienation are at once his crime and his punishment; for he commits a kind of suicide when he steps outside of society by deciding to live in unrepented sin; and he can only return to haunt the world of ordinary men like a ghost. Every major protagonist of *The Scarlet Letter* is such a specter. Of Hester, we are told that "she was as much alone as if she inhabited another sphere," and that "It was only the darkened house which could contain her. When sunshine came, she was not there." Dimmesdale asks of himself, "Then what was he?—a substance?—or the dimmest of shadows?"; and Hawthorne tells us of Chillingworth that "he chose . . . to vanish out of life as completely as if he indeed lay at the bottom of the ocean." Pearl, born of the original sin which has obliterated the substance of her elders, begins as "a born outcast of the infantile world. . . . Mother and daughter stood in the same circle of seclusion from human society."

Neither hate nor love can penetrate the spheres of unreality to which Hester, Dimmesdale, and Chillingworth have consigned themselves. The old physician proves incapable of believing himself a fiend or the two lovers sinners except in a "typical illusion"; and meeting after seven years, the minister and Hester "questioned one another's actual and bodily existence, and even doubted of their own. . . . Each a ghost, and awe-stricken at the other ghost!" Indeed, Hawthorne has the same trouble believing his characters real that they have themselves. "But to all these shadowy beings, so long our acquaintances," he says by way of valedictory, "we would fain be merciful." And we realize the sense in which he himself was, like Dimmesdale or Hester, alienated, removed to a sphere from which like some ghostly Paul Pry he peered down on the ghosts of his imagining. We have spoken of Hester and Dimmesdale as more actual than their shadows; but their actuality is a thin and tenuous thing, though the best at the command of a writer whom Poe advised, in critical impatience, to get a bottle of visible ink! Incapable of portraying full-bodied characters in thickly specified social contexts, Hawthorne just once in his life, in *The Scarlet Letter,* invented a fable within which his pale protagonists seemed apt symbols of alienation through sin.

Not only alienation, however, defines Hawthorne's Faustian protagonists. They dream also of being *free*—uncommitted and unbound by history or moral responsibility. "Let us not look back," says Hester, playing the tempter to Dimmesdale, "the past is gone. . . . With this symbol, I undo it all. . . ." It is an American creed which she espouses, and like a good American, she looks to the world of nature for its consummation: "Doth the universe lie within the compass of yonder town. . . . Whither leads yonder forest track? Deeper it goes, and deeper, into the wilderness. There thou art free!" It is the dream already old by the time of Hawthorne of "lighting out for the territory," pursuing the endlessly retreating horizon of innocence into an inexhaustible West: the seed of a million Saturday matinees. "Begin all anew. . . . There is happiness to be enjoyed. There is good to be done. . . ." Really to believe this, however, is to leave behind the world of moral responsibility inhabited by Puritan saint and sinner alike, and to become a make-believe cowboy.

Here is the critical point at which the sons of Natty Bumppo part company with the descendants of Faust. The former cry out with their mythic progenitor in *The Deerslayer:* "When the colony's laws, or even the King's laws, seem agin the laws of God, they get to be onlawful and ought not to be obeyed." But who is qualified to say what God's laws are: a half-educated trapper without a cross in his blood, an unrepentant adulteress, an orphan boy on a raft with a stolen slave? *Vox dei, vox populi,* says the sentimental populist, and dissents in happy innocence; but the gothic rebel revolts against the will of God itself, saying a little naively with Huck, "All right, then, I'll *go* to Hell!" or shouting melodramatically with Ahab, "From hell's heart I strike at thee"; or, at least, insisting desperately with Dimmesdale, "But now,—since I am irrevocably doomed,—wherefore should I not snatch the solace allowed to the condemned culprit before his execution?"

Yet Dimmesdale is finally incapable of maintaining the Faustian stance, wondering if Hester is not right, after all, in her assurance that flight leads to a better life; half praying that God will somehow forgive him in the end. If *The Scarlet Letter* is, indeed, an American *Faust,* Dimmesdale is not really Faust himself but Gretchen, a secondary sinner lured on to destruction by a stronger one whom he loves, a tremulous victim led astray by daring arguments. It is true that in the end his weakness proves stronger than Hester's strength, leading him to repentance and public confession, while she dreams still of flight; but his is a Christian triumph, which cheats both the Devil who would damn him and the Faustian woman who considers that damnation bliss! Chillingworth is no more Faust than he, only a self-made Mephistopheles, the nearest thing to a real Devil Hawthorne could permit himself in his cautiously gothic tale; but he is a timid Devil at that. He and Dimmesdale are, at any rate, portrayed in one scene, ranging wide in their terrible intimacy over the whole field of faith, and approaching the brink of apostasy: "It was as if a window were thrown open, admitting a freer atmosphere into the close and stifled study. . . . But the air was too fresh and chill. . . . So the minister, and the physician with him, withdrew within the limits of what their church defined as orthodoxy." Neither the Devil-doctor in his hate nor the guilty pastor in his ambivalent vanity dares throw himself into the uncertain depths of Faustian speculation or quarrel with the Calvinist God.

Hester, however, has no such scruples, but during her seven years of outward chastity and inward turmoil of the soul, leaves all limits behind: "she cast away the fragments of a broken chain. The world's law was no law for her mind." Ideas "as perilous as demons" became her familiars, persuading her to question the basic tenets of her faith, the place of woman, the very sanctity of life itself. "At times a fearful doubt strove to possess her soul, whether it were not better to send Pearl at once to heaven, and go herself to such futurity as Eternal Justice should provide." Met in the "vast and dismal forest" by the minister whom she has not confronted for seven years, except in his official role as defender of the religion against which they both have sinned, Hester greets him in the name of a rival, a pagan faith. He is at a loss in the "untamed forest," but she secure; for "her intellect and her heart had their home, as it were, in desert places, where she had roamed as freely as the Indian in his woods." How naturally the metaphor occurs to Hawthorne for whom the woods are haunted and the redskin a Satanic figure. "She had wandered, without rule or guidance, in a moral wilderness," and consequently regarded "whatever priests or legislators had established . . . with hardly more reverence than the Indian would feel. . . ." It is a final satisfactory touch that a woman be not only the first Faust of classic American literature, but also the wildest Indian of them all!

Austin Warren

THE SCARLET LETTER

I

In structure, *The Scarlet Letter* is rather a monody, like *Wuthering Heights* (its closest English analogue for intensity) or *The Spoils of Poynton* (with its thematic concentration), than like the massively rich and contrapuntal Victorian novel—say *Middlemarch* or *Bleak House*. And, conducted almost entirely in dialogues between two persons, or in tableaux, with something like the Greek chorus in the commenting community, it is also much nearer to a tragedy of Racine's than to the Elizabethan drama, of which the three-volumed Victorian novel was the legitimate successor.

This purity of method, this structural condensation and concentration, prime virtues of *The Scarlet Letter,* disturbed, while they obsessed, its author. He regretted not being able to intersperse the gloom of his novel by some chapters, episodes, or passages in a lighter mode. "Keeping so close to its point as the tale does, and diversified no otherwise than by turning different sides of the same idea to the reader's mind," he wrote his publisher, would, he feared, bore, disgust, or otherwise alienate the reader.

But the enduring power of the book lies in its "keeping so close to its point," lies in its method: looking at the "same idea" (the situation or theme) from "different sides." Hawthorne's phrase, "different sides," is not synonymous with the Jamesian "point of view," though there is a degree of overlap. Hawthorne is the nineteenth-century omniscient author; and it is he who shows us the "different sides," now a character's public behavior, now the same character's private introspection; who presents two characters operating on each other; who gives us the shifting attitudes of the community to the actions of the central figures; who provides settings and symbols and generalizing comments. It is none the less true that the author does not

From *Connections* (Ann Arbor: University of Michigan Press, 1970), pp. 45–69. First published in *Southern Review* n.s. I, No. I (Winter 1965): 22–45.

flit from character to character. Each chapter has not only a center of interest, commonly indicated by its title, but tends to be seen through a single or central consciousness. As we remember the novel, the interpolations and other deviations fall away, and we retain the impression of a massive construction in terms of centers of interest and of consciousness.

The first eight chapters of the novel are seen through Hester's consciousness; even though the minister appears from time to time it is in his public capacity as her "pastor." The next four concern the minister, two of them close studies of "The Interior of a [Dimmesdale's] Heart." Hester again engages the next four. The Forest chapters represent the only real meeting, the only real converse between the two.

This is an eminently proper mode of telling the story. The two characters are joined by an act which occurred before the novel opens. They never meet again save twice, ritualistically, on the scaffold, and once, rituals dispensed with, in the Forest. Otherwise, these are tales of two isolated characters, isolated save for the attendant spirit of each—Pearl for Hester; for Dimmesdale, Chillingworth. Hester's story, as that of sin made public, must begin the novel; the telling of Dimmesdale's, as that of sin concealed, must be delayed till its effects, however ambivalently interpreted, begin to show. The last chapters must present both characters to our consciousness, even though Dimmesdale recedes into something like the public figure of the early chapters, lost in his double role of preacher and dying confessor.

The composition of the novel, deeply as it stirred Hawthorne, was creatively easy, for (as he wrote his publisher), "all being all in one tone, I had only to get my pitch and could then go on interminably." But this high, or deep, tragic pitch made him uncomfortable—as, I dare say, did Melville's praise of his *Mosses from an Old Manse,* in which the new friend, who was beginning to write *Moby-Dick,* spoke of "the blackness in Hawthorne . . . that so fixes and fascinates me," singling out from that collection "Young Goodman Brown," a piece "as deep as Dante." Hawthorne, waiving the question of his 'best,' preferred *The House of the Seven Gables* as "more characteristic" of him than *The Scarlet Letter;* and doubtless among his tales, too, he would have preferred the "more characteristic" to the 'best.' A critic may be pardoned if he prefers the 'best.'

And certainly *The Scarlet Letter* resumes, develops, and concentrates the themes which Hawthorne had already essayed in some of his chief and greatest short stories—"Roger Malvin's Burial," "The Minister's Black Veil," and, especially, "Young Goodman Brown": concealment of sin, penance, and penitence; the distinction between the comparatively lighter sins of passion and the graver sins of cold blood—pride, calculated revenge; the legacy of sin in making one detect, or suspect, it in others.

II

In reading Hawthorne's masterpiece, one should be careful to distinguish the 'story,' 'fable,' or 'myth' from the author's commentary. Even in his own lifetime, the

now forgotten but good Boston critic, E. P. Whipple, wrote, acutely, that Hawthorne's "great books appear not so much created by him as through him. They
have the character of revelations,—he, the instrument, being often troubled with
the burden they impose upon his mind." *The Scarlet Letter* seems preeminently
such a case. The 'myth' was a delivery; the commentary was an offering.

The novelist, whether the later James of the strict point of view constructions,
or Jane Austen and E. M. Forster and Dostoevski, has an enviable 'dramatic' privilege. If his characters act out their willed destiny and utter the views appropriate to
their characters, the novelist (who is also a nonwriter, a man whose divided self
approves but in part of what his *personae* say and do) has the immunity of
dissociating himself from a position which he can empathize or entertain but to
which he does not wish to commit himself. Hawthorne could, if necessary, let his
latent 'moral'—that of his powerfully presented 'myth'—go one way while he
safeguarded his other self by uttering, in his own person, words of warning or
reproof.

What the author says through his characters cannot 'legally' be quoted as his
attitude; but, on the other hand, what he says as commentator must, almost equally,
be regarded as not the view of his total self. As commentator, he may say what he
thinks he believes or what is prudential. The blessed immunity and gift, thus, is to
be able to give voice to all the voices in him, not, finally, attempting to suppress any
of them—not, finally, feeling the need to pull himself together into the tight doctrinal consistency at which a theologian or philosopher must aim.

One cannot, in *The Scarlet Letter,* take 'proof-texts' out of their context or
utterances away from their speakers. Hence, the 'moral' of the novel is not contained, as an eminent critic once asserted, in Hester's avowal to her "pastor" in the
pagan Forest, that "What we did had a consecration of its own." Nor, since so many
morals can be drawn from Dimmesdale's misery, are we to think that they can be
summed up in the novelist's choice from among them, "Be true! Be true! Be true!"
Because there are, in Hawthorne's phrase (doubtless half-ironic, half-satiric of Sun-
day School books and tracts), "many morals," the book has no 'moral.' At the least,
half-true, and importantly true, is Henry James's conception that it was not as a
'moralist' that Hawthorne was drawn to his tales and novels of sin, that "What
pleased him in such subjects was their picturesquesness, their rich duskiness of
color, their chiaroscuro. . . ."

Certainly, his literary fascination with sin was quite as much aesthetic and
psychological as moral. As Henry, brother of William, so truly says of Hawthorne,
"he cared for the deeper psychology." Such comparatives as "deeper" left sus-
pended without what they are "deeper" than, I dislike; but I can't pretend, at least
in this instance, not to know what is meant: deeper than analysis of manners,
deeper than consciousness, deeper than normal normality—deeper also than 'uni-
valent' judgments. Ambivalence and plurivalence are the "deeper psychology" open
to the novelist even when, speaking in his own person, he too, casts a vote: I do not
want to say a 'decisive vote,' since I doubt that, as commentator, his 'view' of his
own work has any more authority than that of another critic: it may even have less.

III

Two of the characters in *The Scarlet Letter* certainly engaged Hawthorne in his 'deeper psychology,' and are richly developed.

About Hester, her creator had—as he did about his other brunettes, Zenobia and Miriam—ambivalent feelings. Twice, in *The Scarlet Letter*, he compares her to that seventeenth-century feminist Anne Hutchinson, whom, in *Grandfather's Chair*, his chronicle of New England history written for children, he calls, half or more than half ironically, "saintly"—that is, she who was regarded by many as saintly. 'Strong' women, whether sirens, seers, or reformers, were not, in his judgment, womanly.

For Hester, he provides some Catholic similitudes—the most striking in the description of her first appearance on the scaffold. "Had there been a Papist among the crowd of Puritans, he might have seen . . . an object to remind him of Divine Maternity . . ." But it would have reminded him, indeed, "only by contrast, of that sacred image of sinless motherhood, whose infant was to redeem the world. Here . . . the world was only the darker for this woman's beauty, and the more lost for the infant that she bore."

And, again: after seven years, Hester's life of charity gave her "scarlet letter the effect of the cross on a nun's breast." But Hawthorne draws back from taking the view which her life of self-abnegation might seem to entitle her to receive and him to take; for such a view would be based on Hester's Stoic pride and courage, not on her inner life of motive and thought. She has, to be sure, done penance, and done it with dignity—but she has done it with a *proud* dignity, for she is not penitent.

Her rich and luxuriant hair, though closely hidden by her cap, has not been cropped. Seven years after her act of adultery she still believes that what she and her lover did had "a consecration of its own." It is one of Hawthorne's shrewdest insights and axioms that "persons who speculate the most boldly often conform with the most perfect quietude to the external regulations of society. The thought suffices them. . . ." And so Hester, outwardly penitent and charitable, allowed herself "a freedom of speculation which our forefathers, had they known of it, would have held to be a deadlier crime than that stigmatized by the scarlet letter." Some of these doubts and theorizings concerned the position of woman; and Hawthorne, anti-feminist that he was, says of Hester that, her heart having lost its "regular and healthy throb," she "wandered without a clew in the dark labyrinth of mind. . . ."

Hester has her femininities: her loyalty to her lover and to her child and the love of her craft ("Her Needle"). But her needle, like her mind, shows something awry. For Hawthorne bestows upon her—a kinswoman in this respect to Zenobia and Miriam—a "rich, voluptuous, Oriental characteristic." Despite her self-imposed penances of making "coarse garments for the poor"—gifts to those poor who often but revile and insult her, she allows her fancy and needleship free play in designing clothes for Pearl, her "elf-child."

Even more signally, she shows, in the badge of shame she herself wears—and that from her first appearance on the scaffold—a pride triumphing over her shame.

It does not pass unnoticed by the women spectators at the scaffold: one remarks that the adulteress has made "a pride" out of what her judges meant for a punishment. And "at her needle," though clad in her gray robe of coarsest material, Hester still wears on her breast, "in the curiously embroidered letter, a specimen of her delicate and imaginative skill, of which the dames of a court might gladly have availed themselves. . . ."

Appropriate as it is for the pious Bostonians to think Hester a witch, Hester has not signed with her own scarlet blood the Devil's book. Better, from an orthodox Puritan stance, that she had done so. But she has by-passed all that. She belongs in the Forest, where, in the one recorded conversation between the Pastor and his Parishioner, she meets Dimmesdale; she belongs in the Forest not because it is the Devil's opposing citadel to the Town but because she is pagan—as we might now say, because she is a 'naturalist.' To the Forest she belongs as does "the wild Indian." For years she "has looked from this estranged point of view at human institutions"—human, not merely Puritan—"criticizing all—with hardly more reverence than an Indian would feel for the clerical bands" (the prenineteenth century equivalent of the priest's collar), "the judicial robe, the pillory, the gallows, the fireside" (wedded, domestic, and familial bliss), "or the church."

"Like the wild Indian" (Hawthorne is in no danger of saying or thinking of the 'noble savage'), Hester has not judged men by their professional vestments or their status, nor institutions by virtue of their ideal rank in the hierarchy of some philosopher like Plato or Edmund Burke.

That her judgment was thus disillusioned was both good and bad: indeed, there are two seemingly contradictory truths both of which must be asserted and maintained. One is respect for persons in their representative capacities; for church, state, and university represent, with varying degrees of adequacy, the Ideas of holiness, civic virtue, and learning. The other is a dispassionately critical judgment which distinguishes between the personal and institutional representatives of the Ideas and the Ideas themselves. A third, doubtless, is the passionately critical judgment as to when particular persons and particular institutions so inadequately represent their respective Ideas as no longer to be sufferable—to require reform, expulsion, substitution; this is the Revolutionary judgment.

The difficulty of keeping these three truths—or even the first two of them—before one's mind in steady equipoise is as difficult as it is necessary. Hawthorne never attempted to formulate explicitly, even briefly, what I have just said; but such a conception seems clearly implicit in his characterization of Hester. Hester has been taught by shame, despair, and solitude; but, though they "had made her strong," that had "taught her much amiss."

Hester's exemplary conduct in the years which follow her first scene on the scaffold must be interpreted not as penitence but as stoicism, especially, a stoical disdain for the 'views' of society. She is bound to her Boston bondage partly by a kind of instinctive or romantic fatalism—not of the theological kind but fatalism of being bound to the place where she 'sinned' and to her lover. I put the word 'sinned' in quotes because Hester has not repented, not thinking that she has done anything of which she should repent. She still loves Dimmesdale, or at any event pities him, as weaker than herself; and, upon Dimmesdale's appeal to her, when (by her design and his accident) they meet in the Forest, that she advise him what to do, she is immediately purposeful and practical. Let him go into the forest among the Indians, or back to England, or to Europe. She is imperative: "Preach! Write! Act! Do anything save to lie down and die!" Chillingworth's persecutions have made him too "feeble to will and to do"—will soon leave him "powerless even to repent! Up, and away!" And she arranges passage to England on a ship soon to leave Boston.

After Dimmesdale's death, Hester and Pearl disappear—Pearl, 'for good,' Hester, for many years. Yet Hester finally returns to Boston and to her gray cottage and her gray robe and her scarlet letter, for "Here had been her sin; her sorrow; and here was yet to be her penitence." The "yet to be," ambiguous in isolation, seems, in the rest of the penultimate paragraph, to mean that at the end of her life she did repent. In part, at least, this repentance was her renunciation of her earlier fanciful hope that she might be "the destined prophetess" of a new revelation, that of a sure ground for "mutual happiness" between man and woman. Here Hawthorne the myth-making creator and Hawthorne the Victorian commentator get entangled one with the other. Till the "Conclusion," the last few pages, Hester had remained, in ethics, a 'naturalist,' for whom 'sin,' in its Judaeo-Christian codification, had been a name or a convention. Now she is represented as comprehending that "no mission of divine and mysterious truth" can be entrusted to a woman "stained with sin, bowed down with shame, or even burdened with a life-long sorrow. The angel and apostle of the coming revelation must be a woman indeed, but lofty, pure, and beautiful, wise "through the ethereal medium of joy." Though this future "comprehension" is assigned to Hester, it is said in the voice of Hawthorne, the commentator, the husband of Sophia.

Whether applied to Hester specifically or to the mysterious new revelation to come—reminiscent of Anne Hutchinson, Mother Ann Lee, or Margaret Fuller, the pronouncement seems falsetto. Hawthorne's 'new revelation,' which seems (so far as I can understand it) not very new, is certainly not feminist but feminine and familial. Yet Hawthorne, I think, would allow Jesus His temptations and His sufferings: it is woman who is not permitted to be a *mater dolorosa,* whose nature is damaged, not illuminated and enriched, by sorrow.

Hester's voluntary return to the bleak cottage and the life of good works is intelligible enough without Hawthorne's 'revelation'—perhaps even without postulating her final penitence—which must mean her rejection of a naturalistic ethics, her acceptance of some kind of religious belief. Ghosts haunt the places where they died; college alumni return to the campuses where they spent, they nostalgically believe, the 'happiest years of their lives'; we all have 'unfinished business' which memory connects with the 'old home,' the town, the house, the room where we were miserable or joyful or, in some combination, both. There was a time, and there was a place, where, for whatever reason—perhaps just youth—we experienced, lived, belonged (if only by our *not belonging*).

Pearl, freed (like an enchanted princess) from her bondage, has married into some noble, or titled, European (not British) family and is now a mother; but Hester is not the grandmotherly type, nor to be fulfilled in the role of dowager, knowing, as she does, that—whatever the state of Continental ignorance or sophisticated indulgence—her pearls are paste, her jewels, tarnished. There can be no autumnal worldly happiness for her. Without Christian faith, she must work out, work off, her Karma—achieve her release from selfhood.

I V

Hester's conceptions were altered by her experience; Dimmesdale's were not. Unlike her—and (in different and more professional fashion) the nineteenth-century agnostics Clough, Arnold, Leslie Stephen, and George Eliot—Dimmesdale was never seriously troubled by doubts concerning the dogmas of Christianity, as he understood them, and the ecclesiastical institution, the church, as he understood it. He was by temperament a "true priest": a man "with the reverential sentiment largely developed." Indeed, "In no state of society would he have been called a man of liberal views; it would always have been essential to his peace to feel the pressure of a faith about him, supporting, while it confined him within its iron framework."

Some aspects of Dimmesdale's rituals would seem to have been suggested by those of Cotton Mather, whom Barrett Wendell, in his discerning study, aptly called the "Puritan Priest." Though Mather's Diary was not published in full till 1911, striking extracts from it appeared as early as 1836 in W. B. C. Peabody's memoir, likely to have been read by Hawthorne. Dimmesdale's library was "rich with parchment-bound folios of the Fathers and the lore of the Rabbis and monkish erudition ..."; and Mather (possessor of the largest private library in New England) was, as Hawthorne could see from the *Magnalia,* deeply versed in the Fathers and the Rabbis. Those aptitudes were, among the Puritan clergy, singular only in degree. But the "fastings and vigils" of Dimmesdale were, so far as I know, paralleled only by Mather's.

To fasts and vigils Dimmesdale added flagellations, unneeded by the thrice-married Mather. Dimmesdale's sin, one of *passion* and not of *principle* or even of *purpose*—these three possible categories are Hawthorne's—had been an act committed with horrible pleasurable surprise, after which (since the sin had been of passion) the clergyman had "watched with morbid zeal and minuteness ... each breath of emotion, and his every thought."

It is by his capacity for passion—on the assumption that passionateness is a generic human category, and hence the man capable of one passion is capable of others—that Chillingworth first feels certain that he has detected Hester's lover.

Having sketched a psychosomatic theory that bodily diseases may be "but a symptom of some ailment in the spiritual part," the "leech" declares that his patient is, of all men he has known, the one in whom body and spirit are the "closest conjoined"; Dimmesdale turns his eyes, "full and bright, and with a kind of fierceness," on the 'leech,' and then, with a "frantic gesture," rushes out of the room. Chillingworth comments on the betraying passion: "As with one passion, so with another! He hath done a wild thing erenow, this pious Master Dimmesdale, in the hot passion of his heart!"

If a common denominator between a burst of anger and a fit of lust is not immediately apparent, some sharedness there is: in both instances, reason and that persistence we call the self are made temporarily passive. A man's passions are—by contextual definition at least—*uncontrollable;* they 'get the better of' the habitual self. The man 'lets himself go'; is 'beside himself.' It is in this breakdown of habitual control that Chillingworth finds corroboration of what he suspected.

He finds more positive verification when he takes advantage of Dimmesdale's noonday nap to examine his "bosom," there finding, or thinking he finds, the *stigma* of the scarlet letter branded on the priestly flesh. In view of Hawthorne's emphasis—or, more strictly, Chillingworth's—on the close connection between soul and body in Dimmesdale, this *stigma* appears to be like (even though in reverse) the *stigmata* of Christ's wounds which some Catholic mystics are said to have manifested.

Hawthorne turns now to other aspects of Dimmesdale's 'case.' Consciousness of concealed sin may, like physical deformities, make one feel that everyone is watching him. And inability to give public confession to one's sin, the fact that (through cowardice or whatever) one cannot trust his secret to anyone, may make one equally suspicious of everyone—thus deranging one's proper reliance on some gradated series of trusts and confidences.

"Have a real reserve with almost everybody and have a seeming reserve with almost nobody; for it is very disagreeable to seem reserved, and very dangerous not to be so" is counsel bitter, but not unsage, of Lord Chesterfield. Dimmesdale has a real reserve with everyone and a seeming one, too, save when his passion briefly breaks down his habitual caution. But his cautious guard, his ever vigilant consciousness of what he conceals, has made him incapable of distinguishing between friend and foe, has broken down any confidence in what he might otherwise properly have relied upon, his intuitions. Dimly perceiving that some evil influence is in range of him, and feeling doubt, fear, sometimes horror and hatred at the sight of the old leech, he yet, knowing no rational reason for such feelings, distrusts the warnings of his deep antipathy.

Doubtless what most engaged Hawthorne's creative concern for Dimmesdale was the feature of ambivalence in his situation. Dimmesdale's sin and suffering had, in their way, educated the pastor and the preacher. Without his sin of passion and his sin of concealment, Dimmesdale would have been a man learned in books and theological abstractions but ignorant of 'life,' naive, unself-knowing. It was the self-education forced upon him by his sin which made him the pastor, the 'confessor,' the powerful preacher he is plausibly represented as becoming.

At the end of his seven years, Dimmesdale is a great—of as the American vulgate would have it, "an eminently successful"—pastor and preacher. By way of comparison, Hawthorne characterizes the categories into which his fellow-clergymen could be put—all types illustrated by Mather in the 'saints' lives' of the *Magnalia*. Some were greater scholars; some were "of a sturdier texture of mind than his, and endowed with a far greater share of shrewd, hard, iron, or granite understanding" (the preceding epithets show the noun to be used in the Cole-ridgean, or disparaging, sense); others, really saintly, lacked the Pentecostal gift of speaking "the heart's native language," of expressing "the highest truths through the medium of familiar words and images."

To the last of these categories Dimmesdale might, save for his "crime of anguish," have belonged. This burden kept him "on a level with the lowest," gave him his sympathy with the sinful—and his sad eloquence, sometimes terrifying, but oftenest persuasive and tender. These sermons made him loved and venerated; but their preacher knew well what made them powerful, and he was confronted with the old dilemma of means and ends.

In the pulpits Dimmesdale repeatedly intends to make a confession, and repeatedly he does; but it is a vague, a ritual confession—like that of the General Confession at Anglican Matins, except that the "miserable sinner" in whom there is no health is violently intensified by a consistently Calvinist doctrine of total depravity. No difference: Calvinist and Wesleyan and revivalist accusations against the total self can, with equal ease, become ritual. Dimmesdale never confesses to adultery or any other specific sin—only to total depravity: "subtle, but remorseful hypocrite," he knows how the congregation will take his rhetorical self-flagellation: as but the greater evidence of his sanctity; for the more saintly a man, the more conscious he is of even the most venial sins.

So the clergyman was fixed in his plight. At home, in his study, he practiced not only his physical act of penance, his self-scourging; but he practiced also a "constant introspection" which tortured without purifying. To what profit this penance un-preceded by penitence, this torturing introspection which led to no resolution, no action?

As he later told Lowell, Hawthorne had thought of having Dimmesdale con-fess to a Catholic priest (presumably some wandering French Jesuit) as he did, indeed, have Hilda confess to a priest in St. Peter's, not her sin (for she was 'sinless') but her complicity by witness to a sin and a crime. Such an idea might have crossed the mind of a Protestant "priest" of Dimmesdale's monkish erudition and practices. But, had he acted upon the impulse, and had the Jesuit been willing to hear the confession, there could have been no absolution, either sacramental or moral. Quite apart from having to change his religion, Dimmesdale would have had to do real penance, make real amends, and, had public confession been enjoined, not of his general sinfulness but of his specific sin, confess to the committing of adultery, and of that deeper, more spiritual, sin in which he had persisted for years, that of concealing the truth.

What has kept Dimmesdale from confession? Hester has herself been partly at fault, has made a serious error in judgment. At the beginning of the novel, Dimmesdale, her pastor, has, publicly in his professional capacity, enjoined her to speak. His injunction that she name her child's father reads ironically when one reverts to it after the chronicle of the "seven years" which ensue. "Be not silent from any mistaken pity and tenderness for him; for, believe me, Hester, though he were to step down from a high place, and stand there beside thee, on thy pedestal of shame, yet better were it so, than to hide a guilty heart through life. What can the silence do for him, except it tempt him—yea, compel him, as it were—to add hypocrisy to sin? . . . Take heed how thou deniest to him—who, perchance, hath not the courage to grasp it for himself—the bitter, but wholesome, cup that is now presented to thy lips!"

Already Dimmesdale had, perhaps, begun to master the art he showed in his sermons—that of speaking the truth about himself to others (Hester excluded) in seeming to utter a salutary generalization. Arthur Dimmesdale is, "perchance," a coward, weak beside Hester, whose feeling toward him, never contemptuous, partakes certainly of the maternal. Would, she says, "that I might endure his agony as well as mine."

With all men, surely, the longer confession is delayed the more difficult it becomes. The procrastination is 'rationalized'—even though the 'rationalization' never really satisfies the 'rationalizer.'

Dimmesdale, as we see him seven years after, appears to offer his basic rationalization in his speech to Chillingworth—expressed (like his injunction to Hester in the third chapter) in generalized, in hypothetical, terms: there are guilty men who, "retaining, nevertheless, a zeal for God's glory and man's welfare, . . . shrink from displaying themselves black and filthy in the view of men; because, thenceforward, no good can be achieved by them; no evil of the past be redeemed by better services."

There is some truth in what he says. And the Catholic Church, which consistently holds that the unworthiness of a priest does not invalidate the sacrament he administers, which conducts its confessionals not in the presence of a congregation, sees the degree of truth in Dimmesdale's position.

But, for all his Puritan priestliness, Dimmesdale is a Protestant; and the Catholic half-truth is not for him to appropriate. It is given to Chillingworth to utter the 'Protestant' truth. If men of secret sin "seek to glory God, let them not lift heavenward their unclean hands! If they would serve their fellow-men, let them do it by constraining them to penitential self-abasement!"

After her interview with her pastor on the midnight scaffold, Hester is shocked to reflect upon his state. "His nerve seemed absolutely destroyed. His moral force was abased into more than childish weakness." She reflects on her responsibility. Whether Hester's or Hawthorne's—two of her reflections appear to be intended as those of both, the commentator phrasing what Hester feels—the sentences read: "Here was the iron link of mutual crime, which neither he nor she could break. Like all other ties, it brought along with it its obligations." She must disclose to him Chillingworth's identity; must shield her lover.

So Hester assumes her maternal responsibility to her pastor and lover. In "The Pastor and his Parishioner" the titular roles are ironically reversed. The two meet in the "dim wood," "each a ghost, and awe-stricken at the other ghost." One chill hand touches another almost as chill; yet the grasp of the chill and the chill took away the penultimate chill of isolation which had separated them from all mankind. Their conversation "went onward, not boldly, but step by step...." They "needed something slight and casual to run before and throw open the doors of intercourse, so that their real thoughts might be led across the threshold."

Their first "real thoughts" to find expression are the mutual questions—"Hast thou found peace?" Neither has. Hester tries to reassure Dimmesdale by taking the line, the pragmatic line, which the pastor has already used, in rationalized self-defense, to Chillingworth. He is not comforted. "Of penance I have had enough. Of penitence there has been none!"

Hester sees him, whom she "still so passionately loves," as on the verge of madness. She sees her worse-than-error—originally disguised from her, as an impulse generous and protective—in not letting her lover know that his fellow lodger, physician, and torturer was her husband; she confesses it. Dimmesdale is at first violent against her for her long silence, violent with all that "violence of passion" which first gave Chillingworth the notion that the pastor had, despite his purity, inherited "a strong animal nature from his father or his mother." Then he relents: "I freely forgive you now. May God forgive us both!" But he goes on to extenuate this sin by comparison with Chillingworth's: "We are not, Hester, the worst sinners in the world. There is one worse than even the polluted priest! That old man's revenge has been blacker than my sin. He has violated in cold blood the sanctity of a human heart. Thou and I, Hester, never did so!"

Then follow the famous words of Hester. The lovers, like Dante's yet more illustrious couple, had acted in hot blood, not in cold. And—"What we did had a consecration of its own. We felt it so! We said so to each other! Hast thou forgotten it?"

Dimmesdale replies, "Hush, Hester!... No; I have not forgotten!" That Hester had said so is credible. It is difficult to credit the 'priest's' ever having used, even in the heat of romance, any such sacred word as "consecration," though Hester remembers the word as used by both; but Dimmesdale, though his "Hush" presumably implies that he in some way now thinks it wrong, does not contradict her recollection.

Then he appeals to Hester to rid him of Chillingworth and what Hester calls the "evil eye": "Think for me, Hester! Thou art strong. Resolve for me!" "Advise me what to do." And Hester accepts the responsibility. She fixes "her deep eyes" on her lover, "instinctively exercising a magnetic power" over his spirit, now "so shattered and subdued...."

Dismissing Dimmesdale's talk about the Judgment of God, Hester immediately—like a sensible nineteenth-century physician or practical nurse—recommends a change of scene, an escape from an oppressive situation, and begins to outline alternatives. At first she speaks as though her lover (or former lover—one does not know which to call him) might escape alone: into the Forest to become, like the Apostle Eliot, his recent host, a preacher to the Redmen; or across the sea—to England, Germany, France, or Italy. How, exactly, a Calvinist clergyman, is to earn his living in Catholic France and Italy is not clear; but Hester seems to have unbounded faith in her lover's intellectual abilities and personal power, once he has shrugged off New England; she seems to think of his creed—and even of his profession—as historical accidents. These Calvinists, these "iron men, and their opinions" seem to her emancipated mind to have kept Arthur's "better part in bondage too long already!" He is to change his name, and, once in Europe, become "a scholar and a sage among the wisest and the most renowned of the cultivated world." He is bidden, "Preach! Write! Act! Do anything save to lie down and die!"

In all this appeal, Hester seems to project her own energy into Dimmesdale and, what is more, seems to show little understanding of her lover's nature: could he, eight years ago, have been a man to whom changing your name, your creed, your profession could have been thus lightly considered? Can Dimmesdale ever have been a man of action in the more or less opportunist sense of which Hester sees him capable? If so, as an Oxford man (Hawthorne should have made him, as a Puritan, a Cantabrigian), he could have submitted to Archbishop Laud instead of coming to New England. What positive action do we know him to have committed in 'cold blood'? He committed a sin in hot blood once—it is tempting to say 'once,' and I have sometimes thought (unfairly perhaps) that Hester may have been the seducer. Otherwise his sins have been negative and passive—cowardice and hypocrisy.

False in its reading of his character and rashly oversanguine of programs as Hester's exhortation may be, Dimmesdale is temporarily aroused by her strength, by her belief that a man can forget his past, dismiss its 'mistakes' and 'debts,' and start again as though nothing had happened, as though he had neither memory nor conscience. For a moment indeed he believes he can start all over again, if only, invalid that he is, he has not to start alone. But Hester tells him that he will not go alone: her boldness speaks out "what he vaguely hinted at but dared not speak."

Hester and Arthur part, but not before she has made plans for passage on a vessel about to sail for Bristol. When the minister learns that it will probably be on the fourth day from the present, he notes but to himself, not to Hester, on the fortunate timing.

It is "fortunate" because three days hence Dimmesdale is to preach the Election Sermon, the highest civic honor a Bay Colony clergyman could receive. That Dimmesdale should still be pleased, should still look to this ending of his career as a dramatic close, that he should still think of his public duty more than of his private morality shocks Hawthorne as, of all Dimmesdale's doings and not-doings the most "pitably weak." What is it, finally, but professional vanity? "No man, for any considerable period can wear one face to himself, and another to the multitude, without finally getting bewildered as to which may be the true."

The minister walks home from the Forest "in a maze," confused, amazed. Hester's bold suggestions have temporarily released him from that iron framework which both confines and supports him. His habitual distinctions between right and wrong have broken down; and all that survives is his sense of decorum.

"At every step he was incited to do some strange, wild, wicked thing or other, with a sense that it would be at once involuntary and intentional; in spite of himself, yet growing out of a profounder self than that which opposed the impulse"— 'profounder' in a sense Hawthorne does not define. It may be a man's subconscious or his "total depravity" left to himself—the Dark Forest in man, the Satanic.

All of his impulses are rebellions against his habitual mode of life and even, one would say, of thought and feeling. Meeting with one of his elderly deacons, he has the impulse to utter "certain blasphemous suggestions that rose in his mind respecting the communion supper." And, encountering the oldest woman of his church, pious and deaf and mostly concerned with recollecting her 'dear departed,' he can think of no comforting text from Scripture but only what then seemed to him an "unanswerable argument against the immortality of the soul" which, happily, she is too deaf to hear. To a pious young girl, he is tempted to give "a wicked look" and say one evil word, and averts the temptation only by rudeness; and to some children, just begun to talk, he wants to teach "some very wicked words." Lastly, meeting a drunken seaman from the ship upon which he plans to sail, he longs to share with the abandoned wretch the pleasure of "a few improper jests" and a volley of good round oaths; and it is not his virtue but his "natural good taste" and still more his "habit of clerical decorum" which dissuade him.

These temptations exhibit a Dimmesdale I should not have guessed to exist even in unvoiced capacity—and for which Hawthorne has given no preparation: indeed, we are never given any account of the pastor's English prehistory at all comparable to that which is furnished for Hester. "The Minister in a Maze" is, indeed, something of a brilliant sketch, a 'set piece'—something which occurred to Hawthorne as he was writing his novel, yet does not wholly fit it. Can the pastor once have been a young rake?

It is unlikely. To be sure, some of the Puritans, including the Puritan clergy, were converted not only from their ancestral Anglicanism but from worldliness if not anything more precisely sinful. And at Oxford and elsewhere Dimmesdale may have heard oaths and smutty stories, even though his principles and taste have forbidden him to use them. Likely Hawthorne meant us to see in this amazing scene a brief resurgence of that inherited "strong animal nature" which had for a lifetime, but for a lapse of act and another of feeling, been so rigorously repressed.

This brilliant chapter, if defended, will have to be defended on psychological considerations more general than specifically relevant to Hawthorne's clergyman. In the benign phenomenon called 'conversion'—the selves of a divided self reorder themselves: the self which was dominant is exorcised, or at any event decisively subordinated; the self which existed as subordinate—the 'good self'—becomes supreme, or nearly supreme. And there is a corresponding shift of positions which we may call perversion. Both of these changes with certain types of men, can occur—or show themselves—suddenly, in a moment. Some of these reorganizations persist; some are brief, impelled as they oftenest appear to be, by the 'magnetism' of an emotionally powerful propagandist—such an one as Hester.

In yielding to Hester's proposals of escape, Dimmesdale, says Hawthorne, had, in effect, made such a bargain with Satan as the witch-lady, Mistress Hibbins, suspected him of. "Tempted by a dream of happiness, he had yielded himself with deliberate choice, as he had never done before, to what he knew was deadly sin." This he now has done. Hester, out of one generous impulse, spared identifying Chillingworth to her lover and *concealed* her lover's name from Chillingworth, and now out of another 'generous' impulse she had bade her lover to escape his concealed sin not by revealing it but by abandoning his adopted country, his profession, even his name. And what have been the results of these 'generous' impulses—not wholly disinterested, perhaps, since she thinks of being reunited to her lover? What have been the results of these attempts modern Americans understand so well—attempts to help, by sparing, those we love, or think we love?

Dimmesdale returns to his study, conscious that his old self has gone. The man who returned from the Forest is wiser—wiser about himself, than the man who entered it. But—like Donatello's—what a "bitter kind of knowledge." He throws the already written pages of his sermon into the fire, and, after having eaten "ravenously," works all night on another.

What, the attentive reader speculates, is the difference between the unfinished sermon written before the Forest and the finished one of the night that followed? That difference, like the nature of the sermon delivered, seems curiously irrelevant to Hawthorne. We are told that the new discourse was written "with such an impulsive flow of thought and emotion" that its writer "fancied himself inspired." Which is the word to be stressed: *fancied* or *inspired?* We are told that he wrote with "earnest haste and ecstasy": which of the three words are we to stress? Had he something to say in the sermon which was the result of his intention (premeditated at some time before he delivered the sermon) or there after taking his stand beside Hester on the scaffold? Did the sermon have some new tone in it, some tragic or bitter wisdom wrested from that gross lapse into illusion which so bemused and amazed him as he returned from the Forest?

Melville once wrote a masterly and prophetic sermon for Father Mapple. Hawthorne writes none for Dimmesdale. During the delivery of the sermon, we readers, with Hester, are outside the meeting house. We but hear the preacher's voice, are told of its great range of pitch, power, and mood. Yet, says Hawthorne, if an auditor listened "intently, and for the purpose," he would always have heard throughout the "cry of pain," the cry of a human heart "telling its secret, whether of guilt or sorrow...." Yet in this respect, surely, the present sermon was not unique; for it had always been "this profound and continual undercurrent that gave the clergyman his most appropriate power."

When, after the sermon, we learn dimly from the admiring congregation its burden, we discover, strange to say, that it had ended with a prophetic strain. It had not been a Jeremiad—a denunciation of the Chosen people, but a foresight of New England's "high and glorious destiny." This is puzzling to interpret. That the preacher, about to declare himself an avowed sinner, cannot (like Cotton Mather) denounce his New England's sins, I can see; but why need he celebrate its high destiny? Is it that Hawthorne, to whom the 'subject matter' of the sermon does not seem to matter, has inserted and asserted, his own strong regional loyalties?

What ought to matter to the constructor of so closely constructed a novel seems not to have mattered to Hawthorne. What matters to him, and evokes his harsh rebuke, is that, seeing the error of escape, Dimmesdale has planned first to give the sermon, thus triumphantly ending his professional career, and then to make his public confession. The giving of the sermon as such, and the content of the sermon, do not really concern him—unless the giving of the sermon contributes the publicity and the drama of the scaffold confession requisite to counterpart the publicity and the drama of that first scaffold on which Hester stood—save for her baby on her arm—alone.

Implied is some final clash of wills and 'philosophies' between Hester and Arthur. Dimmesdale bids Pearl and Hester toward the scaffold. Pearl, birdlike, flies and puts her arms around his knees; but Hester comes slowly, "as if impelled by fate and against her strongest will," and pauses before she reaches him. Only when Chillingworth attempts to stop the pastor's public confession and the pastor again appeals does Hester come. But Dimmesdale has assumed the man's role at last—or a man's role: he asks Hester for her physical strength to help him onto the scaffold, but in asking her strength enjoins, "let it be guided by the will which God hath granted me." When they stand together, he murmurs to Hester, "Is not this better than what we dreamed of in the Forest?" Hester cannot assent. She palliates with "I know not"; then adds what seems to mean 'better, perhaps, if we two and little Pearl can die together.' But that, though human, is melodramatic. Hester must see that her lover is dying and that there is no way save a supernatural intervention—an 'act of God,' as insurance companies put it—which can kill her and the child concurrently with him.

After his confession to his parish and the revelation of his *stigma*, he says farewell to Hester. She speaks of their having "ransomed one another" by their consequent miseries, speaks of spending their "immortal life" together. He replies, as he did to her words in the Forest about the private "consecration" of their adulterous union. "Hush, Hester.... The law we broke!—the sin here so awfully revealed.—let these alone be in thy thoughts! I fear! I fear!" What he fears is not for his own salvation—assured, to his perception, apparently, by this, his deathbed repentance and confession—but for any reunion of the lovers after death.

V

It seems, to so close a reading as I have given to Dimmesdale, a pity that Hawthorne's "deeper psychology," and his own commentary, stop at this point. What is one to think of deathbed repentances, and of repentance so dramatic as this? And was not the repentance, if repentance there was and not yet another form of proud illusion, finally produced not by Chillingworth's malign sleuthing but by Hester's 'generous' and—in view of her lover's theology and character, if not indeed judged by any kind of absolute ethic—immoral advice that he escape from the consequences of his deed?

These are questions partly casuistical, partly universal, all of which one would expect to have interested Hawthorne. That they are not 'worked' out is partly, perhaps, Hawthorne's judgment that from earlier comments might be inferred the comments here relevant; partly, I think, a felt conflict between aesthetic and ethico-psychological considerations: aesthetically, he wants a firm, dramatic finale—something at all times difficult for him to manage, and here one which must be reconciled as best he can with his ethically psychological concerns, his probings and questionings.

Lastly, his 'conclusion' must give the modes of interpretation which the community apply to the phenomenon of the *stigma* which "most," though not all, of the spectators testified to having seen when the dying 'priest' bared his breast. In *The Scarlet Letter,* even more than in his later romances, Hawthorne sees life from inside the consciousness of a few persons—those of an introspective and meditative turn; but these persons, however insulated, are not solipsists: they believe, as Hawthorne believes, in a world they have not created by their own consciousness but merely interpreted.

The community forms, in terms of literary tradition, a Greek chorus, to the happenings in his protagonists' inner lives. Like the utterances in the choruses of Sophocles, it doesn't provide what a novice enamored of classical antiquity expects—the voice of true wisdom, the sure guide by which to interpret the too intense, and hence probably aberrative, views of the protagonists. When such a novice reads Arnold's famous praise of Sophocles that he "saw life steadily and saw it whole," the novice looks to the chorus to give that steady and whole interpretation. But the expectation is vain: the chorus partly comments, half empathetically, on what goes forward at the center of the stage, partly utters traditional maxims and apothegms.

In Hawthorne's choruses the same is true. In *The Scarlet Letter,* there are many auctorial comments on the community—comments frequently not limited to that seventeenth-century Puritan community in which Arthur and Hester lived. It is impossible to reduce them to any unitary and propositional form. Hawthorne is no Utopian, whether of the Brook Farm or any other variety; he is equally free from any extravagant individualism, even of the Emersonian variety: I say 'Emersonian' because Emerson himself was no such individualist as the half-gifted, half-eccentric people who appealed to his ears and sheltered themselves under his name.

Hawthorne's 'community'—or 'society'—is now kind, now persecuting; now foolish, now wise. Perhaps his most characteristic view of it is that, given time enough, 'the people' will show wisdom and do justice. *Given time enough,* it will forget initial suspicions and hostilities—do justice to the relatively heretic individualists—Edwards, Emerson, Thoreau, Garrison, Anne Hutchinson. What if it has not time?

The relation between individual truth (that of existential insight) and the community's slowly shifting 'wisdom' can never be either perfectly or permanently adjusted. Seneca wrote, "As often as I have been among men, I returned home less a man than I was before." But Aristotle opens his *Politics* with the maxim that "A man who can live alone must be either a god or a beast." *Society and Solitude* (the title of Emerson's last collection of essays) names two resorts, the two forces which must ever be 'checking' and 'balancing' each other.

Hawthorne's 'absolute truth' and 'ultimate reality' are not to be identified with any of their adumbrations. They are not imparted in their wholeness to Dimmesdale, or Hester, or to the chorus of the community, nor to Hawthorne as commentator on his own myth, nor to the author of this essay. We all know but in part, and prophesy but in part. Generalizations without case histories are commonplaces; case histories without the attempt at formulating 'first principles' are but (in the pejorative sense) casuistries.

This dialectical nature of truth-finding and truth-reporting Hawthorne was too honest to evade; it is to his literary as well as his 'philosophical' credit.

Michael Davitt Bell

ANOTHER VIEW OF HESTER

In Hawthorne's fiction of Puritan New England, as compared to that of his contemporaries, women are relatively rare and relatively unimportant. To be sure, the exception to this statement—*The Scarlet Letter*—is a major exception. But in the short tales . . . women play subordinate roles. They function mainly as symbols of the bonds of human sympathy rejected by such misanthropes as Parson Hooper or Young Goodman Brown. These women, in all their docility and submissiveness, are the very antithesis of the high-spirited natural heroines of Hawthorne's contemporaries. Yet one of Hawthorne's first published works, appearing in the Salem *Gazette* in 1830, was a biographical sketch of the greatest female rebel of them all, Anne Hutchinson. Like Hope Leslie or Naomi Worthington, Mrs. Hutchinson stands before a gathering of stern Puritan judges. This is the conventional situation of the natural heroine. But it is important to note how completely, in "Mrs. Hutchinson," Hawthorne reverses the meaning of this conventional situation. Rebellion, for Hawthorne, is a noble thing in a severe Endicott or a patriarchal Gray Champion. In a Mrs. Hutchinson it is a quality to be attacked in horror. Anne Hutchinson's judges, in Hawthorne's view, are not persecutors, but rather exemplary founding fathers— "those blessed fathers of the land, who rank in our veneration next to the evangelists of Holy Writ."[1] Mrs. Hutchinson draws her strength from the conventionally appropriate psychological source. "Her heart," Hawthorne writes, "is made to rise and swell within her, and she bursts forth into eloquence." But her eloquence is not that of an innocent Naomi or Hope Leslie. "There is a flash," we are told, "of carnal pride half hidden in her eye, as she surveys the many learned and famous men whom her doctrines have put in fear" [224].

The sources of Hawthorne's hatred of Mrs. Hutchinson are not hard to find. Left fatherless and brotherless at the age of four, Hawthorne grew up surrounded by women. Not surprisingly, he seems to have found it difficult to maintain his

From *Hawthorne and the Historical Romance of New England* (Princeton: Princeton University Press, 1971), pp. 173–90.

masculine identity in these surroundings. All his life he resented any attempt on the part of women to do a man's work, to challenge his distinct role as a male. He particularly disliked female reformers and writers—including apparently his sister-in-law, Elizabeth Peabody, and Margaret Fuller. It is of such women, and not of American "liberty," that Hawthorne's Mrs. Hutchinson is the type. "There are portentous indications," Hawthorne writes in the first paragraph of the sketch, "changes gradually taking place in the habits and feelings of the gentle sex, which seem to threaten our posterity with many of those public women, whereof one was a burden too grievous for our fathers" [217]. Hawthorne's attacks on female writers in his letters to Ticknor and Fields in the 1850's have become notorious.[2] But already in 1830 we can see the same sentiments, along with the personal anxiety of the young writer that lies behind them. "As yet," Hawthorne continues in the opening paragraph of the sketch, "the great body of American women are a domestic race; but when a continuance of ill-judged incitements shall have turned their hearts away from the fireside, there are obvious circumstances which will render female pens more numerous and more prolific than those of men, though but equally encouraged; . . . the ink-stained Amazons will expel their rivals by actual pressure, and petticoats wave triumphantly over all the field" [218]. As opposed to this despised race of man-threatening women, Hawthorne had an ideal of feminine loveliness and domesticity—that is to say of subordination—which was exemplified, so he thought, by his wife, Sophia. But Hawthorne had the ideal long before he met Sophia in 1838. He writes at the close of the first paragraph of "Mrs. Hutchinson" that "woman, when she feels the impulse of genius like a command of Heaven within her, should be aware that she is relinquishing a part of the loveliness of her sex, and obey the inward voice with sorrowing reluctance, like the Arabian maid who bewailed the gift of prophecy" [218–19].

Hawthorne was not, in short, predisposed to treat rebellious or self-willed women in the conventional manner. Like the Quaker Catharine in "The Gentle Boy," Mrs. Hutchinson follows the dictates of her heart at the expense of her domestic obligations. Of course many of Hawthorne's contemporaries, notably Mrs. Lee, were aware of the excesses of Anne Hutchinson and the Quakers. But the fact remains that they regarded these faults as excesses, as errors which did not invalidate the essence or principle of female self-assertion as represented by their heroines. For Hawthorne it was the very essence or principle that was to be deplored. The chief manifestation of the conventional heroine's rebelliousness was to love and marry a man of whom her father and her society did not approve. Her rebelliousness led quite naturally to marriage. For Hawthorne such rebelliousness is by its very nature incompatible with the subordinate role and domestic obligations of the wife. Catharine abandons her child. And Hawthorne is convinced that Mrs. Hutchinson's marriage cannot have been natural. The husband, Hawthorne insists, must have been "(like most husbands of celebrated women) a mere insignificant appendage of his mightier wife" [255]. Marriage and femininity were absolutely antithetical to feminism. Thus Hawthorne wrote rather nastily, in 1855, to his maiden sister-in-law, the reformer: "the conjugal relation is one which God never meant you to share, and which therefore He apparently did not give you the instinct to understand."[3]

In *Hope Leslie* the natural heroine is contrasted with Esther Downing, who "attained the age of nineteen," so we are told, "without one truant wish straying beyond the narrow bound of domestic and religious exercises."[4] It is important to note that Hawthorne's ideal woman has a good deal more in common with Esther Downing than with Hope Leslie, and that in his stories the characteristics of Hope— "this having our own way" [II, 68]—inevitably lead to evil consequences. Hawthorne would certainly have sided with Esther in declaring to Hope, "You do allow yourself too much liberty of thought and word: you certainly know we owe implicit deference to our elders and superiors; we ought to be guided by their advice, and governed by their authority" [I, 262]. Hawthorne's female rebels, disregarding this sort of advice, become as extreme in their fanaticism as a Parson Hooper or a Young Goodman Brown. If Hooper and Brown reveal their inhumanity by repudiating such "domestic" women as Elizabeth and Faith, Mrs. Hutchinson and Catharine reveal their inhumanity by refusing to *be* such women. They are indelicate because they are insubordinate. The young woman's defiance of authority, great emblem of liberty in the conventional historical romance of New England, is for Hawthorne an emblem of the very worst in female pride.

Twenty years separate the publication of *The Scarlet Letter* from the publication of "Mrs. Hutchinson." But the romance begins with the same conventional situation—a proud woman stands before her stern Puritan judges.[5] And Hawthorne seems to have his 1830 heroine very much in mind: the rosebush beside the prison door from which Hester emerges is associated, in the first chapter, with "the sainted Ann Hutchinson" [48]. This phrase suggests that Hawthorne's attitude toward Anne Hutchinson and her kind may have softened since the 1830's. Hester is certainly treated with greater sympathy than Mrs. Hutchinson, and her judges are both more harsh and less qualified than were the Puritans of the 1830 sketch. But one should be careful to avoid exaggerating Hawthorne's sympathy with his heroine. A popular reading of *The Scarlet Letter* sees it as a tragedy of true love crushed by an unfeeling society. This line of criticism, in a curious way, turns Hester completely into a conventional natural heroine, unjustly persecuted by an intolerant society. But it falsifies the reality of the book. Hawthorne may pity Hester, he may sympathize with her, but he does not accept her values as his own. She is not his spokesman in the book. Hawthorne's position is made quite clear, not only in his frequent criticisms of Hester, and in the seriousness of her crime, but also in Hester's voluntary return to Boston at the close. This is not the same woman who proudly maintained herself on the scaffold, who passionately exhorted Dimmesdale to flee.

It is of crucial importance to note that what Hawthorne approves in his heroine is not her rebelliousness, however splendid that quality may sometimes seem, but rather her ability to *overcome* that rebelliousness and assume the feminine qualities of domesticity. For the great difference between Hester and Hawthorne's earlier female outcasts is that Hester returns to her obligations and subordinate position. Unlike Catharine in "The Gentle Boy," Hester Prynne does not abandon her child. Hawthorne surely agrees with Dimmesdale's argument, at Bellingham's mansion, that there is "a quality of awful sacredness in the relation between this mother and this child." Hawthorne believes with Dimmesdale that the child was meant, "above all things else, to keep the mother's soul alive, and to preserve her from blacker depths of sin into which Satan might else have sought to plunge her!"[6]

What these "blacker depths" are is made clear in Chapter XIII, entitled "Another View of Hester." Hester, we learn, is on the verge of falling into feminism, into an open defiance of tradition and authority.[7] "The world's law," we are told, "was no law for her mind" [164]. Hester envisions a change in the role of women, a change Hawthorne regards with horror. For with this change, Hawthorne insists, "the ethereal essence, wherein [woman] was her truest life, will be found to have evaporated" [165–66]. Hester risks being transformed permanently into a Catharine or an Anne Hutchinson. "She might," Hawthorne writes, "have come down to us in history, hand in hand with Ann Hutchinson, as the foundress of a religious sect. She might, in one of her phrases, have been a prophetess. She might, and not improbably would, have suffered death from the stern tribunals of the period, for attempting to undermine the foundations of the Puritan establishment" [165]. All this might have happened, we are told, "had little Pearl never come to her from the spiritual world." Hester is saved by Pearl. "Providence," Hawthorne continues, "in the person of this little girl, had assigned to Hester's charge the germ and blossom of womanhood, to be cherished and developed amid a host of difficulties" [165]. Like Catharine in "The Gentle Boy," Hester has a choice between following the whims of her fancy or following her duties as a mother. But unlike Catharine she chooses the latter. No more than "Mrs. Hutchinson" does The Scarlet Letter glorify female self-assertion. To the extent that Hester forges something positive out of the aftermath of her sin, her success represents a triumph not of rebellion but of subordination.

The ethic embodied in the conventional natural heroine is, at least by implication, profoundly revolutionary. The historical romancers of New England would, so it seems, set up nature over civilization, the heart over the head, impulsive youth over sober age. And yet the writers who propounded this revolutionary ethic were themselves usually quite conservative—in general outlook and often in political belief as well. One would expect such people to fear, rather than recommend, the triumph of nature and the heart. How, one wonders, did they deal with the possibility that the abandonment of restraint—of civilization or of reason—might lead not to progress but to chaos? How, in short, could civilization follow nature without running the risk of destroying itself?

Most of the great writers of this period—Cooper and Melville for example—

were agonized by this problem. For them "the problem of American self-recognition" became, as Perry Miller has put it, "essentially an irreconcilable opposition between Nature and civilization—which is to say, between forest and town, spontaneity and calculation, heart and head, the unconscious and the self-conscious, the innocent and the debauched."[8] But the lesser writers had a way of getting around this contradiction—a kind of semantic trick that allowed them to follow something called "nature" without braving the hazards of excess. These writers simply assumed that there were two kinds of nature, two ways of following the heart. We can see this sort of distinction in Mrs. Lee's two kinds of Quakerism—which are, finally, two kinds of religion of the heart. In the actual Quakers Mrs. Lee embodies the real dangers of obeying impulse without restraint. "The principle of their religion," she writes in *Naomi,* "flattered self-esteem and fostered spiritual pride."[9] And yet in the heroine exactly the same "principle" is somehow purged of its dangerous connotations. Naomi "held nothing in common with the Quakers of that day," we are told, "but the essential principle of their faith" [336]. Mrs. Lee's curiously contradictory use of the word "principle" makes it clear that for her at least the dangers of excess were overcome—or evaded—by distinguishing between two sorts of impulse, two ways of following the heart, one dangerous and the other somehow safe.

Similarly there are two kinds of "nature" in these books—one wild and therefore (like the Quakers) dangerous, the other tame and therefore safe. It is the latter that is associated, in these romances, with the natural heroine. It is to this tame nature that Mrs. Lee refers when she says of Naomi that "Nature had endowed her with a vigorous reason, a strong good-sense" [41]. Book after book draws the important distinction between the forest, on the one hand, and the meadow or garden on the other—between wild nature and the "natural." Catharine Sedgwick deals with this distinction in *Hope Leslie* by means of a device much honored in nineteenth-century romance, though for some reason relatively rare in the historical romance of New England. Hope's rebelliousness is brought out by contrast with the obsequiousness of Esther Downing. But Hope is also contrasted with another girl, an Indian named Magawisca. Magawisca grows up with the hero, Everell Fletcher, and at one point saves his life. But such a match is obviously out of the question. Magawisca finally leaves Boston for good before the marriage of Everell with the true heroine, Hope Leslie. For as Hope represents the safe "nature" of the natural heroine, so Magawisca is marshaled forth to represent the perils of the forest, of wild "nature." Just as there are two kinds of nature, so there are two kinds of heroine: fair and dark, Scott's Rowena and Rebecca, Cooper's Alice and Cora, Melville's Lucy and Isabel. The dark heroine (like Mrs. Lee's Quakers) represents the nature that cannot be reconciled with civilization, the nature that cannot safely be followed. Everell Fletcher, in *Hope Leslie,* turns from the dark Magawisca to marry Hope. Since marriage is always the final symbol of the new civilization in these books, the hero cannot marry the dark heroine. But he can reconcile civilization with the other kind of "nature" simply by marrying the fair natural heroine, the blonde. There is something terribly tenuous and circular about all this: the blonde is both "safe" and "natural" because she is *by definition* both "safe" and "natural." She represents not the resolution of a contradiction but the longing for such a resolution. But she is still important, because so many of these authors treat the longing as an accomplished fact. Thus for Catharine Sedgwick there is no danger of chaos at the end—no danger that the whim of Hope Leslie, our only guide after rejecting all the wisdom of Boston, may lead us only farther astray. Her nature is tame, and therefore safe.

Hawthorne thoroughly repudiates this convention in *The Scarlet Letter*. But his repudiation is carried out by means of the very symbols that other writers used to *support* the convention. Thus Hawthorne does not simply ignore the conventional opposition of fair and dark heroine; he subverts it by making Hester, his natural heroine, dark rather than fair. He does not reject the conventional association of the heroine with nature. Rather he radically subverts the meaning of this association: he attacks the cult of nature through the figure usually used to support it. And Hawthorne does not reject the ideas of civilization and nature that so perplexed his contemporaries; he does not ignore the question of whether civilization should (or could) follow nature. The difference is that he answers this question so unequivocally in the negative. What Hawthorne does reject, in all his skepticism, is the precarious semantic distinction between wild nature and tame nature. *All* nature, for Hawthorne, is wild. In *The Scarlet Letter* there is only the forest. There are no meadows and the only garden, with the somber exception of the graveyard, is being overrun by wild pumpkins. And as the only nature in *The Scarlet Letter* is wild, so the only heroine is dark. There are no blondes in Hawthorne's romance.[10]

The point is not that Hester is *particularly* wild, as compared with other "natural" women, but that *all* natural women are necessarily wild by virtue of their association with nature. By denying the existence of a tame nature Hawthorne is denying the whole concept represented by the blonde.[11] Hester is clearly a composite blonde and brunette—both devoted mother and passionate temptress. And surely much of her impact results from combining these characteristics in an age so firmly committed to distinguishing them. For if the natural heroine was really a temptress, then following nature could be a dangerous business indeed. If all nature was wild, then, following the conventional iconography to Hawthorne's anti-conventional conclusion, all natural heroines must have been dark. As Hester counsels freedom and escape in the forest, it is crucial to note that her dark, glossy hair is there to warn us that all is *not* well, that her advice is suspect, that the forest path is dangerous.

The forest scene, the climactic moment of *The Scarlet Letter*, is also the moment at which Hawthorne is most clearly subverting the convention—letting its own imagery throw its deepest values into question. It is extraordinary how nearly this scene seems to follow the convention. Dimmesdale, true to his role as hero, even as he violates one of Hawthorne's deepest prejudices, subordinates himself utterly to Hester. This conventional subordination of hero to heroine becomes as well the emblem of the conventional victory of heart over head. "Think for me, Hester!" Dimmesdale cries, significantly pressing his hand to his heart as he does throughout the book. "Thou art strong. Resolve for me!" [196]. When she has convinced Dimmesdale to flee with her Hester becomes in appearance the innocent natural heroine. "There played around her mouth," Hawthorne writes, "and beamed out of her eyes, a radiant and tender smile, that seemed gushing from the very heart of womanhood. . . . Her sex, her youth, and the whole richness of her beauty, came back from what men call the irrevocable past, and clustered themselves, with her maiden hope, and a happiness before unknown, within the magic circle of this hour" [202].

Here, to digress for a moment, we can see how Hawthorne has fused his own themes with his critique of the convention. For these qualities of "richness" and "beauty" are at once the conventional qualities of the natural heroine and the qualities of life whose exclusion from New England Hawthorne treats in story after story. In his earlier tales Hawthorne examines the traits of the New England character that caused it to reject, to cut itself off from, the richness and beauty of English life. This is also an important theme in *The Scarlet Letter*. But Hawthorne is also, in *The Scarlet Letter*, approaching this same question from another point of view. As he does more briefly in the young couple in "The Maypole of Merry Mount" so here, too, he examines the characteristics of the European life style itself which inevitably exclude it from the American future. Edith and Edgar, who at the outset of their story represent the life style of the "flower decked" Anglican, function in much the same way as the rebellious young couple of the convention— except, of course, for the outcome of their rebellion. Similarly Hester Prynne, the representative of richness and passion, is also the natural heroine. In revealing the inconsistencies embodied in this conventional figure Hawthorne is also, finally, showing why Hester has to deny the values of the convention in order truly to become an American.

Hester's passionate rebellion, like that of the conventional heroine, finds its equivalent in the joyous gaiety of nature:

> And, as if the gloom of the earth and sky had been but the effluence of these two mortal hearts, it vanished with their sorrow. All at once, as with a sudden smile of heaven, forth burst the sunshine, pouring a very flood into the obscure forest, gladdening each green leaf, transmuting the yellow fallen ones to gold, and gleaming adown the gray trunks of the solemn trees. The objects that had made a shadow hitherto, embodied the brightness now. The course of the little brook might be traced by its merry gleam afar into the wood's heart of mystery, which had become a mystery of joy.
>
>   Such was the sympathy of Nature—that wild, heathen Nature of the forest, never subjugated by human law, nor illumined by higher truth—with the bliss of these two spirits! [202–203]

Here again Hester is differentiated from the conventional heroines, not by what she represents—for she is as natural as they are—but by Hawthorne's judgment of what she represents. There is no tame nature for Hester. There is only the "wild, heathen Nature of the forest." Hester's nature, like that of the conventional heroine, is "never subjugated by human law." But Hester's nature is also, as Hawthorne writes, not "illumined by higher truth." In relation to a convention that set up nature as the ultimate ethical value such a statement is heresy. What Hawthorne is saying is that there must be a balance between head and heart, between civilization and nature. And his constant implication is that the balance should tip—if it tip at all—in the direction of the head and of civilization. Hawthorne may deplore the Puritans' excessive reliance on the dictates of the head, he may pity the plight of Hester and Dimmesdale, and he may even (though hardly so much as his contemporaries) lament the excessive strictness of the magistrates. But he rejects firmly (as do both Hester and New England, finally) the extreme alternative offered by the convention—subordination of all to the heart, to romantic love, to nature.

Hawthorne thus rejects, finally, the whole notion of historical progress that lies behind so many of the works of his contemporaries. Hester Prynne, again like the conventional heroines, opposes to the severity of the Puritans, to the mistakes of the past, a glowing American vision of a new start, a liberated future. "Begin all anew!" she shouts to Dimmesdale, and her comment could apply not only to Dimmesdale's failure but to the failure of the whole American experiment; "Hast thou exhausted possibility in the failure of this one trial? Not so! The future is yet full of trial and success. There is happiness to be enjoyed!" [198]. "Let us not look back," Hester insists. "The past is gone! Wherefore should we linger upon it now!" To prove her point she removes the token of her identity from her breast and throws it among the "withered leaves." "See!" she explains, "with this symbol, I undo it all, and make it as it had never been!" [202]. Yet within nine pages Hester has had to reassume her scarlet letter, and Hawthorne's reading of the event hardly supports the notion that the future holds either happiness or liberation. "An evil deed," Hawthorne writes, "invests itself with the character of doom" [211].

Hester cannot escape her past, as she demonstrates at the close by voluntarily returning to Boston to wear the scarlet letter to her grave. The American experiment, as the opening paragraph of *The Scarlet Letter* makes clear, has failed to achieve its Utopian goals. Hawthorne sees this as the great, inescapable fact about America—as it is the full meaning of Hester's return to Boston. "An evil deed invests itself with the character of doom." Hawthorne will not accept the assurance that progress has restored, or will restore, the possibility of success. As the claims of the head or the claims of "higher truth" should control the "wild, heathen Nature of the forest," so the claims of the past, Hawthorne believed, were not lightly to be dismissed. By subverting the symbolic values of the natural heroine, Hawthorne was rejecting not simply the belief in nature or in the liberation of the heart but also the notion that history, and especially American history, were to be comprehended as the glorious triumph of nature and the heart over the past. In rejecting the assumptions behind the conventional historical romance of New England, Hawthorne was rejecting the essential pattern by which the writers of that convention understood the movement, the direction, and the nature of history.

NOTES

[1] Nathaniel Hawthorne, "Mrs. Hutchinson," *Standard Library Edition of the Works of Nathaniel Hawthorne*, ed. George Parsons Lathrop, 15 vols., Boston, 1882–1891, XII, 223. Subsequent references to this work will appear in brackets in the text.
[2] Perhaps the best known of these attacks is the contention, in a letter to Ticknor, that "America is now wholly given over to a d——d mob of scribbling women." (*Letters of Hawthorne to William D. Ticknor, 1851–1864*, 2 vols., Newark, N.J., 1910, I, 75). Even more picturesque is the protest written to Fields (December 11, 1852): "*All* women, as author's [*sic*], are feeble and tiresome. I wish they were forbidden to write, on pain of having their faces deeply scarified with an oyster shell." ("Letters from Nathaniel Hawthorne to James T. Fields," MS Copies by Several Hands. By permission of the Harvard College Library.)
[3] Quoted by Mark Van Doren, *Nathaniel Hawthorne*, New York, 1957, pp. 106–107.
[4] Catharine Maria Sedgwick, *Hope Leslie; or, Early Times in the Massachusetts* [1827], New York, 1842, I, 198. Subsequent references to this work will appear in brackets in the text.
[5] In a recent article on *The Scarlet Letter*, John C. Stubbs has also noted briefly the resemblance between Hester's situation and that of the conventional romance heroine—"the situation of the heroine with a warm, loving nature alienated from, or in conflict with, Puritan severity." ("Hawthorne's *The Scarlet Letter*: The Theory of the Romance and the Use of the New England Situation," *PMLA*, LXXXIII [1968], 1445.)
[6] Nathaniel Hawthorne, *The Scarlet Letter*, *The Centenary Edition of the Works of Nathaniel Hawthorne*, Columbus, Ohio, 1962, p. 114. Subsequent references to this work will appear in brackets in the text.
[7] Hester's relationship to nineteenth-century feminism has been noted by a number of critics. See, for example, Neal F. Doubleday, "Hawthorne's Hester and Feminism," *PMLA*, LIV (1939), 825–28.
[8] Perry Miller, "The Romantic Dilemma in American Nationalism and the Concept of Nature," *Nature's Nation*, Cambridge, Mass., 1967, p. 199. In this article Professor Miller also speculates on the reasons why these are particularly American oppositions. "The crucial difference between the American appeal to Romantic Nature and the European," he writes, is that "in America, it served not so much for individual or artistic salvation as for an assuaging of national anxiety" (p. 203). The European turned to nature as an individual fleeing civilization. The American wanted his whole civilization to flee with him, and his effort was thus, on every level, fraught with contradictions.
[9] Eliza Buckminster Lee, *Naomi; or, Boston, Two Hundred Years Ago*, Boston, 1848, p. 336. Subsequent references to this work will appear in brackets in the text.
[10] Pearl is as close as we come to having a blonde here, but we learn that she eventually became as dark as her mother. She has, we are told, "hair already of a deep, glossy brown, and which, in after years, would be nearly akin to black" [101].
[11] But if Hawthorne has rejected the blonde in *The Scarlet Letter* why, one might ask, does he return to her with Phoebe in *The House of the Seven Gables*, and to the blonde-brunette pairing in *The Blithedale Romance*, *The Marble Faun*, and the unfinished *Septimius Felton?* It is usually argued that the blondes of *The Blithedale Romance* and *The Marble Faun* are to some extent parodies of the convention—which somewhat removes from Hawthorne the onus of mere conventionality. But it seems to me that we cannot so easily remove this onus. I think that Hawthorne, in many respects, *does* become more conventional in the works that follow *The Scarlet Letter*. Many conventional symbols are simply taken over and used uncritically in these later works. It is certainly true, as we will see in the next chapter, that *The House of the Seven Gables* is much more conventional than *The Scarlet Letter*. The appearance of Phoebe, exemplar of a convention examined so critically only a year before, is one of a number of ways in which *The House of the Seven Gables* represents a falling off from the intensity and clear-headedness of Hawthorne's masterpiece. (For a discussion of Hawthorne's blondes see Virginia Ogden Birdsall, "Hawthorne's Fair-Haired Maidens: The Fading Light," *PMLA*, LXXV [1960], 250–56).

Robert Penn Warren

HAWTHORNE REVISITED: SOME REMARKS ON HELLFIREDNESS

*T*he *Scarlet Letter* is another example of Hawthorne's inclination to treat violent materials in the long perspective of the past. In this work Hawthorne not only takes his materials from the past, in which the violence may be regarded at arm's length, but omits what might have been the most violently emotional phase of the story—the account of the growth of passion, the temptation, and the fall. Indeed, he does not even begin with the story itself, but with the introductory discussion of the custom house, which serves as a screen between the reader and the possible intensity of action, as a distancing device. Then, when he does enter the story proper, he opens with the first stage of the long train of consequences, the moment when Hester steps forth from the jail to face public shame. Even this is introduced by a kind of prologue, which puts the event in the perspective of meaning as contrasted with a direct shock to the emotions: the scene of the throng of men in "sad-colored garments" contrasted with the wild rose bush blooming at the very door of the jail, "in token that the deep heart of Nature could pity and be kind". So we have here in this contrast the first indication of the thematic tension, which represents an intellectualizing of emotion.

The same contrast is to be developed, more deeply and ironically, in the fact that the women waiting at the jail, who, as women, should "naturally" exhibit some sympathy and understanding for Hester's plight, are more savage than the men in their condemnation: that is, there is a contrast between their natural rôle and their social rôle. To continue, when Hester does appear, the scarlet *A* on her bosom presents a variation on the same thematic line; for, embroidered in gold thread with a "gorgeous luxuriance of fancy", it is—"naturally", shall we say?—an object of beauty, while socially considered it is a badge of infamy.

This set of contrasts, we shall see as the story develops, will lead us to another and deeper paradox, in that the act which is a "sin" is also presented as the source of deepened understanding and development. This, however, is to run ahead of

From *Sewanee Review* 81, No. 1 (January–March 1973): 95–111.

ourselves, and for the moment what we see is that the woman who, we have learned from the crowd, is a creature to be reviled steps forth, surprisingly enough, in a beauty and pride which make "a halo of the misfortune and ignominy". The point here is simply to observe how freighted with meaning are the details of the narrative and how coherently these suggestions will be developed.

If we look at the first three chapters, we find a marvelously compact and exciting introductory section; for *The Scarlet Letter* is, in point of fact, the first American novel to be truly "composed", in the sense that we shall find Henry James using the term; that is, the first novel to consider form as, in itself, an expression of emotion and meaning. In connection with the structure of the novel, we must note that in this first scene Hester stands on the scaffold. This fact is of the deepest significance, for the scaffold is crucial to the whole conception. With this opening scene, the great scene of Dimmesdale's midnight vigil on it (in Chapter 12, at the middle of the novel), and the denouement and Dimmesdale's death on it at the end, the scaffold becomes the seminal image of the novel, the locus of both agony and vision.

Now, at the beginning, Hester, standing on the scaffold, experiences, in a flash of memory, the "entire track along which she had been treading since her happy infancy"—aware, however vaguely, of a pattern in her fate. Across the crowd she suddenly sees the old man who is her husband, and who, as though an incarnation of her past, seems to be summoned by her thoughts of it. His identity is not yet divulged to us, but from the sinister tone of his questioning of a bystander, we get what exposition we need, getting it as an action thrusting forward (as the old man, referring to Hester's unknown partner in guilt, threatens, "He will be known"), not as mere exposition. Then, as the apex of this "triangular" scene, we first see Dimmesdale, placed high with the great and powerful of the state who judge and administer judgment: poor Dimmesdale, whose sermon to Hester now, with all its doubleness of motivation and of meaning, is a dynamic development of, and a guide to, his private drama.

Chapter 4, with the scene between Hester and Chillingworth, may be taken as the last phase of the first movement of the novel. Here Chillingworth defines for himself, and for us, his rôle, and forces Hester into her decision to keep silent about his identity, a decision which gives the key to the future action. The novel is now in train: we have a masterful piece of exposition, the characters established in their archetypal stances, with a maximum of economy in presenting the past and a maximum of suspense in the thrust toward the future.

After the essentially dramatic exposition of the first four chapters, there is a second movement, this of generalized narrative rather than scene, analytical rather than dramatic. Here we have a description of the kind of life Hester works out for herself in the "charmed circle" of her moral isolation and, as a corollary, a further presentation of her character. Why has she remained in Boston to be a "type of shame"? Because here she has encountered reality; "her sin, her ignominy, were the roots which she had struck in the soil." But there was another motive, although she "hid the secret from herself". Dimmesdale is here, with whom "she deemed herself connected in a union ... that would bring them together before the bar of final judgment, and make that their marriage altar, for a joint futurity of endless retribution". So in the very idea of "endless retribution" with her lover there enters an element of sexual gratification, torment as ecstasy, a thing totally removed from the idea of true penitence; it was an idea that "the tempter of souls" thrust upon her, and then "laughed at the passionate and desperate joy with which she seized, and then strove to cast it from her".

Meanwhile, Hester lives by doing sewing and performing acts of charity, even for those who revile her in the moment of accepting it. She was a "martyr", but she "forbore to pray for her enemies lest, in spite of her forgiving aspiration, the words of blessing should stubbornly twist themselves into a curse". She felt, too, that the letter had "endowed her with a new sense", that it "gave her a sympathetic knowledge of the hidden sin in other hearts". In regard to this she was torn between the temptation to believe that all "purity" was a "lie", and the impulse to "believe that no fellow mortal was guilty like herself". (But she will, at the end, develop another option in which she will rest: that of using the knowledge coming from "sin" as a means to assist and comfort others.)

The only society possible to her is little Pearl. She dresses the child gorgeously, the richness of color being an expression of that part of her own nature otherwise suppressed. The child, often presented as little more than an allegory, is a kind of elf, outside the ordinary world, a child of "nature" who says to Hester, "I have no Heavenly Father". There comes a time when the authorities are about to remove Pearl from Hester's care, and only the arguments advanced by Dimmesdale prevent this, a fact which confirms Chillingworth in his suspicions of the minister's guilt.

In the second movement of the novel, too, the course of the relation of Dimmesdale and Chillingworth is traced. Dimmesdale is living in anguish. Tormented by his guilt and by his weakness in not bringing himself to confess it, he can still self-deceivingly argue that there are men who, though guilty, retain "a zeal for God's glory and man's welfare", and therefore "shrink from displaying themselves black and filthy in the view of men", because by such a course "no evil of the past can be redeemed by better service". He keeps a scourge in his closet and pitilessly brings blood to his own shoulders, all the while laughing bitterly. But all his acts of penance are fruitless; there is, he says, "penance" but not "penitence", only a "mockery of penitence". In other words, as in Hester's thought of union in the torture of "endless retribution", there is, in Dimmesdale's pangs of penance, a kind of sexual gratification.

Even as he suffers, Dimmesdale "has achieved a brilliant popularity in his sacred office", having "won it indeed by his sorrows", for, in a kind of parallel to Hester's notion that she could intuit the guilt in the hearts of others, Dimmesdale's "burden" is what makes "his sympathies so intimate with the sinful brotherhood of mankind" that his pain issues in "gushes of sad, persuasive eloquence".

As a result of his torment, Dimmesdale's health fails, and the learned stranger

Chillingworth moves into the same house with him, ostensibly to save him for the greater glory of God and of New England. Chillingworth is there, of course, out of his desire for vengeance, which now amounts to a mania, a mania intertwined with his intellectual passion for anatomizing the soul and body of the sufferer. Dimmesdale, out of the morbidity of his sensibility, is aware of an inimical agency but cannot identify it.

With Chapter 12, the second movement of the novel ends, the long section of generalized narration and analysis being concluded by the night scene in which Dimmesdale, forecasting the climactic scene at the end of the novel, mounts the scaffold. Now, "in this vain show of expiation", Dimmesdale is "overcome with a great horror of mind, as if the universe were gazing at a scarlet token on his naked breast", where in fact there had long been "the gnawing and poisonous tooth of bodily pain". In his agony Dimmesdale shrieks, and then, being sure that his voice has summoned the whole town to see his shame, he exclaims, with an echo of the Biblical account of the crucifixion, "It is done!" The town does not rouse itself to witness Dimmesdale's agony (as it will in the end), but there is the ghostlike appearance of the old governor at his window and at another the head of his sister, the witch, and then, in the street, unaware of him, the Reverend Mr. Wilson, who has been praying by the deathbed of old Winthrop, the former governor.

It is the passing of Mr. Wilson that stirs up the wild self-torturing humor in Dimmesdale that is to appear again after the forest scene with Hester; and this "grisly sense of the humorous" summons up his vision of what the morning will reveal:

> The neighbourhood would begin to rouse itself. The earliest riser, coming forth in the dim twilight, would perceive a vaguely defined figure aloft on the place of shame; and, half crazed betwixt alarm and curiosity, would go, knocking from door to door, summoning all the people to behold the ghost—as he needs must think it—of some defunct transgressor. A dusky tumult would flap its wings from one house to another. Then—the morning light still waxing stronger—old patriarchs would rise up in great haste, each in his flannel gown, and matronly dames, without pausing to put off their night-gear. The whole tribe of decorous personages, who had never heretofore been seen with a single hair of their heads awry, would start into public view, with the disorder of a nightmare in their aspects. Old Governor Bellingham would come grimly forth, with his King James's ruff fastened askew; and Mistress Hibbins, with some twigs of the forest clinging to her skirts, and looking sourer than ever, as having hardly got a wink of sleep after her night ride; and good Father Wilson, too, after spending half the night at a death-bed, and liking ill to be disturbed, thus early, out of his dreams about the glorified saints. Hither, likewise, would come the elders and deacons of Mr. Dimmesdale's church, and the young virgins who so idolized their minster, and had made a shrine for him in their white bosoms; which, now, by the by, in their hurry and confusion,

they would scantly have given themselves time to cover with their kerchiefs. All people, in a word, would come stumbling over their thresholds, and turning up their amazed and horror-stricken visages around the scaffold.

At this Dimmesdale, "to his own infinite alarm", burst out into wild laughter, and this laughter, as by the logic of dream, evokes the "light, airy, childish" laughter of Pearl, the "good" witch (unlike the sister of Governor Bellingham), the child who is of nature, who has "no Heavenly Father". And there is Hester, who, with Pearl, ascends the scaffold to stand by his side. Then the red meteor flames in the sky, and in that red glare appears Chillingworth, who has come, he says, to lead Dimmesdale home.

The scaffold scene not only brings to focus, there at the middle of the novel, all the forces that, in their complexity and ambiguity, are at work, but also provides a new thrust of plot. For the scene impels Hester to seek out her husband to persuade him to have mercy on his victim. Chillingworth refuses, but he offers an insight into himself and his private story. He is, he says, now a "fiend", and he demands: "Who made me so?" To which, Hester, shuddering at a new sense of guilt, replies: "It was myself." But even the "fiend" can see the pity of their situation: "Peradventure, hadst thou met earlier with a better love than mine, this evil had not been. I pity thee for the good that has been wasted in thy nature."

But when Hester says that she pities him for the same reason and makes a last plea that, to save his own soul, he release Dimmesdale, he can only reply that "it has all been a dark necessity." And in one of the most important thematic statements of the novel, he continues: "Ye that have wronged me are not sinful, save in a kind of typical illusion; neither am I fiendlike who have snatched a fiend's office from his hand. It is our fate. Let the black flower blossom as it may!"

The refusal of Chillingworth to relinquish Dimmesdale justifies Hester, she feels, in breaking her promise not to divulge his identity, and so prepares for the end of the third movement of the novel in the forest scene (Chapter 17), in which the strong and vital Hester attempts to save Dimmesdale by persuading him to flee from America and seek a new life, and which comes to a climax when she snatches the A from her bosom and casts it away.

This scene, in the beautiful interpenetration of elements in the structure of the work, not only provides a forward thrust for action (it prepares for the end), but interprets the past. We had never seen, or been told anything about, the relation of the lovers before the opening of the novel, but now, in this "natural" forest scene, we understand how Hester, in her "natural" strength and vitality, is the "seducer" of Dimmesdale, and we understand that it must have been this way, however unconsciously, in the beginning of their story before the novel opens. We understand more precisely than before another element of both structure and meaning: the tension, in life and in man, between "nature" and "idea", the doom of man's essential division of flesh and spirit.

Other elements are to emerge in the fourth movement. In the forest scene itself we notice the reaction of little Pearl, who will not cross the brook to her mother and Dimmesdale until the A is restored to its place—to declare Hester's identity (and, for that matter, Dimmesdale's too). The forest scene throws a special light on the split between flesh and spirit. It would seem that man, in seeking the freedom of nature (discarding the A and preparing to flee), loses his identity, that is, his moral history. But, at the same time, in the ambiguity of experience, we see that the most immediate consequence of this decision to discard the mark of guilt and to flee to make a new life (by discarding penance without having achieved penitence) is the great burst of "natural" energy for the nearly moribund Dimmesdale.

Associated with this energy as he rushes homeward is a kind of diabolic humor, like that observed on the midnight scaffold, which now amounts to a parody of Dimmesdale's gift of intuitive sympathy for the sinful hearts of others and which now expresses itself in a desire to entrap others in their own corruption—to whisper a wicked joke in the ear of a young girl or an atheistical argument into that of a poor widow who has nothing left but her Christian faith. Dimmesdale experiences, in other words, a sudden release of his suppressed sexual energy (brilliantly analyzed by Frederick Crews in his study of Hawthorne), which had been spent in penance and which now comes out in an anarchic denial of all "purity"; but he is still so much the man of faith that he can think of his new energy only in terms of the joy of Christian conversion—"risen up all made anew, and with new powers to glorify Him that hath been merciful". (And this little passage may be put in balance with the last words of Dimmesdale in the climactic scene of the novel.) This is a parody of conversion, and as such the carrier of a double irony. First, Dimmesdale does not realize the nature of the "joy", not even when it eventuates in the anarchic obscenities. Second, Dimmesdale does not realize that he, being the "religionist" he is, cannot escape into the guiltlessness of pure nature. He is doomed to penitence—doomed, as it were, to be saved. This is his "dark necessity".

Another consequence flows from the forest scene. As the new "joy" of Dimmesdale bursts forth into the obscene comedy on the way homeward, so, once in his chamber, it bursts forth in the composition of the election day sermon that he will give before his flight into "guiltlessness". As he sits in his chamber, and sees his old Bible there, he thinks of himself as he had once been; and he "eyes that former self with scornful, pitying, but half-envious curiosity". Even as he repudiates that old pious self, his pen is racing ahead as though beyond his control. What if this eloquence, which soon all auditors will consider divinely inspired, springs from the same energy that had been bursting out in the anarchic obscenities? Hawthorne would certainly not regard this as a simple irony undercutting the validity and spirituality of the sermon. There is an irony, to be sure, but an irony involving the very doubleness of human nature.

The fifth, and last, movement of the novel begins with a public gathering, which architecturally balances the scene outside the jail at the beginning of the story. Hester and Pearl are now in the crowd waiting for the great procession to the church where Dimmesdale will give his sermon. Here Hester encounters the captain of the Bristol ship that is to take her, Pearl, and her lover away (the captain, let us note, is "outside" society and its values, a creature of the wild ocean like a creature of the unredeemed forest, where the Devil lurks and witches foregather); but from him, the agent of freedom, she gets the news, not of freedom and guiltlessness, but of pursuing guilt in the person of Chillingworth, who has found out the secret of their intended flight and taken passage on the same ship.

A second shock awaits Hester when she sees Dimmesdale in the procession, suddenly seeming far beyond her among the great, his mind "far and deep in its own region" and his eyes not sparing even a glance for her. Her spirit sinks with "the idea that all must have been delusion". And upon her thoughts, to compound this distress, there breaks Mistress Hibbins, the witch, speaking of the Black Man in the forest and how Dimmesdale had signed a bond there with him.

At the time of the sermon, with symbolic appropriateness, Hester is outside the church, standing by the scaffold of the pillory, with the sense in her "that her whole orb of life ... was connected with this spot, as the one point that gave it unity"—as it gives the novel unity. As she stands there, she cannot hear the actual words of the sermon, only the flow of the minister's peculiarly musical and expressive voice, with an "essential character of plaintiveness". The fact that she cannot hear the words has symbolic significance, of course, for, in a sense, she and her lover do not speak the same language. They belong to different dimensions of life that scarcely intersect—only in their "love". His obsessed spirituality, which is his "necessary" story, is not for her. So what she hears is not a message from his dimension, but the "whisper, or the shriek, as it might be conceived, of suffering humanity". And it is the same secret voice of "suffering humanity", not the message, that provokes the "rapture of the congregation—though, ironically enough, they think they are moved by the message which foretells a high and glorious destiny" for the settlers in New England, that "newly gathered people of the Lord".

When, after the sermon, Dimmesdale summons Hester and Pearl to the scaffold with him for the climactic scene of the confession, several features should be remarked. First, the rôle of Chillingworth, we now see, is not to uncover the sinner, but to prevent the confession, for in the confession his victim "escapes" him. Second, in Dimmesdale's penitent confession there is, in the very ecstasy of self-abasement, a kind of egotism; he is, he proclaims, the "one sinner of the world". Third, as a corollary of this egotism, when Hester, from the depth of her feeling, cries out for assurance that they will meet in the immortal life, Dimmesdale replies that the "law" has been broken and it may be vain to hope for a "pure reunion". He does add that God is merciful, but with this reference to mercy, his egotism totally reasserts itself, and the mercy now referred to is to be directed at Dimmesdale alone. If God had not mercifully given Dimmesdale the "burning torture" on his breast, the company of the "dark, terrible old man", and death in "triumphant ignominy", then he "had been lost forever".

Poor Hester is utterly forgotten. In fact, we should add that if the confession is an "escape" from Chillingworth, it is also, in a deeper fashion, an "escape" from Hester—from nature, from flesh, from passion, from sexuality, from, in the end, woman, who is the unclean one, the temptress. So, even in the heroic moment, there is the deepest of all ambiguities.

It is easy to see how, if a reader ignores all the characters except Dimmesdale, if he does not attend very closely to what Dimmesdale does and says, and if he accepts Dimmesdale's values as Hawthorne's, he can take *The Scarlet Letter* as *merely* a story of conscience and redemption. But, clearly, Sophia with her "grievous headache", Emerson with his "Ghastly, ghastly", and Hawthorne with his "hell-fired" saw more. Each in his own way saw the tragic tensions, the pitiful instances of waste, the irremediable askewness of life which the story, taken as a whole, delineates.

Taken as a whole: that is the point. Even in Dimmesdale's story there are ambiguities. How much, for instance, is there of spiritual aspiration, and how much of fear of nature, fear of his own nature, sexual incertitude, and narcissism? But whatever Dimmesdale may actually be taken to be, he is only part of the pattern of the novel. Chillingworth, for instance, is a thematic and psychological counterpoint to him; and even, in the novel, a structural counterpoint, for the relation of each to Hester gives one principle of the action, and one principle of balance to the action. Psychologically and thematically, their rôles are even more significant. Both are men "outside" of nature, Chillingworth with his passion for study (to be directed, of course, to the good of mankind) and Dimmesdale with his aspiration to spirituality (so as to be a model for the redemption of mankind). When Chillingworth comes to the vital Hester he is already old, twisted, withered, and all but impotent, and if Dimmesdale discovers passion with her, there is inevitably the self-loathing we find expressed in the fact that part of his penance is to stare at his own face in a mirror. If Chillingworth, out of envy of what he takes to be the successful lover, and in his outraged vanity, devotes himself to the torture of Dimmesdale, then we find, as a parallel, Dimmesdale's obsessively gratifying process of self-torture. In the end, the two men are more important to each other than Hester is to either; theirs is the truest "marriage"—and a marriage of two perfect egotists.

Hester's story is one of penance, it is clear. She accepts her rôle as the outcast, the revulsion of society and the insults from even those unfortunates whom she succors, but she does this out of pride rather than humility. She has, in fact, stayed here for reasons having nothing to do with penance, to be near Dimmesdale and, perhaps more importantly, to fulfill some obscure sense of what Hawthorne calls the "unity" of her life and what we might call her identity. Further, her isolation has freed her mind to speculate about the nature of society, and to decide that society is not fixed by God in immutable law but is subject to change. This is not penance; and certainly not penitence.

Hawthorne says, indeed, that Hester had in her the making of a harsh prophetess who might attempt to create the future. It is this strain of coldness and harshness developed in her adversity, in her "battle" with the world, which he deplores, even as he admires her courage. This point is reinforced in the last scaffold scene. When Pearl, as though aroused by the "great scene of grief", comes out of the "spell" to kiss at last her father's lips, Hawthorne says that her tears "were the pledge that she would grow up in human joy and sorrow, nor forever do battle with the world, but be a woman in it"—unlike her mother.

The scaffold scene, then, would say that Hester has been forced to do battle with the world and that part of her tragedy lies in the consequent hardening of her womanliness; only in the meeting with Dimmesdale in the forest, where love is again "aroused", does her natural womanliness return: "Such was the sympathy of Nature—that wild, heathen nature of the forest, never subjugated by human law, nor illumined by higher truth."[1]

Hester, strong, vital, beautiful, is indeed the wonderful "natural" creature, one of those dark, passionate temptresses that Hawthorne put into fiction and, apparently, flinched from in life; but even so, another source of her tragedy lies in the fact that she cannot be merely "natural". Here we must consider that the men she has accepted are not men we would reasonably expect as her sexual partners. We can argue that accident and social conditions may well have played a part here, and this is true; but *dramatically* regarded, what we have is the natural woman yearning, as it were, toward a condition beyond her "naturalness". Dramatically, psychologically, and thematically regarded, it is not an accident that Hester takes up with the old and twisted Chillingworth, and when she deserts him, it is for the pale, beautiful Dimmesdale and his pathologically sensitive conscience and narcissistic spirituality, instead of for some strapping officer of militia who would wear his religion more lightly, could gratify her appetites more single-mindedly, and could sleep better o' nights. From the very start there has been an askewness in her fate, an askewness that Chillingworth recognizes when he says, "hadst thou met with a better love than mine, this evil had not been." But what he does not recognize is the possibility that there may also be a reason why "naturalness" yearns beyond "nature".

The last chapter is balanced, as a kind of epilogue, against the first, which, as we have said, serves as a prologue. The climactic scaffold scene must, then, be regarded in the context of this conclusion. The meaning of Dimmesdale's confession is, in this epilogue, subjected to debate, and the mere fact qualifies the interpretation of the whole story. There is, too, considerable complexity in the way the story of Chillingworth is worked out. Deprived of the terrible meaning of his own life, he withers away, but in the very withering he provides means for Pearl to achieve her life. As heiress to his fortune, she goes to Europe, marries a nobleman, and, as we are given to understand, fulfills the prediction that she would not "do battle with the world, but be a woman in it". This may be taken as a happy normality coming out of the distorted lives—but if so, then with what illogicality, and after what waste! Pearl's happiness can scarcely be taken to discount the grief of all the others.

As for Hester, can the final meaning of her life be taken to discount the grief?

She returns from Europe to resume her life in the withdrawn cottage and resumes, by her own choice, the scarlet letter—for only thus could she feel that her own life had found meaning. Now as she distributes comfort and counsel to women suffering from "wounded, wasted, wronged, misplaced, or erring and sinful passion", she assures them that a "brighter period" would come when the relation of man and woman would be "on a surer ground of mutual happiness". This, we must observe, is at the farthest remove from penitence, for the message that Hester, by implication, gives the suffering women is not that they are "sinners" in need of redemption, but that they are victims of a social order that violates nature.

How seriously are we, the readers, to take this prediction that would give to the novel, at least in a qualified way, a "happy ending"? Not very seriously, for, by a last strange irony, Hester, whose identity and vision have been made possible only by her "sin", can say that the prophetess of the new dispensation must be a woman "lofty, pure, and beautiful", and wise too, but, unlike Hester herself, not wise through a "dusky grief". This would be a world freed of all guilt, a world of natural joy. It is her dream, but scarcely the world Hawthorne envisaged.

In this connection, it may be recalled that, just as *The Scarlet Letter* was often misread as a cautionary tale of sin and conscience, it could also be misread as a tract in which Hester is primarily a martyr for the liberation of women—and of men, too—from a sexually repressive society. Such was the interpretation in a transcendentalist discussion of the novel by a certain George Bailey Loring, a young physician, writing in Theodore Parker's *Massachusetts Quarterly Review*—transcendentalist in so far as the doctrine of "self-reliance" and the validity of "intuition" were taken to imply sexual release from the sanctions of both church and state.

This element of conflict between the individual and society is clearly present in *The Scarlet Letter,* and it is reasonable to suppose that the influence of the Transcendentalists may have sharpened it in Hawthorne's mind. But Hawthorne's concern with the rigors of Puritan society, as with the complex tensions of sexual encounters, long preceded the initial meeting of earnest seekers in George Ripley's study that is usually understood to have officially ushered in the movement.

The meaning of *The Scarlet Letter* is far more tangled and profound than Dr. Loring ever imagined, and bears no simple relation to transcendental reformism. The concern of Hawthorne here, as in his work in general, lies in the tension between the demands of spirit and those of nature. Indeed, the Transcendentalists had insisted upon this issue, but Hawthorne's view, profoundly ironical as it was in seeing the tension between the two realms as the very irremediable essence of life, in its tragedy and glory and even comedy, was far different from anything that ever crossed a transcendental mind.

Even nature, which, in the novel, is thematically set against the sanctions of society, cannot be taken simply. The forest is a haunt of evil as well as of good, and the wishes of the heart may be wicked as well as benign. In the tale "The Holocaust," for example, when all the marks of evil and vanity have been consigned to the flames, the world is not purged; there remains the human heart. In that world of ambiguities, there is, inevitably, a terrible illogic. Good and bad may be inter-twined; good may be wasted; accident, not justice, rules. Man is doomed to live in a world where nature is denied and human nature distorted, and—most shatter-ingly of all—in a world where love and hate may be "the same thing at bottom", and even vice or virtue may represent nothing more than what Chillingworth calls "a typical illusion". But men must live by the logic of their illusions, as best they can—Dimmesdale by his, Hester by hers, and Chillingworth by his. That is their last and darkest "necessity". What compensation is possible in such a world comes from the human capacity for achieving scale and grandeur even in illusion—one might say by insisting on the coherence of the illusion—and from the capacity for giving pity. And here we must remind ourselves that Hawthorne found it "almost impossible to throw a cheering light" on the book.

So much for the hellfiredness of *The Scarlet Letter*.

NOTE

[1] This scene has strong parallels with the scene in *Billy Budd* where the chaplain meditates on the "innocence" of the "barbarian" boy.

Judith Fryer

HESTER PRYNNE: THE DARK LADY AS ''DEVIANT''

Hester Prynne is warm, alive, human—so much so that it is difficult to determine just where Hawthorne's sympathies lie. In making her the best—the most "human"—character in the book he is at his most ambiguous in his valuation of both community mores and individual deviance, with Hester's life-giving but threatening sexuality once again standing for the hazard which individuality poses to the very survival of the community. I do not use the word "ambiguous" lightly here; I believe that Hawthorne was not able finally to resolve his own dilemma. He, as his own marriage to the "safe" Sophia demonstrates, needed the security of community; but as alienated artist he felt estranged from that community which defined "masculinity" in terms of success in the commercial world. His profound sense of alienation led him in 1825 to seclude himself in his "owl's nest" from a world in which he perceived no way to acknowledge the "femininity" of his own artistic nature. In an attempt to reestablish contact with the human community, he wrote to Longfellow on June 4, 1837: "By some witchcraft or other—for I really cannot assign any reasonable why and wherefore—I have been carried apart from the main current of life, and find it impossible to get back again. Since we last met . . . I have secluded myself from society; and yet I never meant any such thing, nor dreamed what sort of life I was going to lead. I have made a captive of myself and put me into a dungeon; and now I cannot find the key to let myself out—and if the door were open, I should be almost afraid to come out. . . . For the last ten years I have not lived, but only dreamed about living."[1] His few attempts to find his "place" in the world were futile. He sees himself, in "The Custom-House" preface to *The Scarlet Letter,* as an "idler," an oddity to have sprung from "the old trunk of the family tree, with so much venerable moss upon it," and never regards his sojourn there as anything other than "a transitory life" because in the quest for "Uncle Sam's gold" all "imaginative delight . . . passed away out of my mind."[2] His sojourn at Brook Farm

From *The Faces of Eve: Women in the Nineteenth Century American Novel* (New York: Oxford University Press, 1976), pp. 72–84.

proved no more successful. As he wrote to Sophia in the fall of 1841, "A man's soul may be buried and perish under a dung-heap or in the furrow of a field, just as well as under a pile of money." His salvation was his marriage to Sophia; she provided him with both a link to society and protective solitude—the combination necessary for his creativity. "Thou only hast revealed me to myself," he wrote to her in 1840, "for without thy aid, my best knowledge of myself would have been merely to know my own shadow—to watch it flickering on the wall, and mistake its fantasies for my own real actions. Indeed, we are but shadows—we are not endowed with real life, and all that seems most real about us is but the thinnest substance of a dream—till the heart is touched. That touch creates us—then we begin to be— . . . ." But Sophia was no richly vital, fully sexual Hester Prynne. She is, in the same letter, his "Dove": "I begin to understand why I was imprisoned so many years in this lonely chamber, and why I could never break through the viewless bolts and bars; for if I had sooner made my escape into the world, I should have grown hard and rough, and been covered with earthly dust, and my heart would have become callous by rude encounters with the multitude; so that I should have been all unfit to shelter a heavenly Dove in my arms."[3]

Hawthorne, then, places great value on belonging to the society *through* Sophia, his dove, the preserver of society's standards; yet at the same time, as an artist he is at odds with that very society. Whoever touches Uncle Sam's gold, he warns in "The Custom-House," "should look well to himself, or he may find the bargain to go hard against him, involving, if not his soul, yet many of its better attributes; its sturdy force, its courage and constancy, its truth, its self-reliance, and all that gives emphasis to manly character." His use of the word "manly" here is different from his perception of society's definition of that term elsewhere in "The Custom-House." It suggests the difficulty he has accepting what he feels to be the "unmanly" qualities of his artistic self, and is therefore a clue to his own sexual insecurity. Those "manly" attributes are also the very qualities which both make Hester Prynne attractive and condemn her: "sturdy force," "courage and constancy," "truth," "self-reliance,"—attributes diametrically opposed to those of Sophia, qualities which in a woman cannot preserve the community, but would destroy it.

Hawthorne's ambiguity about Hester, then, is an attempt to work out his ambiguity toward himself, as artist, as man, as member of the human community. When he places her scarlet letter on his own breast in "The Custom-House," he experiences "a sensation not altogether physical, yet almost so, as of burning heat; and as if the letter were not of red cloth, but red-hot iron." The "A" of the alienated artist is *the* subject of most of Hawthorne's tales. This warning from "Wakefield," for example (later echoed by Zenobia in *The Blithedale Romance*), is a warning for Hawthorne the artist and Hester the woman alike: "Amid the seeming confusion of our mysterious world, individuals are so nicely adjusted to a system, and systems to one another and to a whole, that, by stepping aside for a moment a man exposes himself to a fearful risk of losing his place forever."

The importance of "place" must not be discounted by twentieth-century readers who would see Hester Prynne as "androgynous" and Hawthorne as a writer with "feminist" sympathies.[4] If Hawthorne the artist was not sure which values—those of Uncle Sam or those of "truth" and "self-reliance"—were manly, how much less did Hester Prynne lack a context for her androgynous qualities. Hawthorne himself would deny women such a context. He wrote, for example, in his biography of "Mrs. Hutchinson":

> Woman's intellect should never give the tone to that of man; and even her morality is not exactly the material for masculine virtue. [It is] a false liberality, which mistakes the strong division-lines of Nature for arbitrary distinctions. . . . As yet, the great body of American women are a domestic race; but when a continuance of ill-judged incitements shall have turned their hearts away from the fireside, there are obvious circumstances which will render female pens more numerous and more prolific than those of men . . . and the ink-stained Amazons will expel their rivals by actual pressure, and petticoats wave triumphantly over all the field. Fame does not increase the peculiar respect which men pay to female excellence, and there is a delicacy . . . that perceives, or fancies, a sort of impropriety in the display of woman's natal mind to the gaze of the world. . . . In fine, criticism should examine with a stricter, instead of a more indulgent eye, the merits of females at its bar, because they are to justify themselves for an irregularity which men do not commit in appearing there; and woman, when she feels the impulse of genius like a command of Heaven within her, should be aware that she is relinquishing a part of the loveliness of her sex, and obey the inward voice with sorrowing reluctance, like the Arabian maid who bewailed the gift of prophecy.[5]

I have quoted this long passage on Anne Hutchinson because it is necessary to understand Hawthorne's attitude toward strong women in any attempt to decide upon his sympathies for Hester Prynne, and because *The Scarlet Letter* is set in Anne Hutchinson's Boston. There are two deliberate references linking Anne Hutchinson to Hester Prynne. In the initial chapter a wild rose-bush blooms by the prison door from which Hester emerges; it is said to have "sprung up under the footsteps of the sainted Anne Hutchinson." And in the chapter called "Another View of Hester" we are told that had little Pearl not come to her from the spiritual world, then "she might have come down to us in history, hand in hand with Anne Hutchinson as the foundress of a religious sect. She might . . . have been a prophetess. She might, and not improbably would, have suffered death from the stern tribunals of the period, for attempting to undermine the foundations of the Puritan establishment." This is a clue to the whole questions of Hester and of Hawthorne's ambiguity in posing her against a group of grim, intolerant and even un-Christian Puritans, who do, nevertheless, comprise a community. Hester's deviance from its norms represents not an alternative community, not the Garden, but the wildness of the forest.

The Scarlet Letter is a novel about a failed community. Like The Blithedale Romance, the novel specifically about Hawthorne's involvement in a (failed) utopian community, the earlier Scarlet Letter is contemporaneous with that experience. As he saw the attempt to re-create Eden at Brook Farm as a doomed attempt in Blithedale, so he perceived the vision of the founders of the Massachusetts Bay Colony as doomed from the beginning. He believed the roots of evil to exist in the individual, not in social institutions; he was more interested in psychology than in social change. One is prepared by the remark in the preface that "Neither the front nor the back entrance of the Custom-House opens on the road to Paradise" for the opening of The Scarlet Letter: "The founders of a new colony, whatever Utopia of human virtue and happiness they might originally project, have invariably recognized it among their earliest practical necessities to allot a portion of the virgin soil as a cemetery, and another portion as the site of a prison." There is not only death in this New World Garden of Eden; there are deviants who are so obnoxious or dangerous to the community that they must be locked up. Such malefactors might be Antinomians, Quakers or other "heterodox religionists," Indians, or witches, among them Anne Hutchinson and Hester Prynne—the one represented by the wild rose-bush, and the other, in contrast to the "sad-colored garments" of the Puritans, by the "fantastic flourishes of gold thread" of the letter A, embroidered with "much fertility and gorgeous luxuriance of fancy." The community is grim, but it is lawful; the rose-bush is beautiful, but it is wild; and the fantastically embroidered scarlet letter has the effect of taking Hester "out of the ordinary relations with humanity, and enclosing her in a sphere by herself."

Hester's prideful stance upon the scaffold as she faces her judges, then, is deliberately modeled upon Anne Hutchinson's; they pose the same threat to the community. "In the midst, and in the centre of all eyes, we see the woman," Hawthorne wrote in his portrait of Anne Hutchinson. "She stands loftily before her judges with a determined brow; and unknown to herself, there is a flash of carnal pride half hidden in her eye."[6] The members of this "community," in the words of John Winthrop's "A Modell of Christian Charity" of 1629, the written compact for the Massachusetts Bay Colony, entered into a "covenant" with God to do His will, literally to found "a city upon a hill," a New World Garden of Eden. Winthrop himself, in this document, is the Moses who will lead his people to the promised land.[7] As Erikson points out in Wayward Puritans, every community has its own set of boundaries, and its boundaries are determined by the behavior of its members. The boundaries of the Massachusetts Bay Colony were clear; Winthrop defined them in his "Little Speech on Liberty," where "civil" or "federal" liberty is a covenant between God and man, represented politically by the subjection of citizens to those in authority as God's representatives. It is this same kind of "liberty" which makes a wife, after she has chosen her husband through her own free will, subject to him: "a true wife accounts her subjection her honor and freedom."[8] Ostensibly punished for her Antinomian (literally, against the law) beliefs, Anne Hutchinson was a woman who did not keep "in the place God had set her."[9] Witch or feminist, depending on one's point of view—her skills as nurse and midwife indicating her knowledge of the secrets of birth and healing outside the realm of men, and her theological discussion groups our first women's consciousness-raising sessions—she opposed the church fathers, among them the same John Wilson who takes part in condemning and punishing Hester.

Hester, too, has perpetrated a crime against church and state: she has committed adultery and borne an illegitimate child. But her refusal as a woman to keep to her appointed place would have placed her outside the boundaries of the self-righteous community had her conduct been otherwise irreproachable. And Hester is a real, not an imagined threat to the community, as her "natural dignity and force of character"—unusual in a person just emerging from a long prison confinement to face a public humiliation—make clear. Had no stigma attached itself to her, she would have attempted nothing less than revolution. Hester often broods upon the "dark question" of "the whole race of womanhood," and her conclusions—that the "system of society is to be torn down, and built up anew"—are bothersome to Hawthorne because it would mean a modification of "the very nature of the opposite sex" necessary to woman's being "allowed to assume what seems a fair and suitable position." There can be no reforms, he says, until woman shall have undergone a mighty change "in which, perhaps, the ethereal essence, wherein she has her truest life, will be found to have evaporated." A man who himself married a pale maiden can only be at best ambivalent in his admiration for Hester. He calls the "ethereal essence" her "truest life." And he cannot help adding, "A woman never overcomes these problems by any exercise of thought. They are not to be solved, or only in one way. If her heart chance to come uppermost, they vanish."

In Hawthorne's later books the "ethereal essence" of the dark lady will have evaporated; it will belong to the pale maiden, the blonde or brown-haired New England girl. Because Hester is not split into schizophrenic segments, she comes across as a whole person, one who elicits the reader's sympathy and admiration. She is his most perfect Eve, combining sensuality with an "ethereal essence." Like Eve's, Hester's crime was not really in tempting Adam, but in disobeying God the Father. Her exotic beauty, then, is an emblem of her spiritual deviance. She is tall, "with a figure of perfect elegance." Her dark and abundant hair is "so glossy that it threw off the sunshine with a gleam," and her face, "besides being beautiful from regularity of feature and richness of complexion, had the impressiveness belonging to a marked brow and deep black eyes." Her physical appearance "seemed to express the attitude of her spirit, the desperate recklessness of her mood, by its wild and picturesque peculiarity." Most significant, of course, is the fantastically embroidered scarlet letter, an emblem of Hester's extravagant beauty, deviance and alienation.

⟨. . .⟩ What makes Hester so interesting is that she has chosen both her act of illicit love and her feminist philosophy. She is a woman who acts, not a woman who is acted upon. Hester's emergence from prison into the open air "as if by her own free will" is an act of self-reliance both literally and symbolically. "Shame, Despair, Solitude" will make a weak person—like Dimmesdale—weaker, but they have only served to harden Hester's strength. Although the shame of the scarlet letter burns, "the tendency of her fate and fortunes had been to set her free. The scarlet letter was her passport into regions where other women dared not tread."

Hester's self-reliance sets her apart from every other character in the book—with the exception of Pearl, who is a law unto herself. This "infant worthy to have been brought forth in Eden" is part preternaturally wise child, part elfin spirit, but primarily a symbol—"the scarlet letter in another form; the scarlet letter endowed with life." Hester makes deliberate use of this parallel by dressing Pearl in a gorgeous crimson velvet tunic "abundantly embroidered with fantasies and flourishes of gold thread" when they visit Governor Bellingham's house. The beauty of the child so dressed cannot help reminding those present "of the token which Hester Prynne was doomed to wear on her bosom." And just as that token is both Hester's shame and her passport to freedom, so Pearl's illegitimacy is balanced by her "moods of perverse merriment which . . . seemed to remove her entirely out of the sphere of sympathy or human contact."

Chillingworth, the Satan in this Garden of Eden—Hawthorne labels him literally as such and associates him both with snakes and savage Indians, is motivated only by revenge. He feeds off Dimmesdale like a parasite, and when the minister finally escapes the old man's clutches by confessing, Chillingworth's countenance becomes blank and dull, lifeless: "All his strength and energy—all his vital and intellectual force—seemed at once to desert him: insomuch that he positively withered up, shrivelled away, and almost vanished from mortal sight, like an uprooted weed that lies wilting in the sun."

Dimmesdale, Hester's Adam, declines from a "simple and childlike" person, one of "freshness and fragrance, and dewy purity of thought" who "could only be at ease in some seclusion of his own," to a weak and helpless person, one who is dependent on the esteem of his parishioners or, masochistically, on punishment by his evil enemy for his self-concept. Hester is shocked, after their midnight interview, at his disintegration: "His nerve seemed absolutely destroyed. His moral force was abased into more than a childish weakness. It grovelled helpless on the ground." During their forest meeting, she confronts him with his weakness, and he answers her, "Be thou strong for me! . . . Advise me what to do." At first Hester attempts to revive in him the inner strength for which she first loved him: "And what hast thou to do with all these iron men and their opinions? . . . Preach! Write! Act! Do anything, save to lie down and die!" But Dimmesdale has no self-reliance left; he is by this time only half a man, as his eyes indicate, their "fitful light" kindled by *her* enthusiasm, flashing up and dying away. "Thou tellest of running a race to a man whose knees are tottering beneath him," he tells her. "There is not the strength or courage left me to venture into the wide, strange, difficult world, alone!" The minister agrees to leave the community only when Hester, maternally, promises to go with him and arrange all the details of their escape, but he dares defy the universe only in Hester's presence. Away from her, he is afraid. Where he once loved her, he is now threatened by her sexuality; like Young Goodman Brown, he prefers her in fantasy. He would prefer even to see her as an image of "sinless motherhood"; he can no longer accept her as a real woman, nor himself as a real man.

As for the other characters in the book, the townsfolk and officials of the church and state, they are too shadowy to merit much consideration, but unlike Hester, they rely for their self-concepts upon the mores of the community. They judge and scorn Hester because she violates the mores; thus her act of individuality threatens their very identity.

Hester's difference is pointed up in a number of ways. Her physical beauty, obviously, sets her immediately apart, but she is not simply beautiful; her beauty is of "a rich, voluptuous, Oriental characteristic." In Miriam (in *The Marble Faun*) this "Oriental" characteristic becomes "Jewish" hair, and the point that like Miriam, Hester is not typically Protestant American is emphasized by linking her to the hated (and exotic) Catholics: "Had there been a Papist among the crowd of Puritans, he might have seen in this beautiful woman, so picturesque in her attire and mien, and with the infant at her bosom, an object to remind him of the image of Divine Maternity, . . . something which should remind, indeed, but only by contrast, of that sacred image of sinless motherhood." There is no Papist, of course, and Hester is *not* sinless. Her "taint of deepest sin in the most sacred quality of human life" is exactly what Dimmesdale cannot and the Puritan community will not accept; it makes Hester Eve, not Mary. As Chillingworth says, "By thy first step awry thou didst plant the germ of evil; but since that moment, it has all been a dark necessity."

Like her beauty, Hester's house, her shell, physically and symbolically separates her from the rest of the community. It is on the outskirts of the town, not in close vicinity to any other habitation, and "its comparative remoteness put it out of the sphere of that social activity which already marked the habits of the emigrants." Standing for Hester's own self-reliance as well as her isolation, her house looks "across a basin of the sea at the forest-covered hills, towards the *west*" (emphasis added). In fact, she is more at home in the nearby forest than she is in the town; it is there that she removes the scarlet letter and the cap which confines her luxuriant hair. Hester's familiarity with the forest stands for the unrestrained quality of her nature, her "long seclusion from society" which has taught her "to measure her ideas of right and wrong" by no standard "external to herself." Her standards are by no means wrong: her isolation has taught her, unlike her "Christian" neighbors, to be kind. Clearly she is deeply and uniquely human in feeding and clothing the poor, in caring for the sick, in sympathizing with the sufferer. Her nature is "warm and rich; a well-spring of human tenderness, unfailing to every real demand, and inexhaustible by the largest." A "self-ordained Sister of Mercy," her scarlet A comes to mean "Able," to have the effect of a cross on a nun's bosom. Still, she is "not merely estranged, but outlawed from society," largely through her own choice by the end of the book. In her courage and independence, her "latitude of speculation," Hester becomes "altogether foreign" to the rest of the community. She has wandered "without rule or guidance, in a moral wilderness; as vast, as intricate and shadowy, as the untamed forest." For years she has looked "from this estranged point of view at human institutions, and whatever priests or legislators had established; criticising all with hardly more reverence than the Indian would feel for the clerical band, the judicial robe, the pillory, the gallows, the fireside, or the church."

It is the forest, finally, that points up the difference not only between Hester and the rest of the townspeople, who regard it as the province of the Devil, but between Hester and Dimmesdale as well. If the forest is *her* home, it is not his. He, like Sophia, is society's representative; he stands for culture and civilization as the estranged Hester does not. The minister, Hawthorne is careful to point out, has "never gone through an experience calculated to lead him beyond the scope of generally received laws." He stands at "the head of a social system" which upholds the judicial robe, the pillory, the gallows, the fireside, the church. Hester, on the other hand, has been taught by "Shame, Despair, Solitude"; these "stern and wild" influences have "made her strong, but taught her much amiss." He is "the sainted minister in the church"; she is "the woman of the scarlet letter" in "that magic circle of ignominy." His "sin" with her in the forest, then, is a sin of "principle," committed in weakness, not a "sin of passion" like their first adulterous love. That love, they tell each other, "had a consecration of its own"; it was not a crime like Roger Chillingworth's violation "in cold blood [of] the sanctity of a human heart." But in the forest Hester persuades Dimmesdale to leave the community where he is a leader and become an outlaw, to breathe the "wild, free atmosphere of an unredeemed, unchristianized, lawless region," even to take on another name—to give up his very identity. And "tempted by a dream of happiness, he . . . yielded himself, with deliberate choice, as he had never done before, to what he knew was deadly sin." What may be right for Hester is not right for Dimmesdale. What happens to him after he and Hester decide to flee is that he becomes quite literally mad. At every step he takes homeward, in the chapter called "The Minister in a Maze," he feels "incited to do some strange, wild, wicked thing"; he can barely restrain himself from uttering blasphemies, insulting deacons and parishioners, teaching wicked words to children. When he reaches home, he stays up all night writing his Election Sermon, a masterpiece inspired by a maniacal frenzy, which is the triumph of his career. Once he delivers the sermon, however, his strength is gone; he resembles "the wavering effort of an infant with its mother's arms in view"—Hester, the agent of his destruction and of his salvation.

Hester is both. Hawthorne means seriously the last line of the book, the inscription on the common tombstone of Dimmesdale and Hester: "On a field, Sable, the Letter A, Gules." The red A on a black background: individual passion against the restraints of the community. He deliberately set out to create the kind of balance Whitman achieves in equating the "I" with the "en Masse," and in a way the balance works because one senses he is exactly divided between the attraction and the repulsion he feels for his wonderfully individualistic heroine. Surely Hawthorne intends Hester to stand for a contrast to the sinful Puritan community which represses all human emotions; but when he is confronted with the choice of alienated individualism or communal repression, his final sympathies are ambiguous. Hawthorne *might* have created our first androgynous heroine, but within the context of *The Scarlet Letter* and of his own nineteenth century there is no place for all that energy of Hester Prynne's, and when she tempts others to her own brand of lawlessness, she threatens with destruction the society in which the Dimmesdales and the Hawthornes do live and serve.

NOTES

[1] Cited in Allen Flint, "The Saving Grace of Marriage in Hawthorne's Fiction," *Emerson Society Quarterly* XIX (1973), 112.

[2] Nathaniel Hawthorne, *The Scarlet Letter*, 1850 (New York: Rinehart, 1960). Subsequent references are to this edition.

[3] Cited in Malcolm Cowley, *The Portable Hawthorne* (New York: Viking, 1948), pp. 611–18.

[4] See Carolyn Heilbrun, *Toward a Recognition of Androgyny* (New York: Alfred A. Knopf, 1973); and Nina Baym, *"The Blithedale Romance:* A Radical Reading," *Journal of English and Germanic Philology* LXVII (Oct. 1968), 545–69; "Hawthorne's Women: The Tyranny of Social Myths," *Centennial Review* XV (Summer 1971), 250–72; "Passion and Authority in *The Scarlet Letter,*" *New England Quarterly* XLIII (June 1970), 209–30; "The Romantic *Malgré Lui:* Hawthorne in the Custom House," *Emerson Society Quarterly* XIX (1973), 14–25.

[5] Nathaniel Hawthorne, "Mrs. Hutchinson," in *Biographical Sketches of Nathaniel Hawthorne,* vol. XII (Boston: Houghton Mifflin, 1883), pp. 217–19.

[6] Ibid., p. 224.

[7] John Winthrop, "A Modell of Christian Charity," *Winthrop Papers,* vol. II (Massachusetts Historical Society, 1931), pp. 283–94.

[8] John Winthrop, *Journal,* vol. II, James K. Hosmer, ed. (New York: Scribners, 1908), p. 239.

[9] These are the words of John Winthrop explaining why a woman of his acquaintance had become mentally ill (*Journal,* vol. II, p. 225). For a discussion of woman's place in the Puritan community see Edmund S. Morgan, *The Puritan Family: Religion and Domestic Relations in Seventeenth-Century New England* (New York: Harper & Row, 1944). For a discussion of this problem with specific reference to Anne Hutchinson see Kai T. Erikson, *Wayward Puritans: A Study in the Sociology of Deviance* (New York: John Wiley & Sons, 1966), pp. 71–107.

Kristin Herzog

THE SCARLET A: ABORIGINAL AND AWESOME

It might be that a sluggish bond-servant, or an undutiful child ... was to be corrected at the whipping-post. It might be, that an Antinomian, a Quaker, or other heterodox religionist, was to be scourged out of the town, or an idle and vagrant Indian, whom the white man's fire-water had made riotous about the streets, was to be driven with stripes into the shadow of the forest. It might be, too, that a witch, like old Mistress Hibbins, the bitter-tempered widow of the magistrate, was to die upon the gallows.[1]

The Scarlet Letter is a story set at the rough edge of civilization. The dark forest is still ominously near, and the dark dangers from foreign servants, untamed children, stubborn heretics, idle Indians, or hell-bound witches seem to threaten the progress of Puritan civilization's sacred new orders. The passage quoted above foreshadows in a variety of images Hester Prynne's emergence from the prison: while she is not a bond-servant, she is bound by the bonds of marriage to an unloved, old husband who sent her alone to a foreign continent. She also binds herself in love to a man whose name she will not utter. She is certainly no child, but the gruff English-born matrons who gossip about her fate and her character call her "brazen hussy" (54) and "naughty baggage" (51), and the image of the "undutiful child" prepares us for getting to know Pearl. Her lonely exile at the border of the town will later make her an Antinomian in thought, and the author has already reminded us of another freethinker, "sainted Anne Hutchinson," with whom Hester is symbolically identified through the wild rosebush at the prison door (48). Hester herself might have become the foundress of a religious sect or a prophetess if she had not borne a child and had lived a purer life (165, 263). She certainly is as much an outcast as any Quaker in the Puritan colony, and she bears public abuse with a

From *Women, Ethnics, and Exotics: Images of Power in Mid-Nineteenth-Century American Fiction* (Knoxville: University of Tennessee Press, 1983), pp. 7–16.

Quaker's dignity. Her freedom of speculation makes her as dangerous as any "heterodox religionist" who was "then common enough on the other side of the Atlantic" (164).

The image of the Indian appears at the beginning and at the end of the novel, and throughout the story a certain wildness and passion in Hester's character is, directly or indirectly, identified with the American Indian. This "aboriginal" aspect of Hester's femininity is not the only trait, however, which separates her from the Puritan women around her. She is also an alien with a touch of the exotic, in spite of her apparently uneventful childhood in rural England. "She had in her nature a rich, voluptuous, Oriental characteristic,—a taste for the gorgeously beautiful" (83). In her "otherness," she is a woman of awesome power.

Hester's Indian or "aboriginal" characteristics have been strengthened by social isolation which caused her to wander "without rule or guidance, in a moral wilderness; as vast, as intricate and shadowy, as the untamed forest" (199). Arthur Dimmesdale, after the climactic union in the forest, is filled not only with hope and joy, but "with fear betwixt them, and a kind of horror at her boldness." In part Hester's attitude grew out of her "native courage and activity," but it was also a consequence of her outlaw existence. "Her intellect and heart had their home, as it were, in desert places, where she roamed as freely as the wild Indian in his woods" (199). At the beginning of the novel, she is described as "impulsive and passionate" (57) and yet showing a "natural dignity and force of character" (52). The "desperate recklessness of her mood" (53) is hidden behind a "serene deportment" (55). This description parallels a portrayal of the Indians toward the end of the story, when they have flocked to town at the New England holiday.

> A party of Indians—in their savage finery of curiously embroidered deer-skin robes, wampum-belts, red and yellow ochre, and feathers, and armed with the bow and arrow and stone-headed spear—stood apart, with countenances of inflexible gravity, beyond what even a Puritan aspect could attain. Nor, wild as were these painted barbarians, were they the wildest feature of the scene. This distinction could more justly be claimed by some mariners. (232)

Inwardly passionate, outwardly composed—this describes Hester as well as the Indians. Her garment is "curiously embroidered" like theirs, and she stands apart, like them, from the crowd (232, 234). A "combative energy" in her character enables her to turn the scene of her public ignominy "into a kind of lurid triumph" (78). She is free to return to her birthplace, and she has "the passes of the dark, inscrutable forest open to her, where the wildness of her nature might assimilate itself with a people whose customs and life were alien from the law that had condemned her" (79), but she decides to stay at the place of her shame, to submit "uncomplainingly to the worst usage of the public" (160). She gives an impression of "marble coldness" (164) and, at times, of humility, even though it might actually be pride (162); like the Indians she keeps her emotions to herself.

The primeval forest, an image of the "moral wilderness in which she had so long been wandering" (183), and an image always connected with the Native Americans, also expresses Hester's deepest hope and joy. "That wild, heathen nature of the forest, never subjugated by human law, nor illuminated by higher truth" harbors a "heart of mystery" which at the reawakening of love between Hester and Dimmesdale becomes a "mystery of joy" (203). But the joy is transient. "In itself good, Nature is not a sufficient support for human beings."[2]

The most splendid image for the wild, untamed aspect of Hester's nature is her "elf" child, Pearl. In her dress, her looks, and her behavior she is a part of wild nature.

> A fox, startled from his sleep by her light footstep on the leaves, looked inquisitively at Pearl, as doubting whether it were better to steal off, or renew his nap on the same spot. A wolf, it is said,—but here the tale has surely lapsed into the improbable,—came up, and smelt of Pearl's robe, and offered his savage head to be patted by her hand. The truth seems to be, however, that the mother-forest, and these wild things which it nourished, all recognized a kindred wildness in the human child. (204–5)

This description of the child expresses a part of Hester's nature as well. Among the crowds at the holiday,

> Pearl, who was the gem on her mother's unquiet bosom, betrayed, by the very dance of her spirits, the emotions which none could detect in the marble passiveness of Hester's brow.
>   This effervescence made her flit with a bird-like movement.... She broke continually into shouts of a wild, inarticulate, and sometimes piercing music. (228)

The Puritans are inclined to consider Pearl a "demon-offspring" (244), just as they consider the Indians to be "powerful enchanters" skilled in the "black art" (127). At the holiday, when Pearl runs to look a wild Indian in the face, he becomes "conscious of a nature wilder than his own" (244). Just like Hester, Pearl combines "native audacity" with "a reserve as characteristic" (244). The vivid natural images that describe her confirm her as a part of nature. Besides being repeatedly compared to a bird, she is associated with an April breeze and a brook, and likened to a nymph-child or infant-dryad, a fairy, and an elf. She is so "aboriginal" that she declares in public "she had not been made at all, but had been plucked by her mother off the bush of wild roses that grew by the prison-door" (112).

Pearl is not only an image of her mother's passionate, yet restrained, "Indian" nature; she is also a picture of Hester's "taste for the gorgeously beautiful" (83), of her rich, Oriental, luxurious traits that make her awesome among Indians as well as Puritans. Pearl's garments are the product of the "fertility and gorgeous luxuriance of fancy" expressed in Hester's needlework (53) and make the child look as exotic as "a wild tropical bird" (111). Hester's exquisite needlework is her art, an outlet for her passion and imagination. Through it she converts her badge of shame into a symbol of triumph and defiance.

Hester's exotic Oriental traits contribute also to her awe-inspiring elevation and isolation. Throughout the novel she is repeatedly seen as pedestaled on the scaffold.[3] With her child in her arms she seems an "image of Divine Maternity" (56) as the crowd beholds her for the first time. At the end, after having stood "statue-like" at the foot of the scaffold (244), she appears almost like a Pietà at the moment of Dimmesdale's death of "triumphant ignominy" (357), although the scene is ambiguous: "Then, down he sank upon the scaffold! Hester partly raised him, and supported his head against her bosom. Old Roger Chillingworth knelt down beside him" (255).

As an image of Divine Maternity Hester is, in archetypal terms, not the aboriginal adulteress but the awesome, adored, and redeeming Magna Mater. She inspires a vague "horror" in Dimmesdale (199) as well as in Chillingworth (61), and yet she is Dimmesdale's "better angel" (201). In the forest scene, he is exhilarated by breathing the same "wild, free atmosphere of an unredeemed, unchristianized, lawless region" as Hester (201), and yet the flood of sunshine brightening the "magic circle" of this hour (202) indicates that their love is also redeeming and healing, even if it will not in the end prevent Dimmesdale's death or Hester's suffering.

Again it is Pearl who images most clearly the redemptive aspect of Hester's nature, just as she also expressed her untamed, precivilized life-force. In spite of her wild elf nature, "there was love in the child's heart" (115). Had the authorities taken Pearl away from her mother, Hester might have been lost to the Black Man. "Even thus early had the child saved her from Satan's snare" (117). In the forest scene, Dimmesdale and Pearl for the first time really meet each other. There was "an awe about the child as she came onward" (207). She shares in Hester's alien, exotic nature. Dimmesdale "dreads this interview, and yearns for it" (207). When Pearl has decked herself out with flowers, her "brilliant picturesqueness" is intensified. The sunshine is "attracted thitherward as by a certain sympathy" (208). But the germ of love in her does not grow prematurely. She withholds her affection as long as she detects falsehood, which she scorns bitterly (180). She senses that Hester's throwing off the scarlet letter means throwing off part of what has shaped her identity, and she might also sense that the minister is not ready as yet to "go back with us hand in hand, we three together, into the town" (212). And so she throws a temper tantrum which for Dimmesdale has as "preternatural" an effect as Mistress Hibbins's "cankered wrath" (210). This is the "aboriginal" trait of the "witch-baby" in Pearl, a name the shipmaster gives her (245). The same potentially demonic force unites Hester herself with weird Mistress Hibbins. The witch-baby Pearl becomes an image of love and liberation at the scaffold when she flies to the staggering Dimmesdale with "bird-like motion" and when just before his death she kisses his lips and breaks the spell of guilt and estrangement. Redemption comes from the very forest powers which the Puritans considered fiendish.[4]

Pearl is not the only evidence of Hester's identity as a redemptive figure. The aura of Divine Maternity is reflected in various ways. To some of the townspeople, "the scarlet letter had the effect of the cross on a nun's bosom. It imparted to the wearer a kind of sacredness.... It was reported, and believed by many, that an Indian had drawn his arrow against the badge, and that the missile struck it, but fell harmless to the ground" (163). Hester is a "self-ordained Sister of Mercy"; her nature "showed itself warm and rich: a well-spring of human tenderness, unfailing to every real demand, and inexhaustible by the largest" (161). At the turning point of the novel, when Hester, Dimmesdale, and Pearl meet during the night at the scaffold, there seems to appear in the sky an *A* which some observers take as standing for "Angel"; and although they refer to Governor Winthrop who was "made an angel this past night" (158), the reader knows that the *A* refers first of all to Hester Prynne, adulteress as well as "angel of mercy."

Hester, then, is described in images that form two clusters: the aboriginal and the awesome (to spin out farther the mystical meaning of the letter *A*). In the first aspect, she represents subhuman nature, as it is usually associated with the American Indian, with wild forest places, and with witch-like persons such as Mistress Hibbins. In the second, she represents an almost supernatural figure of Divine Maternity, exotic beauty, Oriental richness, and angel-like mercy. The two clusters of imagery merge and overlap. Pearl, for example, is in the end the humanizing force which unites the subhuman and the superhuman in a redeeming center. She is both the witch-baby and the child mediating divine grace.

Hester's inner spiritual and emotional struggle shows the same polarity. On the one hand, she is a typical romantic heroine who can say after a meeting with her husband, "Be it sin or no ... I hate the man!" (176). She can remind Dimmesdale that what they did had "a consecration of its own" (195). When she broods about the dilemma of womanhood, she wanders "without a clew in the dark labyrinth of her mind." At times, a fearful doubt strives to possess her soul "whether it were not better to send Pearl at once to heaven, and go herself to such futurity as Eternal Justice should provide" (166). When she finds new hope after the reunion with Dimmesdale in the forest, she is ready to flee with him on a ship that significantly is an outlaw vessel with a crew of "rough looking desperadoes" who are guilty of "depredations on the Spanish commerce" (233). Hester is at times a "Fausta," boldly or desperately overstepping all boundaries of faith and tradition.[5]

But there is a self-restraining side to Hester also. She upbraids herself for hating Chillingworth, though she cannot overcome her hate (176); she patiently bears insults, even from the poor whom she is helping; she is "a martyr indeed," although she does not pray for her enemies "lest, in spite of her forgiving aspirations, the words of the blessing should stubbornly twist themselves into a curse" (85). Before as well as after Dimmesdale's death, she is free to go back to England but remains to do of her own free will what society had forced her to do. She becomes a Mary figure to whom people bring "all their sorrows and perplexities" (263).

Thus Hester is not just a fallen Eve; she is a divine mother, a Sister of Mercy, a nun, a saint, an angel, a potential prophetess or foundress of a religious sect, and a martyr. Hester is an "able woman" (161), a woman of strength "almost majestic in . . . despair" (173). She is a queenly figure who may have gotten her name from the biblical Esther. Queen Esther is a woman of courage, beauty, dignity, selflessness. Hester Prynne has all these qualities. In contrast to many pliable, submissive women figures in the fiction of the 1850s, Hester has "combative energy" (78), a "desperate recklessness of . . . mood" (53), "freedom of speculation" (164), and "a mind of native courage and activity" (199). She explores realms unimagined by Dimmesdale and by her society.

Dimmesdale lacks the strength which had borne up Hester under the burden of the scarlet letter (171), and he begs her, "Twine thy strength about me! Thy strength, Hester" (253). In contrast to her, Dimmesdale is often described in feminine terms. He "kept himself simple and childlike; coming forth . . . with a freshness, and fragrance, and dewy purity of thought, which, as many people said, affected them like the speech of an angel" (66). "The creator never made another being so sensitive as this" (171). Dimmesdale himself admits his weakness in the forest scene: "Think for me, Hester! Thou art strong. Resolve for me!" (196). And she urges him desperately: "Preach! Write! Act! Do any thing, save to lie down and die!" (198). Although Dimmesdale agrees to flee with Hester, he returns immediately and guiltily, "pitiably weak" (215), to his public duties after their meeting.

Hester combines the strength of a Squaw Sachem (described earlier in Hawthorne's historical sketch "Mainstreet") with the awesomeness of a Hebrew queen, but the primitive strength of these two types is tempered by Hester's suffering and faith which convince her that a life of loving service will give her existence new meaning.[6] While she appears at first as a kind of Arminian who wants to expiate her sins by quiet good works without public confession, her final views amount in effect to the same public confession which Dimmesdale felt urged to make as a true Puritan. The important difference between the two, however, is that Hester embodies a life-force and creativity whereas Dimmesdale exemplifies "mere" spirituality. In her maturity, Hester represents an early, lively Puritanism that emphasized the heart's turning away from itself toward others and discovering God's grace in human action.[7]

Romantic primitivism tempered by suffering and faith—this aspect of the novel's meaning is also reflected in its structure. Of Hawthorne's works, it has been said that "theme . . . is structure."[8] In *The Scarlet Letter* the scaffold is the central symbol and, like the scarlet *A*, it stands for shame as well as elevation. The action of the first three chapters and the last three (except for part of the Conclusion) is centered around the scaffold, and in the central chapter 12 Hester, Dimmesdale, and Pearl mount the scaffold in the night. During the procession at the New England holiday, when Hester stands "statue-like" at the scaffold, she has "a sense within her . . . that her whole orb of life, both before and after, [is] connected with this spot, as with the one point that gave it unity" (244). This "scaffolding" in structure and theme of the novel is related to its concern with divine and human law. It could be

summarized by James Russell Lowell's simple line, "Truth forever on a scaffold."
Divine truth is forever crucified on the scaffolds of human authorities. The same
paradox of theme and structure is mirrored in the stylistic scaffolding of romantic
and realistic elements. Hawthorne and Melville use the romance pattern in its
primitive or archetypal form. They do not make use of a realistic "displacement" of
the basic romance but consciously write "a more primitive and archaic sort of
fiction."[9] In *The Scarlet Letter* Hawthorne uses allegory, witchcraft, superstitions,
Indian Black Art, or the popular assumption that dark Oriental or European heroines are fallen or dangerous women.[10] Hawthorne, however, weaves a measure of
realism, in setting and psychological detail, into this romantic primitivism and so
makes the reader aware of an element of illusion. He thereby invites us to use our
own imagination and draw our own conclusions. If we are told of the folk belief that
an Indian had drawn his arrow against Hester's badge, but that it struck and fell
harmless to the ground, we are compelled to think about the incredible power of
a social stigma.[11]

Hester's "lawless passion," then, "turns her into a kind of white Indian, and she
becomes in Hawthorne's mind a focus for all those associations of knowledge with
sexual power which we have . . . observed in Cooper's mythic red men and dark
ladies."[12] But besides her "Indian" or primitive side, Hester has a Puritan side. As a
member of a Puritan colony and in love with a Puritan minister, she fights the
demonic forces of the forest in herself when she tries hard not to hate or curse,
not to take her own life or that of her child, not to join in with Mistress Hibbins's
insane forest rites, and to keep love and mercy alive in her. Her Indianness,
however, is also her strength. Her return to her old abode and her taking up the
scarlet letter again of her own free will are the best expression of the two forces
in her: an aboriginal freedom and an awesome power of commitment.

In the early Puritan tradition, the colonist is either a captive or a destroyer of
Indians; he has to oppose the primitive elements of human experience he sees
expressed in the Indian enemy. Later in the history of the Puritan colonies, this
attitude changes. After the threat of the real Indian is removed from the more
established American civilization, Indian life and lore turns into myth, and the
colonists adopt "a more favorable attitude toward the Indians, beginning with a
more objective treatment of them and ending (in 1773–1800) in the advocacy of
a systematic imitation of the Indian way of life." The transformation of Indian culture
into myth culminates in Thoreau's work and in Longfellow's "Hiawatha."[13] Hawthorne, especially in his tales, describes the early Puritan view of the Indian, but as
a romantic writer he cherishes the vitality of the primitive life-force expressed in
the American Indian. Therefore, on the one hand, Chillingworth's worst traits,
according to Puritan rumors, were intensified by his contact with the Indians' Black
Art (127), and Hester wanders in a "moral wilderness" like the Indian who roams
in desert places; on the other hand, Hester's Indian-like qualities of strength, passion, endurance, dignity, and independence are deemed admirable and are contrasted with the narrow-mindedness of the Puritan system and the weakness of

Dimmesdale. The Indian of the nineteenth century was alternately the symbol of humanity's childhood and Golden Age innocence and the lustful, cruel violator of American pastoral peace. But to Hawthorne, the Puritans are the more cruel violators. Throughout the Hawthorne canon, the Puritans' martial prowess against the Indian is exposed as inhuman.[14]

Hester, then, is an example of a new American Eve. Her similarity to primitive Indians is not, as it would be in popular sentimental novels, a similarity in terms of childlike behavior, docility, and self-effacing nobility. It is instead a kinship on grounds of an unquenchable thirst for freedom, a vital power of imagination, as expressed in her needlework art, and a strength in endurance which looks merely stoic on the outside but allows her to turn the prejudices of society, the images of the "old" Eve, into symbols of victory. Hester does not use her inner freedom in an individualistic fashion; she builds community instead of destroying it, as her final way of life indicates.[15] No American writer before Hawthorne had described a woman as powerful as Hester Prynne.

NOTES

[1] Hawthorne, *The Scarlet Letter,* The Centenary Edition of the Works of Nathaniel Hawthorne (Columbus: Ohio State Univ. Press, 1962), 49. Hereafter, page numbers in parentheses within the text refer to the work under discussion.

[2] Richard Harter Fogle, *Hawthorne's Fiction: The Light and the Dark,* rev. ed. (Norman: Univ. of Oklahoma Press, 1964), 136.

[3] See Robert E. Todd, "The Magna Mater Archetype in *The Scarlet Letter,*" *New England Quarterly,* 45 (Sept. 1972), 423. "In the first third of the book (chs. i–viii) Hester is referred to at least a half dozen times as pedestalled."

[4] See Claudia D. Johnson, *The Productive Tension of Hawthorne's Art* (Tuscaloosa: Univ. of Alabama Press, 1981), 49, 58, 63, 65. Claudia Johnson rightly sees that this is the same demonic power that Hawthorne felt within himself as a writer of fiction. He could identify with Hester as the narrator of "The Custom-House" trying on the burning red letter *A* in a lifeless world of "customs" which did not understand him. His "pearl" is always some "devil in manuscript," as he titled one of his sketches. But, just like Hester, he turns demonic into creative forces.

[5] See William Bysshe Stein, *Hawthorne's Faust: A Study of the Devil Archetype* (Gainesville: Univ. of Florida Press, 1953), 112.

[6] In Nina Baym's estimation, Hester is meant as an "admirable character, . . . while of course in Christian terms she is from first to last an unredeemed sinner." However, an unredeemed sinner can be, in human terms, an admirable character. Hester has sinned, is admirable, and is redeemed, as far as redemption is humanly possible. The "virtual absence of God from the text" does not imply at all that Hester's and Dimmesdale's relationship is nothing but "a social crime" unrelated to divine law. Interestingly, the biblical book of Esther also does not mention God even once, and that certainly does not imply that it is not concerned with divine law. We cannot impose on Hawthorne a secularized 20th-century world view, however ambiguous his religious ideas may have been. Especially the last pages of the novel point in another direction. See Baym, *The Shape of Hawthorne's Career* (Ithaca, N.Y.: Cornell Univ. Press, 1976), 9, 125–26, and *The Westminster Dictionary of the Bible* (Philadelphia: Westminster Press, 1944), s.v. "Esther."

[7] See Michael T. Gilmore, *The Middle Way: Puritanism and Ideology in American Romantic Fiction* (New Brunswick, N.J.: Rutgers Univ. Press, 1977), 93–112; and Johnson, *Productive Tension,* 130.

[8] Kenneth Dauber, *Rediscovering Hawthorne* (Princeton, N.J.: Princeton Univ. Press, 1977), 38.

[9] Richard Brodhead, *Hawthorne, Melville, and the Novel* (Chicago: Univ. of Chicago Press, 1976), 22, 60.

[10] See Henry Nash Smith, *Virgin Land: The American West as Symbol and Myth* (New York: Vintage Books–Random House, 1950), 127. Charles W. Webber was one of the first to introduce the custom

of making a heroine of questionable repute a European instead of an American. The violation of propriety was less shocking when the girl was not an American.

[11] On the causes and implications of stigmatizing, see Marjorie Pryse, *The Mark and the Knowledge: Social Stigma in Classic American Fiction* (Columbus: Ohio State Univ. Press, 1979).

[12] Joel Porte, *The Romance in America: Studies in Cooper, Poe, Hawthorne, Melville, and James* (Middletown, Conn.: Wesleyan Univ. Press, 1969), 104.

[13] Richard Slotkin, *Regeneration through Violence: The Mythology of the American Frontier, 1600–1860* (Middletown, Conn.: Wesleyan Univ. Press, 1973), 205, 356, 363–65, 519–23.

[14] See Louise K. Barnett, *The Ignoble Savage: American Literary Racism, 1790–1890* (Westport, Conn.: Greenwood Press, 1975), 150.

[15] Cf. Judith Fryer, *The Faces of Eve: Women in the Nineteenth-Century American Novel* (New York: Oxford Univ. Press, 1976), 84, who maintains that Hester is "wonderfully individualistic" and that "her own brand of lawlessness . . . threatens with destruction" the society of her day.

Evan Carton

THE PRISON DOOR

*T*he *Scarlet Letter* is about representation; every major aspect of the novel reflects or re-creates the tension of Hawthorne's representative situation. The subordination of historical event to imaginative construction 〈...〉 is *The Scarlet Letter*'s enabling (and constraining) condition. At the outset, its essential and determinative event has already occurred and cannot be recovered by the reader, by the Puritan community, or even by Hester herself. Neither, however, can it be escaped. It can only be represented—multiply, incompletely, transformatively. The "A" is the sign by which the colonial authorities seek to fix the crime and the criminal, but this mark—the alphabet's first letter and its initial—also signifies its own symbolic or representational character, its arbitrariness and its ambiguity. The letter is both limited—no more sufficient to produce in full the never-named adultery than is the magistrates' power to produce both adulterers—and wildly accommodating, susceptible to the multiple readings that begin in the course of Hester's textual history and continue to accumulate throughout her career in criticism. Pearl is another representative of the unpresented original event, but although it is, literally, her origin, she remains an alternative "token" (i, 52), an "emblem" (i, 93), "the scarlet letter in another form" (i, 102). Despite Chillingworth's suggestion that an analysis of her character and mold might reveal the father, she is, like the letter, too elusive or too overwhelming a symbol to yield her source. For the reader and for Hester herself, Pearl's volatile and contradictory significances unsettle the meaning of the generative act; the questions that Pearl is typically and repeatedly asked, however playful or rhetorical they seem, point up her problematic representational status: "Child, what are thou?" (i, 97); "Canst thou tell me, my child, who made thee?" (i, 111). Finally, the novel's event[1] is encoded in Dimmesdale's conduct and Chillingworth's plot; it is at once obscured and allegorically re-enacted in their behavior, and it is represented as well in the interpretive constructions that the letter's readers (both within and without the book) apply.

From *The Rhetoric of American Romance: Dialectic and Identity in Emerson, Dickinson, Poe, and Hawthorne* (Baltimore: Johns Hopkins University Press, 1985), pp. 192–216.

Hawthorne's representative situation, as it poses the problem of representation itself, not only finds multiple analogues in *The Scarlet Letter* but becomes the crux of the novel. It is a situation that is replicated in the relationship between each principal and the social matrix (the Puritan state remains a matrix, no matter how forbiddingly patriarchal), but its central exemplar is Hester Prynne. Hester is Hawthorne's entry to his Puritan past; her story provides the intimate association with the society of his ancestors that he desires, but it also affords him some distance, for, like Hawthorne, Hester is both a representative and a deviant, a product and a subversive reproducer of her community's meanings. Hawthorne's association with Hester is variously indicated between the moment in "The Custom-House" when the letter first burns on his breast and the moment in the "Conclusion" when he confesses that it still burns in his brain. The simultaneous emergence of Hawthorne from the customs house and Hester from the jail; the "spell" (i, 11), or "fatality" (i, 79) that compels both "to linger around and haunt, ghost-like, the spot where some great and marked event has given color to their lifetime" (i, 79–80), as if Salem or Boston were "the inevitable center of the universe" (i, 12); the shared effort to sustain and transform the past through its representation and to win one's proper strength in one's relation to a community—all of these convergences identify the author with his character. But such an identification, as the self-division of both Hawthorne and Hester might suggest, can only be an ambivalent one. Insofar as her enterprise models his, Hester is made to suffer the consequences of the doubt, suspicion, and guilt that attend Hawthorne's acts of imagination; as he censures himself in the voice of his ancestors early in "The Custom-House," so Hawthorne censures Hester in the same representative capacity. If William and John Hathorne distinguish themselves by the persecution of deviant women, their descendant in some sense follows suit. Redemption and repetition often cannot be differentiated in *The Scarlet Letter*'s representations.

The opening words of the story proper are those of the title to chapter I, "The Prison Door." Appropriately, Hawthorne's first image suggests the dialectical relations of inner and outer space, solitude and community, bondage and freedom, that generate the novel. Moreover, the uncertain significance (however plain the reference) of the prison door points up the shifting and problematic nature of these relations as their terms harden into mere opposition (the door is a barrier) or collapse into identity (the door is a passage). Here, then, the tension between overdetermination and indeterminacy that informs *The Scarlet Letter* and accounts for much of its power is initiated. Hawthorne enhances this tension in his equivocal treatment of the rosebush and in his assertion that the prison door is "the threshold of our narrative, which is now about to issue from that inauspicious portal" (i, 48). At once assuming a burden of guilt and announcing its release or even its redemption, the narrative proceeds to the marketplace for a scene in which each major character is simultaneously liberated and bound.

The first scaffold scene marks Chillingworth's release by his Indian captors and his entrapment by the spectacular situation that greets him in Boston. More significantly, though, it marks his escape, and Dimmesdale's, from social stigma, from the kind of external determination of personal identity that the community attempts to impose upon Hester. Hester is, ironically, the only potential agent of such determination for both men. "Recognize me not, by word, by sign, by look!" (i, 76). Chillingworth later instructs her, and when she agrees to "keep thy secret, as I have his" she ensures that he, like Dimmesdale, will be able to go unrecognized by the society at large. Paradoxically, however, Dimmesdale's and Chillingworth's apparent avoidance of socially (and historically) determined identities involves more of a loss than a gain of personal autonomy. Both begin to mortify their former selves, to behave compulsively, and to become consumed by their roles as representatives of the society they are deceiving. Hester, on the other hand, suffers ritualized and perpetual public recognition by word, by sign, and by look. Yet such attention invests her with a potential for significance that is not absolutely regulable from without; it engages her in symbolic exchange and thus affords her a vocabulary for self-representation. Like the act that Pearl represents, this vocabulary at once binds and frees, requiring Hester to formulate an identity that resists both detachment from and consumption by it.

In "The Custom-House," Hawthorne first notes his "true position as editor, or very little more" of *The Scarlet Letter,* but later claims to have allowed himself, "in the dressing up of the tale, . . . nearly or altogether as much license as if the facts had been entirely of [his] own invention." Hester's ambivalent relation to her letter mirrors Hawthorne's to his book; she is charged merely with presenting to the public a text that others have determined and authorized, yet in the dressing up of that text she can exercise imaginative license and assume a measure of control over its appearance and meaning. In taking possession of the symbol of her disgrace (and of the disgrace itself), Hester at once realizes and transforms it. It is, in fact, this tension between realization and transformation, obedience and defiance, public and private authority, that produces the shock of Hester's entry into the marketplace:

> On the breast of her gown, in fine red cloth, surrounded with an elaborate embroidery and fantastic flourishes of gold thread, appeared the letter A. It was so artistically done, and with so much fertility and gorgeous luxuriance of fancy, that it had all the effect of a last and fitting decoration to the apparel which she wore; and which was of a splendor in accordance with the taste of the age, but greatly beyond what was allowed by the sumptuary regulations of the colony. (i, 53)

Hester's apparel, "in accordance" with the community's taste yet in violation of its rules, exhibits the mingled compliance and transgression of parody, thus complicating the spectators' understanding of her and, perhaps, of themselves. This wild publication of the letter also reflects the common judgment of Hester's nature, but it constitutes a more aggressive and unsettling confession than the people of Boston had bargained for; its "fertility and gorgeous luxuriance of fancy" suggestively re-create her crime before their transfixed gaze. In short, the "A" on Hester's breast both indicates and thwarts the community's authority over her identity. It makes her "the type of shame"—forces her to "[give] up her individuality" and "become the general symbol at which the preacher and moralist might point, and in which they might vivify and embody their images of woman's frailty and sinful passion" (i, 79), but it also has "the effect of a spell, taking her out of the ordinary relations with humanity, and inclosing her in a sphere by herself" (i, 54). It serves as "the chain . . . of iron links" (i, 80) that keeps her "within the limits of the Puritan settlement" (i, 79) and as "her passport into regions where other women dared not tread" but where "she roamed as freely as the wild Indian in his woods" (i, 199).

The question of control over the letter, and consequently of the susceptibility of Hester's identity to social determination, is most explicitly posed at the end of the long first scene, when the Reverend Mr. Wilson attempts to coerce Hester to name her lover by suggesting that the information "may avail to take the scarlet letter off [her] breast." Hester's response is openly revolutionary: "Never. . . . It is too deeply branded. Ye cannot take it off" (i, 68). Taking her punishment more radically to heart than her judges could have anticipated or intended, Hester subverts their sentence by her very faithfulness to it. In so doing, she makes herself the battleground of social and personal authority, of determinate and indeterminate meaning, of letter and spirit. Hester's reply to Wilson out-allegorizes the Puritan magistrates, for if they reduce her to a "type," if they displace her material being by identifying her as "the figure, the body, the reality of sin" (i, 79), she abstracts and displaces the material sign of their allegorical interpretation. Her re-interpretation of the letter does not free her from it or from them, however, but engages her in the play of significances that the magistrates' sentence similarly inaugurates rather than concludes. This is the serious play of the novel, the play on which social order and personal identity are staked and by which each constrains and empowers the other. As Julia Kristeva has noted in another context, "to interpret" means "to be mutually indebted";[2] *The Scarlet Letter* observes this definition and rigorously pursues its implications.

In her claim that the letter "is too deeply branded" for the magistrates to remove, Hester acknowledges their power, even internalizes it, while she announces their constraint. The authority she exercises, moreover, binds her as well—a fact that she discovers seven years later, when, not in the town but in the forest and not for Puritan law but for romantic love, she finally speaks the name "Arthur Dimmesdale" and briefly imagines that this act can take the scarlet letter off her breast. "The past is gone!" (i, 202), she cries as she discards its mark, ⟨. . .⟩ contravening the principle upon which, in "The Custom-House," Hawthorne establishes his novelistic career. Significantly, it is Pearl, alive and at hand, who demands that Hester "take it up" (i, 210) again. For Pearl not only embodies the letter but also enforces its double authorization, identifies it as the product of intercourse, and reveals the limits of Hester's freedom and power. Throughout, Pearl's character and function are those of the letter; she is at once a mutable and ungovernable enigma and—in her repeated demands for explanations of her origin, the letter, and Dimmesdale—a relentless agent of the Puritan order; she represents both Hester's distinction from the community and her connection with it. The extent to which she remains alien to Hester until the novel's final scene is the extent to which she is not "mother's child" (i, 110), as she identifies herself in the governor's hall, but father's—the child of Arthur Dimmesdale, the local minister and representative of the Puritan patriarchy.

Although Hester vehemently takes Pearl to herself, as she does the letter, she is the independent author of neither, and over neither can she "win the master word" (i, 93). She can only dress them up, "as if [they] had been entirely of [her] own invention." This she does, replicating her initial exhibition of the letter in the ornamentation of her daughter. Hester "bought the richest tissues that could be procured," Hawthorne notes, "and allowed her imaginative faculty its full play in the arrangement and decoration of the dresses which the child wore, before the public eye" (i, 90). Through the play of what Hawthorne repeatedly calls "her art," Hester distinguishes Pearl and herself, indulges the "rich, voluptuous, Oriental characteristic" (i, 83) in her nature, and symbolically asserts her indomitability by the social judgment and strictures that have been imposed on her. Thus, again, she metaphorically re-enacts her crime in her needlework: in "the gorgeously beautiful, . . . the exquisite productions of her needle," she finds "a mode of expressing, and therefore soothing, the passion of her life" (i, 83, 84). Yet, if Hester's art preserves her difference, it also constitutes her bond to the Puritan community, for it is the means by which she supports herself and Pearl and participates in communal affairs. This dual significance, in fact, is reflected both in the character of Hester's needlework and in her attitude toward it. The "exquisite productions" in which she takes "pleasure" are set against "coarse garments for the poor," the "rude handiwork" in which "she [offers] up a real sacrifice of enjoyment" (i, 83). Taken as a whole, then, Hester's art comprises both an expression of her passion and an internalization of its punishment, a mode of penance (i, 83).

It is not simply in her self-mortifying productions, however, that Hester represents, rather than opposing, her society. On the contrary, "deep ruffs, painfully wrought bands, and gorgeously embroidered gloves" (i, 82) are among the most fashionable and lucrative types of her handiwork. "The taste of the age," Hawthorne observes, "demanding whatever was elaborate in compositions of this kind, did not fail to extend its influence over our stern progenitors, who had cast behind them so many fashions which it might seem harder to dispense with" (i, 82). The last clause of this sentence is the crucial one, for it obliges us to ask why embroidery should be an indispensable indulgence for a people that had repudiated so many others. This question and its answer indicate Hester's most profound engagement with the Puritan community.

Embroidery is for the Puritans what it is for Hester: an expression of human presence, human will, human value, a means of laying claim to the world and to oneself. Hence it is "deemed necessary to the official state of men assuming the reins of power," is "a matter of policy" in public ceremonies, is required to "give majesty" to governmental forms, and is "demand[ed]" at funerals "to typify . . . the sorrow of the survivors" (i, 82). Hester's "curiously embroidered letter," then, the first product of her art, both marks her sin and her deviance and follows, even epitomizes, Puritan custom: it is, Hawthorne writes, "a specimen of . . . delicate and imaginative skill, of which the dames of a court might gladly have availed themselves, *to add the richer and more spiritual adornment of human ingenuity* to their fabrics of silk and gold" (i, 81–82; emphasis added). More precious than the fabric of experience itself is the application of a design, the inscription of a purpose, upon it. The insistence upon such a societal inscription lies at the heart of Puritanism, as Hawthorne sees it; indeed, Puritanism depends (with magnificent literalness here) on such embroidery as Hester Prynne's. Hester practices the art of symbolic overlay by which her community gives meaning and distinction to experience, and she suffers from the symbolism that she herself purveys. Thus, her art—an art that represents not only Hester's passion but also the Puritans' social enterprise and Hawthorne's literary one—exemplifies her reality and theirs. Material fact in *The Scarlet Letter* is a matter of embroidery, of "human ingenuity" and "imaginative skill," or perhaps, as the less salutary meanings of the term would have it, of exaggeration, fabrication, specious narration.

Hester's intuition of her art's significance—of its constitutive power, its obliquity, its conduciveness to deception and even self-deception—prompts her to suspect it and to regard her pleasure in it as a sin. This is a judgment that, like the embroidery itself, implicates both Puritan reality and Hawthorne's fiction, and Hawthorne must at once acknowledge and deflect this implication. Thus the narrator contests Hester's guilty sense of her art but takes her scruples as a sign of her deviance from clarity and rectitude: "This morbid meddling of a conscience with an immaterial matter betokened . . . something doubtful, something that might be deeply wrong, beneath" (i, 84). Embroidery, of course, is not an "immaterial matter," and the punning play on the notion of materiality here compromises the authority of the narrator's assertion. Moreover, Hester's imposition of moral significance upon needlework exemplifies the fundamental hermeneutic principle of her society, a principle that neither she nor Hawthorne is able or willing to repudiate entirely. The paragraph that precedes the one in which Hester's judgment is criticized, in fact, suggests several moral explanations for the popularity of her needlework, explanations that assume and endorse a "morbid meddling of conscience with an immaterial matter" on the part of Hester's community. ("Vanity, it may be, chose to mortify itself, by putting on, for ceremonials of pomp and state, the garments that had been wrought by her sinful hands. . . . But it is not recorded that, in a single instance, her skill was called in aid to embroider the white veil which was to cover the pure blushes of a bride. The exception indicated the ever relentless vigor with which society frowned upon her sin" [i, 82–83].) All matters are "material" in Hester Prynne's world; as Hawthorne notes repeatedly during the opening scene of the novel, events that might be dismissed as trivial or taken up as "a theme for jest" by those in "another social state" (i, 56) are "invested with . . .

dignity" (i, 50) in Puritan Boston. Yet, it is also true that no matters are material in this world, for all material facts (to paraphrase Emerson) signify (or are "invested with" the significance of) immaterial, or spiritual, facts.

This paradox of material immateriality, or of overdetermined indeterminacy, attends not only the plot elements of *The Scarlet Letter* but also its characterizations. Leslie Fiedler has argued that "one of the major problems involved in reading *The Scarlet Letter* is determining the ontological status of the characters, the sense in which we are being asked to believe in them." As he elaborates this point:

> Hawthorne ends by rendering two of his five main characters (Hester and Dimmesdale) analytically, two ambiguously (Chillingworth and Pearl), and one projectively (Mistress Hibbins). Hester and Dimmesdale are exploited from time to time as "emblems" of psychological or moral states; but they remain rooted always in the world of reality. Chillingworth, on the other hand, makes so magical an entrance and exit that we find it hard to believe in him as merely an aging scholar, who has nearly destroyed himself by attempting to hold together a loveless marriage with a younger woman; while Pearl, though she is presented as the fruit of her mother's sin, seems hardly flesh and blood at all, and Mistress Hibbins is quite inexplicable in naturalistic terms, despite Hawthorne's perfunctory suggestion that she is simply insane.[3]

The importance of Fiedler's analytical and projective modes to an understanding of *The Scarlet Letter*, I would suggest, lies not in the fact that they are constantly opposed in the text but in the fact that their ostensible opposition is constantly collapsing. Fiedler more or less acknowledges as much in his mediatory category of the ambiguous and in his notation of Hawthorne's tendency to reverse or hedge against both analytical and projective characterization. It must be stressed, however, that the problem of characterization is a function not of Hawthorne's vacillating, imprecise, or obscurant use of two different modes but of his challenge to the presumption (ours, as well as the Puritans') that there is any sensible difference between analysis and projection, between the actual and the imaginary. Time and again, in the novel that grows out of his initial analysis (or projection) of "a certain affair of fine red cloth" in "The Custom-House," Hawthorne offers minute analyses of objects, situations, and characters, only to render them projective by contradiction, equivocation, multiplication, or attribution to tradition, to the community, and to his own or even to the reader's fancy. Indeed, the "world of reality" in which Fiedler claims Hester to be rooted is itself, however defined, a projective construct. If it is Hester's social world, it is, ironically enough, the same world that recognizes her only in the allegorical role it projects for her, that of "the type of shame." If it is the world that Hawthorne creates for his readers, it is one in which Hester exists more tangibly than the other characters only by virtue of the narrative's attentive and (for us) appealing psychological projection of her, its insistence on complicating (and modernizing) the Puritan perspective by regularly articulating, as one chapter title puts it, "Another View of Hester."

The Scarlet Letter, then, is always transforming or threatening to transform Fiedler's ontological and epistemological issue into a sociological and linguistic one. We cannot define the status of characters and objects otherwise than as "the sense in which we . . . believe in them," the terms on which we admit them into our thought, our vocabulary, our community. And this sense may be self-serving or self-deluded; these terms may be arbitrary. Puritan Boston affixes a letter to Hester Prynne's breast that identifies her as a type and an outcast and announces the community's own ability to make moral, social, and ontological determinations. But Hester's representative qualities, along with the undiscovered identities of Chillingworth and Dimmesdale, mock this presumption of competence. While she is taken "out of the ordinary relations with humanity," they, as ministers to the townspeople's bodies and souls, are immersed in such relations. The sense in which Chillingworth and Dimmesdale command belief obscures their falsity; the sense in which Hester commands belief obscures her reality. Deviance and representativeness converge in all three, a convergence epitomized in the figure of Mistress Hibbins, the avowed witch and spectral forest denizen who also happens to be Governor Bellingham's sister and the obtrusive sharer of his mansion.

Hawthorne's treatment of Chillingworth sharply illustrates the narrative's general inclination to withhold or unsettle all the bases for absolute moral, social, or ontological judgments. As he first appears, Chillingworth is a classic outsider: old, deformed, oddly dressed, unnaturally intelligent, he stands as a prisoner of the Indians and a still unransomed newcomer to the colony. Soon, however, he has become an agent of social power and justice, strangely re-enacting in his private punishment of Dimmesdale the sentence passed on Hester by the elected magistrates. Rather than condemning Dimmesdale to death, Chillingworth condemns him to live beneath an ever-burning gaze fixed on his breast. Beyond this, the metaphor that Hawthorne attaches to Chillingworth's retributive enterprise is the metaphor for the enterprise of Puritan justice. "A blessing on the righteous Colony of the Massachusetts, where iniquity is dragged out into the sunshine!" (i, 54), cries the town beadle, as he leads Hester to the scaffold. It is another "inevitable moment," the twin of this one, that Chillingworth seeks—the moment when his probes, as cautious as those of "a treasure-seeker in a dark cavern," will strike their object, and "the soul of the sufferer [will] be dissolved, and flow forth in a dark, but transparent stream, *bringing all its mysteries into the daylight*"[4] (i, 124; emphasis added). Both alien and representative avenger, Chillingworth does also function in the novel's social world as a healer. "But for my aid, his life would have burned away in torments, within the first two years after the perpetration of his crime and thine" (i, 171), he tells Hester, and we are given no cause to doubt his claim.

On his moral function and ontological status Hawthorne provides conflicting indications. Many of the townspeople "see a providential hand," and some enthusiasts proclaim "an absolute miracle" (i, 121), in the timely arrival of a physician possessed of the skill and devotion to preserve their minister's failing life. Hester, undeceived at least about his personal identity, early pronounces: "Thy acts are like mercy. . . . But thy words interpret thee as a terror!" (i, 76). Yet Dimmesdale's own dying words reverse her judgment and, interpreting the terror of Chillingworth's acts as a mercy, ratify the community's initial association of the physician with Divine Providence: "He hath proved his mercy, most of all in my afflictions. By giving me this burning torture to bear upon my breast! By sending yonder dark and terrible old man, to keep the torture always at red-heat!" (i, 256). The narrator, on the other hand, tends to encourage the reader to view Chillingworth as a demon, a devil, the Black Man, but deftly undercuts such a view each time it seems on the verge of confirmation. When Chillingworth, in a paroxysm of self-recognition, labels himself "a fiend," Hawthorne begins the next sentence with the words, "the unfortunate physician," and goes on to note the "look of horror" that accompanied his outburst (i, 172). In one condemnatory sentence, Hawthorne modifies "the avenger" with the parenthetical phrase "poor, forlorn creature that he was, and more wretched than his victim" (i, 141). And, in Chillingworth's most diabolical scene, when the old man uncovers the breast of the sleeping minister and cele-brates with a grotesque and riotous dance what he discovers there, Hawthorne refuses to conclude the chapter with the apparently conclusive Satanic association. Instead, gratuitously, he adds a sentence that unbalances the equation and reopens to interpretation the issue of Chillingworth's character:

> Had a man seen old Roger Chillingworth, at that moment of his ecstasy, he would have had no need to ask how Satan comports himself, when a precious human soul is lost to heaven, and won into his kingdom.
>
> But what distinguished the physician's ecstasy from Satan's was the trait of wonder in it! (i, 138)

In his meticulously equivocal last chapter, entitled "Conclusion," Hawthorne catalogues the popular interpretations of Dimmesdale's dying revelation (a revela-tion not described in the preceding chapter, entitled "The Revelation of the Scarlet Letter"). His list concludes with the testimony of certain "highly respectable wit-nesses" (i, 259) that there had been no material sign on Dimmesdale's breast, no mark to be viewed, but that "he had made the manner of his death a parable" (i, 259) which required a more abstract reading. The narrator disparages this position on the ground that it resists "proofs, clear as the mid-day sunshine on the scarlet letter" (i, 259). But his phrase, in spite of the certainty of Dimmesdale's guilt, is inescapably ironic. Throughout the novel, light and language have repeatedly proved to be anything but clear, constant, and uncomplicated. The broad daylight of Puritan justice and of Chillingworth's knowledge is, in each instance, compro-mised by shades of self-deception and darker motives; Hester's letter is openly displayed at the outset but takes on various significances and remains enigmatic to the end. Above all, it is Dimmesdale's identity that is bound up with the complex-ities of light and language and that is only revealed (insofar as it is revealed at all) by and as their power and their play.

Dimmesdale's first words in the novel are to implore Hester to see "the accountability under which I labor" (i, 67). The accountability is, of course, his obligation as a preacher of the word. But the burden that this role imposes is also its peculiar liberation, much as Hester Prynne's role is one in which bondage and freedom converge. The community requires of—and imposes on—both Hester's letter and Dimmesdale's word a typological significance; in each case it assumes that significance to be exclusively accountable to its interpretive authority, exclusively readable by its lights. But the art of symbolic overlay that Puritan Boston demands and receives from its outcast and its minister is not so easily controlled or interpreted, and the rigidity and predictability of the community's interpretive conventions virtually ensure the duplicity of Hester's and Dimmesdale's "texts." An early example of these conventions, and of the opportunity they afford Dimmesdale for simultaneously orthodox and subversive ministerial service, occurs in the governor's hall. Pearl, who throughout the book plays with light and even is characterized as the embodiment of the play of light (i, 90, 91, 92, 95), has just made an unsettling appearance. Her dazzling and freakish attire has shocked the sensibilities of Governor Bellingham and Mr. Wilson, and her perverse response to their religious examination has confirmed them in their decision to remove her from Hester's care. Dimmesdale, at Hester's command, successfully contests this course by offering a symbolic reading of Pearl's offensive appearance and comportment, one that makes conventional Puritan sense of her and relieves Wilson and Bellingham of the confusions of sensory and emotional response. Pearl is to be regarded not as a poorly raised and shamefully dressed child but as God's living judgment upon Hester, a judgment that replicates and ratifies the sentence of the magistrates by combining mercy, retribution, and the opportunity for limited atonement. Pearl is Hester's blessing and her "ever-recurring agony," Dimmesdale asserts, clinching his argument by explaining the child's embroidered gold and crimson tunic typologically: "Hath she not expressed this thought in the garb of the poor child, so forcibly reminding us of that red symbol which sears her bosom?" (i, 114).

Not in material existence but only by the office of the word is faith in a universe of determinate meaning affirmed and renewed; hence Dimmesdale's colleagues give his formulation greater weight than their own experience of Pearl. Because they see the world in figurative terms, the Puritans cultivate the figurative power of language and tailor their interpretative conventions to the discovery (or production) of the broadest significances. But, paradoxically, the very strategies that guarantee meaning, faith, and social order may threaten to undo them. Dimmesdale's duplicitous self-revelations illustrate the point:

> He had told his hearers that he was altogether vile, a viler companion of the vilest, the worst of sinners, an abomination, a thing of unimaginable iniquity; and that the only wonder was, that they did not see his wretched body shrivelled up before their eyes, by the burning wrath of the Almighty! Could there be plainer speech than this? Would not the people start up in their seats, by a simultaneous impulse, and tear him down out of the pulpit which he

defiled? Not so, indeed! They heard it all, but did but reverence him the more.
(i, 143–44)

More cynically and guiltily than Hester does, Dimmesdale exploits the difference between his "individuality" and his role as a "general symbol," knowing that his confessions will be interpreted as performances of a symbolic kind. His own self-loathing and his congregation's worship of him thus intensify one another in a vicious spiral that progressively diminishes the possibility of communication as it widens the gap between Dimmesdale's private and public identities. "He had spoken the very truth," Hawthorne notes, "and transformed it into the veriest falsehood" (i, 144).

If he worked his transformations in one direction only, Dimmesdale might be conclusively described as a "subtle, but remorseful, hypocrite" (i, 144). This, however, is not the case, for Dimmesdale not only regularly converts his truth into falsehood but, what is more disturbing, converts his falsehood into truth. Alone among New England divines, we are told, he possesses "the gift that descended upon the chosen disciples at Pentecost, . . . Heaven's last and rarest attestation of their office, the Tongue of Flame" (i, 141–42). The man whose words contrive to remain universally misunderstood acquires, by virtue of that contrivance, "the power . . . of addressing the whole human brotherhood in the heart's native language" (i, 142); the man whose inner life is most thoroughly alienated from the world around him acquires through it complete access to that world:

> It kept him down, on a level with the lowest; him, the man of ethereal attributes, whose voice the angels might else have listened to and answered! But this very burden it was, that gave him sympathies so intimate with the sinful brotherhood of mankind; so that his heart vibrated in unison with theirs, and received their pain into itself, and sent its own throb of pain through a thousand other hearts, in gushes of sad, persuasive eloquence. (i, 142)

Not only is Dimmesdale's sin inextricable from his saintliness, but the perpetuation of both states depends on the very same quality of his language: its openness to interpretation in the light of its auditor's own needs, desires, assumptions, and experiences. By the same openness he achieves the pernicious and self-serving deceptions of his public "confessions" and conveys the undiscriminating sympathy, the passionate receptivity, that elicits genuine Christian faith and gives him his Tongue of Flame.

Dimmesdale's Tongue of Flame makes him "the mouth-piece of Heaven's messages" (i, 142) in the eyes of his parishioners. For Hawthorne, however, it is more closely aligned with his own duplicitous discourse and with the "hell-fired story" (as he described it to Melville) of *The Scarlet Letter*. The association of Hawthorne's text and Dimmesdale's expression is implicit in "The Interior of a Heart," where Hawthorne not only reports the minister's duplicity but replicates it—and obliges the reader to do the same in his response—by presenting Dimmesdale in two different yet interdependent lights. This association is confirmed in the next chapter, the novel's pivotal chapter and middle scaffold scene, "The Minister's Vigil." Here, too, the elements of light, language, and interpretation dazzlingly intersect, and—more decisively and dangerously than anywhere else in *The Scarlet Letter*—the imaginary and the actual, the deviant and the representative, the false and the true converge.

Dimmesdale's vigil is the desperate product of his mind's "involuntary effort to relieve itself by a kind of lurid playfulness" (i, 151). As a parody of self-exposure, it incorporates both the genuine impulse to confess and its antithesis; it "intertwine[s] in the same inextricable knot, the agony of heaven-defying guilt and vain repentance" (i, 148). Throughout the first half of the chapter, material fact and spectral fantasy blend and blur in Dimmesdale's tortured and divided consciousness. But, as the scene continues, the "obscure night" (i, 147), Hawthorne's ambiguous, inconclusive, and contradictory narration, and, finally, events themselves begin to conspire in these convergences. When Pearl, having mounted the scaffold with Hester, asks the minister to "take my hand, and my mother's hand, tomorrow noontide," Dimmesdale answers that he shall do so "at the great judgment day," but that "the daylight of this world shall not see our meeting!" (i, 153):

> But, before Mr. Dimmesdale had done speaking, a light gleamed far and wide over all the muffled sky.... And there stood the minister, with his hand over his heart; and Hester Prynne, with the embroidered letter glimmering on her bosom; and little Pearl, herself a symbol, and the connecting link between those two. They stood in the noon of that strange and solemn splendor, as if it were the light that is to reveal all secrets, and the daybreak that shall unite all who belong to one another. (i, 153–54)

Heaven, or Hawthorne's language, here enacts its own bit of "lurid playfulness" which burlesques Dimmesdale's claim. The coincidence of the light and his words seems to reflect a world of immanent meaning, a world capable of confirming and clarifying the human significance intimated in Hawthorne's description of the three linked figures. Yet between the phenomenon and its reading stand the words "as if," which are, like the prison door, at once a passage and a barrier. Dimmesdale, as he has done throughout the chapter, insists on producing meaning and takes the light to be a symbolic revelation of his sin. His boundless self-absorption prompts the narrator to issue an extended and vehement refutation:

> It was, indeed, a majestic idea, that the destiny of nations should be revealed, in these awful hieroglyphics, on the cope of heaven.... But what shall we say, when an individual discovers a revelation, addressed to himself alone, on the same vast sheet of record! In such a case, it could only be the symptom of a highly disordered mental state, when a man, rendered morbidly self-contemplative by long, intense, and secret pain, had extended his egotism over the whole expanse of nature, until the firmament itself should appear no more than a fitting page for his soul's history and fate.

We impute it, therefore, solely to the disease in his own eye and heart, that the minister, looking upward to the zenith, beheld there the appearance of an immense letter,—the letter A,—marked out in lines of dull red light. Not but the meteor may have shown itself at that point, burning duskily through a veil of cloud; but with no such shape as his guilty imagination gave it; or, at least, with so little definiteness, that another's guilt might have seen another symbol in it. (i, 155)

The Scarlet Letter contains few more unequivocal, and no more credible, authorial interjections than this. Not only does the passage differentiate the facts of the narrative from Dimmesdale's fantasies but it affords us the rare security of a normative vantage point from which to judge Dimmesdale's deviant view. It is Hawthorne's interpretative gift to his readers, but two pages later it explodes in their faces. Dimmesdale, on the morning after his vigil, preaches "a discourse which was held to be the richest and most powerful, and the most replete with heavenly influences, that had ever proceeded from his lips," a sermon that brings "more souls than one . . . to the truth" (i, 157). At its conclusion, the sexton closes the chapter by informing the minister of "the portent that was seen last night": "A great red letter in the sky,—the letter A,—which we interpret to stand for Angel. For, as our good Governor Winthrop was made an angel this past night, it was doubtless held fit that there should be some notice thereof!" (i, 158).

That the entire community saw what Dimmesdale saw demolishes the axis of truth and falsity on which we had been evaluating his vision. Indeed, it recasts the phenomenal meteor itself as the multiply and irresolvably interpreted one, the figure, the letter. Beyond their shared perception, the equivalent perceptual behavior of Dimmesdale and the community suggests the minister's representative status at the moment of his wildest perversity. In embroidering his letter, Dimmesdale, like Hester, may not deviate from the right or even from the conventional so much as he sustains a time-honored interpretive tradition. This view, in fact, finds support in a passage which immediately precedes Hawthorne's dismissal of Dimmesdale's egotistical epiphany:

> We doubt whether any marked event, for good or evil, ever befell New England, from its settlement down to Revolutionary times, of which the inhabitants had not been previously warned by some spectacle of this nature. Not seldom, it had been seen by multitudes. Oftener, however, its credibility rested on the faith of some lonely eye-witness, who beheld the wonder through the colored, magnifying, and distorting medium of his imagination, and shaped it more distinctly in his after-thought. (i, 155)

Private fiction and public history, sinful reverie and divine prophecy, disordered imagination and ordered universe—are all cut from the same cloth, "The Minister's Vigil" implies; gratuitous chance, choice, or power affixes the label.

The Scarlet Letter and the meteor of "The Minister's Vigil" are subversive in the same subtle way: each produces an illumination that unsettles the objectivity of objects by revealing the act of perception that figures in their constitution. The virtual identity between the passage that describes the meteor's effect and the passage in the "Custom-House" that depicts the romancer's atmosphere underlines this relationship:

> It showed the familiar scene of the street, with the distinctness of mid-day, but also with the awfulness that is always imparted to familiar objects by an unaccustomed light. The wooden houses, with their jutting stories and quaint gable-peaks; the door-steps and thresholds, with the early grass springing up about them; the garden-plots, black with freshly turned earth; the wheel-track, little-worn, and, even in the market-place, margined with green on either side;—all were visible, but with a singularity of aspect that seemed to give another moral interpretation to the things of this world than they had ever borne before. (i, 154)

> Moonlight, in a familiar room, falling so white upon the carpet, and showing all its figures so distinctly,—making every object so minutely visible, yet so unlike a morning or noontide visibility,—is a medium the most suitable for a romance-writer to get acquainted with his illusive guests. There is the little domestic scenery of the well-known apartment; the chairs, with each its separate individuality; the centre-table, sustaining a work-basket, a volume or two, and an extinguished lamp; the sofa; the book-case; the picture on the wall;—all these details, so completely seen, are so spiritualized by the unusual light, that they seem to lose their actual substance, and become things of intellect. (i, 35)

I quoted part of the second passage here in the discussion of "The Custom-House," in speaking of the self-protective impulse that often prompts Hawthorne to conceal from his readers, and perhaps from himself, the most radical and real implications of his fiction. In that context, I argued that the imputation of insularity and triviality to romance—the suggestion that it can evade or attenuate the pressures of temporality and material circumstance—ignores the dangerous and dynamic engagement with community, time, and physical experience that "The Custom-House" and *The Scarlet Letter* exemplify. By the meteor's light, however, Hawthorne's deceptive characterization of romance begins to appear more revelatory and representative. In "The Minister's Vigil" it is clear that the circumstances of imaginative enterprise are material and the stakes are high. The scaffold is hardly a neutral territory, and, when he ascends to it, Dimmesdale does not leave below his weighty past or his tortured daily life. On the contrary, he seems to draw to him, quite literally, the figures—Hester, Pearl, Chillingworth, Wilson, Bellingham, Hibbins—who dominate or embody both of these realms. The presence of others, moreover, is neither a function of nor a foil for Dimmesdale's imagination. Rather, the entire community shares his visionary experience and takes that experience not as a departure from but as a confirmation of its "actual substance." Thus the cloistered dream pictured in the passage from "The Custom-House" is the social reality of the passage from the novel: like the effects of art, the facts of life are produced by the play of light and the angle of vision and are always subject to "another moral interpretation." Now Hawthorne's prefatory (though composed after the work itself) claim that romance attenuates the most concrete furnishings of actuality and makes them "things of intellect" assumes greater consequence and a different, an anxious, cast. The white light that spiritualizes is the lurid gleam that confounds and consumes.

Hawthorne's own anxiety about his enterprise is succinctly expressed by a writer for the *Church Review* in 1851. *The Scarlet Letter* "saps the foundations of the moral sense," Arthur Cleveland Coxe charged: "We call things by their right names, while the romance never hints the shocking words that belong to its things."[5] Coxe is quite right in his sense that *The Scarlet Letter* challenges a fundamentalist understanding of perception, morality, and language, that it frustrates the attempt to validate them by reference to a reality that exists prior to and independent of their operations. But he miscontrues the force of the challenge and of Hawthorne's book when he implies that its effect is to grant words and thoughts utterly free play in a realm of unencumbered subjectivity. *The Scarlet Letter*'s vision is at once more radical and more conservative than this. If it insists that words and things are not fundamentally joined, it also insists that they cannot be fundamentally disjoined. Such is the equivocal purport of the meteoric letter, that naturalized sign, that conventionalized phenomenon, hurtling through space—a material fact that is no more than a piece of the alphabet, a semantic token that is no less than a piece of the material world. What "The Minister's Vigil" reveals is that the "things of this world" and the "things of [language and] intellect" are neither wholly determinative nor wholly determined; rather, they exist in a relationship of mutual indebtedness. Dimmesdale neither projects the "A" in the sky, as we assume, nor receives it, as he assumes. He interprets it, an act that involves both projection and reception, freedom and constraint. The constraint, moreover, lies not only in the shape of Dimmesdale's object but in the structure of his consciousness, a structure bound to reflect the cultural forms—perceptual, moral, linguistic—of which it is largely composed. Thus, in spying a sign from heaven, Dimmesdale takes his place in the New England tradition of "lonely eye-witness" to divine prophecy; in reading its message as he does, Dimmesdale objectifies the moral principles and psychological pressures of that culture; and in identifying the sign itself as an "A," Dimmesdale sees the same letter that all of Boston sees.

A single mode of expression, even a single token, serves Dimmesdale in his madness, Hester in her defiance, and the society in its orthodoxy. Language enables and enforces their commonality and, in so doing, withholds both determinate reality from Puritan Boston and imaginative indeterminacy from its discontents. At once representative and semantic, language transports history and convention even as it transforms them. This tension manifests itself most elaborately in the lovers' forest rendezvous, a scene that takes place outside of the physical and moral boundaries of society but that Hawthorne wryly introduces in the chapter title, "The Pastor and His Parishioner." Throughout the scene, Hester's and Dimmesdale's language sustains and extends the irony of the title. Their transformations—of social identities to natural ones, of religious meanings to romantic ones, of established truths to subversive ones—are always transportations as well; the terms of their escape are the terms of their return.

"Art thou in life?" and "Dost thou yet live?" (i, 189), the lovers ask each other, as if they shared a belief in, and a recollection of, an alternative ontology whose conditions their obvious physical existence would not satisfy. Like "ghost[s]," they glide "back into the shadows of the woods" (i, 190) to redeem themselves by the words they exchange. Variants of the word "truth" appear over and over in their interview. To save Dimmesdale "eternal alienation from the Good and the True," Hester reveals Chillingworth's identity, prefacing her confession with an appeal for forgiveness: "In all things else, I have striven to be true!" (i, 193). When he absolves Hester of sin against their love, Dimmesdale allows himself to re-value his own sinfulness, to forge "another moral interpretation" of his guilt:

> We are not, Hester, the worst sinners in the world. There is one worse than the polluted priest! That old man's revenge has been blacker than my sin. He has violated, in cold blood, the sanctity of a human heart. Thou and I, Hester, never did so! (i, 195)

The reader, who shares in the long-awaited release of tension and who has witnessed only Chillingworth's crime is moved to agree. Yet, theologically, Dimmesdale's is a shocking doctrine. "Thou shalt not violate the sanctity of a human heart" appears nowhere in the Decalogue. It is only a commandment in the gospel of romantic love, toward which the minister has taken a cautious but decided step. Hester's response ratifies his initiative and announces the new dispensation: " 'Never, never!' whispered she. "What we did had a consecration of its own. We felt it so! We said so to each other!' " (i, 195).

It is a parody of salvation that Hester and Dimmesdale enact in the forest. As sacred language is adapted to profane ends, the relation of pastor to parishioner is also upended. Hester becomes the priestess of romantic love, Dimmesdale her supplicant. "Heaven would show mercy," she pronounces, "hadst thou but the strength to take advantage of it" (i, 196). And she describes to him a new life at whose outset the burdens and stains of this one will melt away:

> Thou art crushed under this seven years' weight of misery. . . . But thou shalt leave it all behind thee! . . . Leave this wreck and ruin here where it hath happened! Meddle no more with it! Begin all anew! . . . Exchange this false life of thine for a true one. (i, 198)

"A Flood of Sunshine" follows, bathing the reconfirmed sinners in the light that they have shunned and that has shunned them throughout. Meanwhile, Hawthorne joins in the production of religious resonances for their halfway convenant. Hester's trials, he tells us, had been "little other than a preparation for this very hour" (i, 200). And of Dimmesdale he remarks: "To this poor pilgrim, on his dreary and desert path, faint, sick, miserable, there appeared a glimpse of human affection and sympathy, a new life, and a true one, in exchange for the heavy doom which he was now expiating" (i, 200). The minister is all but seduced. "O Thou to whom I dare not lift my eyes," he prays, in a final attempt to win some miraculous sanction, "wilt Thou yet pardon me!" (i, 201). But, as the next sentence tersely indicates, the voice he summons and the eyes he meets are Hester's: " 'Thou wilt go!' said Hester calmly, as he met her glance":

> His spirit rose, as it were, with a bound, and attained a nearer prospect of the sky, than throughout all the misery which had kept him grovelling on the earth. Of a deeply religious temperament, there was inevitably something of the devotional in his mood.
> "Do I feel joy again?" cried he, wondering at himself. "Methought the germ of it was dead in me! O Hester, thou art my better angel! I seem to have flung myself—sick, sin-stained, and sorrow-blackened—down upon these forest leaves, and to have risen up all made anew, and with new powers to glorify Him that hath been merciful! This is already the better life!" (i, 201–2)

In his observations on *The Scarlet Letter,* Kenneth Dauber points out the revaluation of Puritan language here and reads the scene as a final opportunity for Hester and Dimmesdale to "unite in a universe that is their own extention" and for Hawthorne to establish creative control over his work and intimacy with his audience. "We have, in effect, a series of puns or pun-like structures, alternative definitions of language from which the couple must choose," Dauber writes.[6] The identities of Dimmesdale, Hester, and Hawthorne are doubly committed, however, and in the forest scene the integration of romantic and religious language, like the union of sexual and spiritual passion that initiates the story, suggests that no choice will constitute an adequate basis for self-definition and moral resolution.[7] Still, the characters, author, and critics of *The Scarlet Letter* are subject to the pressure of its dialectics, a pressure so great that it almost seems to validate any decision to relieve it. Hester's injunction to Dimmesdale—"Exchange this false life of thine for a true one"—expresses the necessary presuppositions of such a decision: that the entangled impulses (or meanings) which are implicit in the self-parodic vocabulary of the scene may be separated and objectified as alternative lives, and that these two lives may be accurately identified as a true one and a false one. These presuppositions are incompatible with the complexity that Dimmesdale's character and the novel itself have exhibited up to this point. As critical pitfalls, though, the arbitrariness and partiality of the kind of separation they underlie may be better illustrated by the relationship between two sophisticated and attractive readings of *The Scarlet Letter* that make opposite choices while observing many of the same textual phenomena and, in general sharing a common critical vocabulary. One of these is Dauber's; the other is contained in a recent essay by John Carlos Rowe.

Dauber reads the novel as an attempt to transform a "house of death" into a "house of life," an opportunity for Hawthorne (through the story of Hester) to escape "alienation in the Salem Custom-House" by "the reaffirmation of intimacy in Salem terms." The opening chapters are rife with possibility as Hawthorne and Hester take "liberties" with established cultural forms. But the alien form of the Fortunate Fall thwarts their chance for self-renewal and affirmation through creative revision. This typical and external story—Dauber calls it "allegory"—"seizes control, and its dominance is firmly established in the middle of the book." The second half of the novel, Dauber observes, simply copies the first half in a way that schematizes the action and sacrifices the potential of romance to allegory's "predictable end."[8] Rowe also sees in The Scarlet Letter "Hawthorne's effort to revivify the static moral categories of Puritanism" by rediscovering "the origins of the communal in the individual." But his Hegelian reading charts a dynamic "transformation of bondage into freedom" through "a narrative that begins with the alienation of the subject from his/her own script and ends with the internalization of language as history." Initially, Rowe argues, "Hester remains fully within the Puritan system of signification" and "is defined also for herself as pure alienation." The first half of the novel, he observes, "perfectly expresses this quality of allegorical externality." Every chapter is "a predicate to the general theological problem of original sin" and the early scenes are mere "allegorical tableaux in which each character plays a predictable role." Conversely, "the second half of The Scarlet Letter shifts noticeably into a dramatic, temporalized mode, in which narrative events no longer govern the characters but are determined increasingly by intentional acts."[9]

One measure of the remarkable pitch and poise of the tensions in The Scarlet Letter is its capacity to elicit interpretations at once so intimately related and so diametrically opposed as these two. This relationship alone casts an unsettling light on the term that Dauber and Rowe apply differently but understand in the same way, the term that marks the intersection of their arguments: allegory. Both critics define allegory as a form of bondage, a sacrifice of the intimate and internal to the abstract and external, an enforcement of a fixed meaning rather than an engagement in the dynamic or dialectical creation of meanings. In so doing, both imply the distinguishability of (true) experience, or (full, unalienated) selfhood, from its (false, partial, alienated) representation. (This implication, I would argue, is present in both readings in spite of the fact that each critic sees the kind of identity or experience he finds most valid as an achievement of the act of representation.) Their radical divergence on the question of what is allegory in The Scarlet Letter and what is not, however, testifies to the novel's implacable resistance to such distinctions. Informed by the structures of language and consciousness, experience is always allegorical, self-divided, at once intimate and abstract, a representation of itself. Its internal difference is, as Emily Dickinson wrote, precisely where the meanings are; that is, the non-identity of its tokens and values both provides for the production of meaning and prevents the absolute establishment of it. In this view, then, allegory, like Hester's letter, is neither submitted to nor overcome. Rather, it is the medium of experience itself, a medium that holds word and thing, spirit and matter, self and other in mutual indebtedness but not in synthesis. As Johnathan Arac has suggested, Hawthorne's use of the allegorical form exemplifies Walter Benjamin's idea that "allegory does not so much enforce any particular meaning as raise the problem of meaning."[10]

Meaning could hardly be more problematic than it is in the concluding chapters of *The Scarlet Letter*. The authorial discomfort that Dauber takes as evidence of Hawthorne's creative frustration by allegory's "final fixing"[11] might be ascribed, at least as convincingly, to Hawthorne's anxiety about the phenomenal inconclusiveness or the moral obliquity of his tale. Rowe's staggeringly sanguine pronouncement that "Dimmesdale's sermon and his confession on the scaffold bring the evanescence of individual self-consciousness into relation with the more enduring values of a social order in which the individual may discover an active, creative role"[12] disregards Hawthorne's uneasiness altogether, as it does the equivocal response that the minister's last performance elicits from Hester and the community alike. Moreover, Rowe ignores the multiple ironies with which Hawthorne laces his description of Dimmesdale's ministerial "triumph," ironies that, as Frederick C. Crews has argued, raise the possibility that the election sermon is the ultimate sublimation of the minister's rekindled passion, that it "is attributable not to Dimmesdale's holiness but to his libido."[13] Indeed, the sermon may be variously characterized, for the crucial fact about it is that it is entirely the product of our characterizations. The novel's climactic piece of language is unwritten and unread. We apprehend it, if at all, only as Hester does, outside "the sacred edifice" (i, 242) and nearer the pillory: "Hester Prynne listened with such intenseness, and sympathized so intimately, that the sermon had throughout a meaning for her, entirely apart from its indistinguishable words" (i, 243). The garbled sermon can only communicate "in a tongue native to the human heart" (i, 243); thus Hester can take it to express her heart's desire. And, in fact, she does understand the sermon and feel its "passion and pathos" (i, 243) in the context of her expectation of imminent reunion with Dimmesdale, an expectation that will soon prove to be a delusion.

When Hawthorne does announce the text of Dimmesdale's sermon, his language is diffident and vague, and the information he offers only draws our attention to the information he withholds: "His subject, it appeared, had been the relation between the Deity and the communities of mankind, with a special reference to the New England which they were here planting in the wilderness" (i, 249). This "relation" is not much clarified by the speech of Dimmesdale's that we do hear, in which his wild self-condemnation as "the one sinner of the world" (i, 254) and his repeated insistence that God's direct and personal attention had all along been focused on the issue of his burning stigma uncomfortably recall the obsessive self-involvement of his midnight trip to the scaffold. Perhaps now they bespeak the fervency of his penitence. Perhaps, too, his cool rebuff of Hester's last hopeful appeal demonstrates spiritual abstraction rather than detached and defensive insularity. In any case, Hawthorne's earlier remark about Hester's deliberate public displays of her letter is an equally apt commentary on Dimmesdale's first and last display of his: "This might be pride, but was so like humility, that it produced all the softening influence of the latter quality on the public mind" (i, 162).

Realization and its parody are balanced in *The Scarlet Letter*'s final scene as they have been in so many earlier ones. The almost comically qualified moral that Hawthorne appends to his tale merely punctuates its ambiguity:

> Among many morals which press upon us from the poor minister's miserable experience, we put only this into a sentence:—"Be true! Be true! Be true! Show freely to the world, if not your worst, yet some trait whereby the worst may be inferred!" (i, 260)

It is not only for the people of Boston, or for Hawthorne's readers, that the truth or falsity of Dimmesdale's salvation remains inferential. The minister, too, can proclaim himself divinely rescued from Chillingworth and yet, in the next moment, turn to Hester "with an expression of doubt and anxiety in his eyes" (i, 254). Questions of meaning and agency persist about the parable that Dimmesdale acts out with a peculiar mixture of willfull effort and entranced compulsion. As he nears the scaffold, Hawthorne compares his movement to "the wavering effort of an infant, with its mother's arms in view, outstretched to tempt him forward" (i, 251). It is a disconcerting image: it offers wavering infancy at the moment of Dimmesdale's manly resolve, the mother's enticement at the moment of his reconciliation to the Father's power, prepubescent sexuality at the moment of his confession to adultery, an emblem of pure affection qualified by the charged and unexpected verb "to tempt." Above all, the image objectifies a state of ontological ambivalence; it suspends a moment in which dependence and independence exist in intimate relation and precarious opposition—a moment that allows a glimpse of the complex texture of freedom and bondage that is human identity.

Hester's will, too, like Dimmesdale's and God's, is placed explicitly at issue in this scene in terms that recall her first description and prefigure her last. When Dimmesdale invites her to the scaffold, Hester goes "slowly, as if impelled by inevitable fate, and against her strongest will" (i, 252). These steps repeat and invert the ones taken seven years and two hundred pages earlier, when, at the prison door, Hester repelled the beadle's inevitable hand "by an action marked with natural dignity and force of character, and stepped into the open air as if by her own free will" (i, 52). In each instance, Hester is at once bound and free, self-alienated and self-possessed; in each, a fiction ("as if") at once reveals and conceals the truth. The only reconciliation of these tensions occurs long after both scaffold scenes: "She had returned, therefore, and resumed,—of her own free will, for not the sternest magistrate of that iron period would have imposed it,—resumed the symbol of which we have related so dark a tale" (i, 263). Hester and her community, liberty and compulsion, truth and fiction are resolved equally here by and into an act of representation. The identity that Hester finally wins from the Puritans comprises her decision, "as their representative, hereby [to] take shame upon [herself] for their sakes" and for her own.

NOTES

All quotations from Hawthorne refer to *The Centenary Edition of the Work of Nathaniel Hawthorne*, ed. Roy Harvey Pearce et al. (Columbus: Ohio State University Press, 1962–   ), cited parenthetically in the text by volume and page number.

[1] The word "event" seems a serviceable reference to *The Scarlet Letter*'s unpresented act of adultery, both for its suggestion of an indisputable yet irrecoverable fact of history and for its explicit association with sexual relations in a relevant passage of *The Blithedale Romance*. There, Zenobia, Hester's descendant, protests to Coverdale that a woman is doomed to discover that "fate has assigned her but one single event which she must contrive to make the substance of her whole life." Coverdale playfully observes that "by constant repetition of her one event, [a woman] may compensate for the lack of variety" (iii, 60). Hawthorne grants lasciviousness unusual latitude in Coverdale's response, but the joke (especially in light of Zenobia's open and, for Coverdale, unsettling sexuality) also images an important structural principle of Hawthorne's work, the tension between overdetermination and indeterminacy.

[2] Julia Kristeva, "Psychoanalysis and the Polis," *Critical Inquiry* 9 (September 1982): 80.

[3] Leslie Fieldler, *Love and Death in the American Novel* (New York: Criterion Books, 1960), p. 512.

[4] The images in this passage further complicate Chillingworth's (and, by extension, the community's) retributive role by their insinuation that Dimmesdale's and Hester's crime is grotesquely replicated in their punishment. Certainly, Fiedler is right to note the curious similarity between the unseen union of Dimmesdale and Hester and the increasingly intimate association of Chillingworth and Dimmesdale, the "dark passion" of their seven-year cohabitation (see ibid., pp. 502–3). The interrelatedness of these two unions remains problematic to the last; Dimmesdale mounts the scaffold and escapes Chillingworth, but, although he calls her to his side, it seems that he has also hit upon the one place guaranteed to afford him escape from Hester.

[5] Arthur Cleveland Coxe, "The Writings of Hawthorne," *Church Review* (January 1851), excerpted in *The Recognition of Nathaniel Hawthorne*, ed. B. Bernard Cohen (Ann Arbor: The University of Michigan Press, 1969), p. 52.

[6] Kenneth Dauber, *Rediscovering Hawthorne* (Princeton: Princeton University Press, 1977), p. 106.

[7] The conflation of religious and sexual impulses is not confined to Dimmesdale's and Hester's relationship and vocabulary or to the minister's equally lurid profane and penitential fantasies. As Hawthorne pointedly indicates, it is the norm among the devout young women of Dimmesdale's congregation: "The virgins of his church grew pale around him, victims of a passion so imbued with religious sentiment that they imagined it to be all religion, and brought it openly, in their white bosoms, as their most acceptable sacrifice before the altar" (i, 142).

[8] Kenneth Dauber, *Rediscovering Hawthorne*, pp. 105, 98, 107, 112.

[9] John Carlos Rowe, "The Internal Conflict of Romantic Narrative: Hegel's *Phenomenology* and Hawthorne's *The Scarlet Letter*," *MLN* 95 (1980): 1210, 1211, 1208, 1214, 1210, 1210–11, 1210.

[10] Jonathan Arac, "Reading the Letter," *Diacritics* 9 (June 1979): 50.

[11] Kenneth Dauber, *Rediscovering Hawthorne*, p. 108.

[12] John Carlos Rowe, "The Internal Conflict of Romantic Narrative," p. 1222.

[13] Frederick C. Crews, *The Sins of the Fathers: Hawthorne's Psychological Themes* (New York: Oxford University Press, 1966), p. 147. Crews goes on to note the multiple ironies that attend Dimmesdale's sermon and confession and unsettle their doctrinal significances (pp. 148–53).

Carol Bensick

DEMYSTIFIED ADULTERY
IN *THE SCARLET LETTER*

Hawthorne's distinctive emphasis on the historical context of moral and psychological experience has somewhat obscured *The Scarlet Letter*'s generic affinities.
Yet there is evident weight in Q. D. Leavis's suggestion, in her classic 1951 essay
"Hawthorne as Poet," that "the just comparison with *The Scarlet Letter* is . . . *Anna
Karenina*."[1] For Hawthorne's tale discovers the same traditional pattern, recurrent
in the European novel since Madame de La Fayette's *Princesse de Clèves* (1678),
that Tolstoy's own novel regards.

But while "the novel of adultery"[2] is evidently *The Scarlet Letter*'s most appropriate genre, studious comparison of Hawthorne and Tolstoy uncovers a basic
anomaly in Hawthorne's relation to their mutual tradition. The classic script, while
deploring society's gratuitous tormenting of the adulteress, nevertheless assumes
misery to be her unavoidable portion; thus *Anna Karenina*, without otherwise
concerning itself with Mosaic law, assumes that somehow "the Lord . . . will repay"
an unfaithful wife. Over the course of *The Scarlet Letter*, by contrast, the issue of
extramarital sex (which Hawthorne conscientiously avoids labeling "adultery")
makes a slow transition from the sphere of mystery to the sphere of marital
sociology: No longer a fateful tragedy to be ritually suffered, adultery emerges as
a practical human problem that the individuals involved have, along with their
society, a common obligation to address.

I

Comparison with the example of Tolstoy verifies Hawthorne's command of
the central elements of the tradition of literary adultery. Beneath the surface, the
seventeenth-century Puritan marriage of Hawthorne's middle-class Anglo-Saxons
incorporates the same basic elements as the nineteenth-century Eastern Orthodox

From *New Essays on* The Scarlet Letter, edited by Michael J. Colacurcio (Cambridge: Cambridge
University Press, 1985), pp. 137–59.

union of Tolstoy's upper-class Russians. Like Aleksey Aleksandrovich Karenin, Roger Chillingworth is considerably older than his wife, and the match, like Karenin's, is an economic arrangement he contracted with her legal guardians. By themselves these factors might seem merely "historical," but by adding, like Tolstoy, the further provision that a vibrantly passionate, sensuous woman has been given to an exceptionally cold and undemonstrative man, Hawthorne sets the stage for the classic literary adultery.

A look at Anna quickly confirms Hester Prynne's proper literary context. Anna is a typical literary adulteress in not having been, before the advent of a suitor, unbearably dissatisfied with married life. Indeed, like the Princesse de Clèves, Anna feels a certain fondness for the older man to whom her relatives sold her girlhood: She "knew [a particular] characteristic in her husband, and liked it."[3] But at Karenin's customary initiation of conjugal lovemaking "with a meaningful smile," and the words, " 'It's time, it's time' " (AK, p. 119), she has, in the classic manner of the literary adulteress, learned to freeze.

Anna's reactions after commencing her affair with Vronsky are also typical. In the fashion of Emma Bovary, the literary adulteress classically attempts to transfer the burden of her afflicted conscience onto the provoking shortcomings of her husband.[4] Anna, comically using Aleksey Aleksandrovich's protruding ears as a pretext, nurses along her sexual indifference to him until it escalates into "a torturing sensation of physical loathing" (AK, p. 446). When Karenin finally confronts her, Anna justifies herself by projecting backward into the past feelings produced by the present situation: " 'I can't bear you, I'm afraid of you, and I hate you' " (AK, p. 225). Overtly, Anna grants that she is " 'a wicked woman, a lost woman' " (AK, p. 220); but in her heart, like Emma Bovary before her, she holds that her husband's intolerable ways exonerate her.

The "generic" elements reproduced in *Anna Karenina*—the wife's apparent content, her sexual incompatibility with her husband, and her final defensive claim of hatred—appear just as clearly in *The Scarlet Letter*. Even the young Hester Prynne was not deceived into thinking that "the utmost passion of her heart" (TSL, p. 176) had been awakened by her husband; when Chillingworth surprises her in the prison immediately after her public ordeal, she reminds him that she " 'was frank' " at their marriage: " 'I felt no love, nor feigned any' " (TSL, p. 74). Yet when Hester is enduring her punishment on the scaffold, the only clear flaw she recalls in her life with her husband ("a man well stricken in years," whose figure, Hester's "womanly fancy failed not to recall, was slightly deformed") was that it was "feeding itself on time-worn materials, like a tuft of green moss on a crumbling wall" (TSL, p. 58).

Seven years later, however, after her momentous talk with Chillingworth on the seashore announcing her intention to unmask him to Dimmesdale, Hester suffers a violent revulsion of feeling. Although in their actual conversation she had at least affected to agree that he had been " 'wise and just' " before she " 'made' " him " 'a fiend,' " she now glowers after him, dwelling morbidly on his "deformity," and says aloud, "bitterly," " 'Be it sin or not, I hate the man.' " Like Anna, Hester in typical literary adulteress fashion ultimately decides that her deepest feeling for her husband is hatred.

In a self-conscious attempt to soften her wicked feelings, Hester goes on to call up memories of her marriage; but although "such scenes had once appeared not otherwise than happy, now, as viewed through the dismal medium of her subsequent life, they classed themselves among her ugliest remembrances." Just as Anna feeds her righteous disgust at Aleksey Aleksandrovich's swollen knuckles, so Hester focuses on Chillingworth's humped shoulder. In an ecstasy of indulged revulsion, Hester "marvelled how such scenes could have been! She marvelled how she could ever have been wrought upon to marry him!" And as Hawthorne spells out what Tolstoy only hints, worst of all to Hester at this point is the idea that "she had ever endured, and reciprocated, the lukewarm grasp of his hand, and had suffered the smile of her lips and eyes to mingle and melt into his own" (TSL, p. 176).

Without analyzing it, the novel of adultery had established the tendency of the literary adulteress to identify her lover, as Emma does Rodolphe, as her true husband, while viewing her husband as a sort of violator.[5] Not content simply to document this classic phenomenon, Hawthorne goes on to articulate its basis. Hester's reactions make clear that what sets up the adulteress's classic inability to see her adultery as "her crime most to be repented of" is the original sexual incompatibility between the husband and wife. Because of her revulsion for her husband, that title is reserved for her wifely acquiescence.[6] From Hester's point of view, "it seemed a fouler offense committed by Roger Chillingworth, than any that had since been done him, that, in the time when her heart knew no better, he persuaded her to fancy herself happy at his side." Her adultery, Hester feels, was a crime only against church and state, but her submission to Chillingworth was an outrage she committed against herself. Thus, the reason the adulteress always concludes "Yes, I hate him," Hawthorne shows, is that she deeply believes "He betrayed me!" (TSL, p. 176).

For his part, Tolstoy too acknowledges that the adulteress's marriage was ill made; indeed, he permits one of his characters to spell out the original error. Anna's brother Stiva tells her, " 'You married a man twenty years older than yourself. You married him without love, not knowing what love was. It was a mistake, let's say' " (AK, p. 449). By contrast with Hawthorne, however, Tolstoy undercuts this rational interpretation by putting it into the mouth of a character elsewhere established as a philanderer. To discredit the position yet further, Tolstoy goes on to stipulate that Stiva experiences a pang of "conscience" while articulating this position: the voice of Jiminy Cricket warning him that, regarding marriage, a rational approach is "wrong" (AK, p. 440). In general, although the novelistic tradition always allowed that the adulteress had been the victim of a mismatch,[7] it was left to Hawthorne to draw an inference from that fact.

Overall, although both *The Scarlet Letter* and *Anna Karenina* visibly attend the same tradition of the incompatible marriage, the two novels' implicit interpretations of this literary phenomenon sharply diverge. Tolstoy's summary comment on all of Anna's shifts is this: Anna recalled "Aleksey Aleksandrovich as she spoke, with all the peculiarities of his figure and manner of speaking, and setting against him every defect she could find in him, softening nothing for the great wrong she was doing him" (AK, p. 201). Although Tolstoy often shows great sentimental pity for Anna herself, he passes unflinching judgment upon her actions. By contrast, although he is rather hard on Hester personally (hinting that Boston comes to show her "a more benign countenance ... than she deserved" [p. 163]), the narrator of *The Scarlet Letter* sees inevitability, if not positive justice, in her position. Indeed, his most general reflection bears, if anything, less on the guilty wife than it does on the husband who went knowingly ahead with a misalliance:

> Let men tremble to win the hand of woman, unless they win along with it the utmost passion of her heart! Else it may be their miserable fortune, as it was Roger Chillingworth's, when some mightier touch than their own may have awakened all her sensibilities, to be reproached even for the calm content, the marble image of happiness which they will have imposed upon her as the warm reality. (TSL, pp. 176–7)

Where Tolstoy so insists on the idiosyncrasies of the characters in his adulterous triangle that it becomes finally impossible to draw any general conclusions from their individual lives, the experience of the members of Hawthorne's triangle distills itself into a pattern that *The Scarlet Letter* convinces us can be stated, however wryly, as something like a law. Which the novelistic tradition had not perfectly observed.

II

"Had Hester sinned alone?" asks the narrator of *The Scarlet Letter*. Of course not; and as the literary adulteress was not alone in her "sin," so is she also not alone in her suffering. Where there is an adulteress, there must of force be a cuckold; and although the whole tradition of the novel of adultery is witness to the predictable course of his behavior,[8] to untangle the feelings behind it was left to Hester uniquely.

Typically a man of substance and standing in his community, the literary cuckold bases his reaction to his wife's infidelity on the assumption that he can be perfectly rational about it. Indeed, the typical cuckold is accustomed to assume he is exempt from merely emotional reactions altogether. Aleksey Aleksandrovich Karenin believes that because, as he thinks, " 'I am not to blame,' " it follows that, in his formulation, " 'I cannot suffer' " (AK, p. 299). Almost parodying this pattern, Roger Chillingworth even convinces himself that he would proceed with tormenting Dimmesdale " 'only for the art's sake' " (TSL, p. 138). If this were true, Chillingworth would indeed be, as he comes to fear, a fiend. As Hawthorne portrays him, however, the cuckold is only a self-deluded man, whose mistaken belief in his own disinterestedness sadly puts the seal on his fundamental misunderstanding with his wife.

Roger Chillingworth's successive reactions to the revelation of his wife's infidelity are clinically charted. Where Tolstoy needs to have his narrator step in to explain that Aleksey Aleksandrovich is really "profoundly miserable" (AK, p. 214), we witness Chillingworth's reactions on his face. As he watches Hester from the crowd, Chillingworth's features "darken" with a "convulsion" of "powerful emotion." It is only "by an effort of his will" that he achieves the calm expression, finger on lips, that Hester herself sees. Although it is integral to the tragedy that Hester cannot know this, Hawthorne makes clear to us that Chillingworth has not gotten over his "horror." His feelings have only "subsided into the depths of his nature" (TSL, p. 61).

That the cuckold is concealing his emotions and not, as his wife thinks, failing to experience any is a crucial provision in Hawthorne's analysis of literary adultery. Anna is typical in her supposition that Aleksey Aleksandrovich is " 'not a man, but a machine, and a spiteful machine' " (AK, p. 201), who simply " 'doesn't care' " what she does because he " 'doesn't know what love is' " (AK, p. 156). But by Chillingworth's reaction in the crowd, *The Scarlet Letter* shows that this assumption by the adulteress is a mistake. Unhappily, it is a mistake the cuckold characteristically does everything to foster.

As *Madame Bovary* makes plain, it is in the adulteress's long-standing assumption that her husband simply lacks feelings that her discontent begins.[9] But by his typical pretense to experience no emotional reaction even to infidelity, the classic cuckold effectively confirms her error; if he fails to react to *that,* then surely nothing she can do will move him. The "Recognition" scene between Hester and Chillingworth is a graphic illustration of this tragicomic pattern. Catching sight of Chillingworth only after he has already arranged his face—missing the "convulsion" of his "horror" but getting the full offensive effect of his shushing finger—Hester, who like Anna habitually assumes that anyone who does not express feelings exactly the same way she does must not have any, is all but forced to conclude that his *only* reaction to herself, letter, and baby is a frigid concern for his good name.

Midway through *Anna Karenina,* Aleksey Aleksandrovich tells his wife that her betrayal has caused him " 'thuffering' " (AK, p. 384); without ever having him make so overt a profession, Hawthorne yet conveys Chillingworth's identical cuckold's pain. It is with a "bitter" smile that Chillingworth tells the Boston townsman, referring to Hester Prynne's husband, " 'So learned a man as you speak of should have learned this too in his books' " (TSL, p. 62). In his succeeding conversation with Hester in the prison, Chillingworth betrays his suffering by fastening morbidly upon the concrete evidence of his wife's rejection: " 'The child is yours,—she is none of mine, neither will she recognize my voice or aspect as a father's' " (TSL, p. 72). And through Chillingworth's revelation that he feels although " 'Elsewhere a wanderer, and isolated from human interests,' " he has now found in Boston " 'a woman, a man, a child, amongst whom and myself there exist the closest ligaments' " (TSL, p. 78), Hawthorne exposes the simple cause of the classic cuckold's complicated reaction to adultery: an exclusive dependence on marriage to fill all emotional needs.

In an extremity, Aleksey Aleksandrovich tells Anna, "I am your husband, and I love you" (AK, p. 156). She does not believe him, and we can see why: Nothing in his behavior gives reality to his claim. But although Chillingworth's behavior through the bulk of *The Scarlet Letter* appears as baffingly heartless as Aleksey Aleksandrovich's, his first conversation with Hester establishes its sufficient emotional basis. Chillingworth never makes Hester an avowal like Aleksey Aleksandrovich's. But having Chillingworth tell her, recalling their married life, " 'I drew thee into my heart, into its innermost chamber, and sought to warm thee by the warmth thy presence made there,' " Hawthorne compels us, with her, to concede that, even in the moral terms of joy and pain that she herself espouses, she " '[has] greatly wronged [him]' " (TSL, p. 74). Masked, inverted, and in a diminished modern world a little absurd, the passion of the novelistic cuckold is recognizable nonetheless: and it is the passion of Othello.

Both *Anna Karenina* and *The Scarlet Letter* testify to the classic phenomenon by which the cuckold steadfastly denies the manifest vindictiveness of his treatment of his wife. As if trying out for *A Woman Killed with Kindness*, Aleksey Aleksandrovich asks Anna sweetly whether she calls it " 'cruelty for a husband to give his wife freedom, giving her the honorable protection of his name, simply on the condition of observing the proprieties?' " But Anna inarticulately feels the charade of his magnanimity: " 'It's worse than cruel—it's base, if you want to know!' " (AK, p. 383). Chillingworth's behavior also displays the characteristic contradiction: Hester, "bewildered and appalled" (TSL, p. 76), cannot at first decide whether his ministrations to her and Pearl in the prison express "humanity or, it may be, a refined cruelty" (TSL, p. 73). But after Chillingworth proceeds dispassionately to elaborate his insane plan of revenge, she confronts him with the discrepancy: " 'Thy acts are like mercy, . . . [but] thy words interpret thee as a terror!' " (TSL, p. 76).

In addition to exposing the passionate impulse behind the cuckold's cold assertions, Hawthorne also accounts for the curious obsession he may develop with his wife's lover. A hypothetic premise of homoeroticism is, it appears, quite unnecessary. Hawthorne makes clear that it is precisely at the moment Hester refuses to identify her lover—the man who, Chillingworth urges, " 'has wronged us both' "—that he makes his avenging vow that " 'Sooner or later, . . . he shall be mine!' " (TSL, pp. 75–6). The connection is plain: Hester, by keeping silent, has shown Chillingworth that she will not be reunited with him on any terms, not even those of vengeance for her own injury. By insisting that it is only when Chillingworth has established the finality of Hester's rejection of them that he turns his attention to her lover, Hawthorne unmasks the cuckold's characteristic obsession with the lover as initially the diverted outlet for his anger at his wife.

Ever since the uxorious Prince de Clèves learned overnight to trick, spy on, and browbeat his wife, it has been a truism in the novel of adultery that the cuckold's reaction to his wife's infidelity transforms his personality.[10] It is this phenomenon Chillingworth is unwittingly articulating when he says of himself, " 'A mortal man, with once a human heart, has become a fiend.' " And Hawthorne goes on to capture the characteristic self-estrangement in a graphic image: " 'the unfortunate physician, while uttering these words, lifted his hands with a look of horror, as if he had beheld some frightful shape, which he could not recognize, usurping the place of his own image in a glass' " (TSL, p. 172). This is no mere gothicism. The "fiend" or, as Aleksey Aleksandrovich experiences it, the "brutal force" (AK, p. 441) impelling these cuckolds to vengeance is the image of their own disinherited humanity come back quite literally to haunt them.

The main reason *The Scarlet Letter* suggests for the cuckold's characteristic lapse into a course of destruction is that he asks too much of his self-control. Chillingworth claims magnanimously to understand that he and Hester " 'have wronged each other' " (TSL, p. 74). His subsequent behavior, however, broadcasts that the mere recitation of this rational formula did not in fact begin to satisfy his wounded feelings. Hardly a surprise: Self-love alone would reject the idea that his marrying Hester was as bad as her deceiving him.

The case of Chillingworth makes clear that the cuckold's mistake is not his outrage at his wife's infidelity. To feel outraged in his situation is simply nature. To repress the feeling as Chillingworth does in the marketplace, however, is not, and it is that willful denial that is the cause of the cuckold's problem. If by the act of saying " 'Between thee and me, the scale hangs fairly balanced' " (TSL, p. 75) Chillingworth could make it so, well and good; but the only circumstances under which that statement could genuinely exhaust all the cuckold's reactions would be if he were impervious to rejection—a condition, of course, no human being ever did or could achieve. In the end, Hawthorne shows, although the literary cuckold can force himself to speak rationally, he cannot enforce rationality upon his feelings. And it is for this reason that the reaction to a literary adultery turns out to be at least as anarchic and destructive as the adultery ever was.

III

The hallmark of the classic novel of adultery is its air of doom. The tradition's mortality rate alone seems to confirm Hester Prynne's passionate declaration that " 'There is no good' " for the literary adulteress, her husband, her lover, or even her child—" 'no path to guide [them] out of this dismal maze' " (TSL, p. 173). A short list of the "casualties" of literary adultery would include, most obviously, Emma Bovary, Stendhal's Julien Sorel, Goethe's Ottilie and Eduard, and Chopin's Edna Pontellier; a slightly longer list would add Charles Bovary, Stendhal's Mme de Rênal, the Prince and Princesse de Clèves, and Rousseau's Julie d'Étanges Wolmar. In addition, the children of Emma, Edna, Julie, and Mme de Rênal end up orphans, whereas the son of Eduard and Charlotte is drowned. Up to and including Edith Wharton's Newland Archer, no member of a classic adultery triangle ever succeeds in marrying his lover; as Goethe's widowed Charlotte tells her suitor, the Captain, " 'We have done nothing to bring about our unhappiness; but neither have we deserved to be happy together.' "[1]

To be sure, a given adulteress may not, like Emma Bovary, positively commit suicide, nor may her cuckolded husband torment himself, like the Prince de Clèves, positively to death; her children may not end up, like Berthe Bovary, consumptive and in the poorhouse; but their unhappiness is assured nonetheless. From their guilt and grief, the literary adulteress and her companions can expect liberation only from death. According to the novelistic tradition, characters touched by adultery are transported by the fatal act to a region where the novelist himself cannot mitigate their doom. Bold to criticize any historical fashion in morals or manners, the traditional novelist of adultery yet perpetuates unquestioned the ideal of wifely fidelity—a transcendent fixture, the single thing in a secular world that Mystery will still bestir itself to repay. The individual husband (suggests the tradition) and the particular society that harass the adulteress are simply the accidental tools of a supernatural justice.

As much as *Anna Karenina*, *The Scarlet Letter* at first seems to be following the traditional drift. Yet by the time of her conversation with Chillingworth on the seashore, Hester Prynne has had a revolutionary idea. Repudiating her earlier assertion of "no good" (itself probably calculated to manipulate Chillingworth anyway), Hester presses her husband to see that he " '[has] it at [his] will to pardon' " (TSL, p. 174). And although Hester does not look this far, Hawthorne clearly implies that the power she attributes to him belongs in equal measure to her. If Chillingworth can forgive her for her betrayal, she can certainly forgive him for his.

That moral issues are at stake in the literary plot of adultery *The Scarlet Letter* is far from denying, but unlike the novelistic tradition, it locates those issues elsewhere than in the breached commandment. The narrator says of Hester that she "ought long ago to have done" (TSL, p. 177) with the idea that Chillingworth betrayed her; and so indeed, the novel implies, ought *all* the characters to have done with the topic of one another's treachery. It is in the willful refusal to forgive and not in the wound blindly inflicted that Hawthorne suggests we seek the crime in the matter of adultery. In adultery as in every other human situation, Hawthorne insists, nursing an injury loses the injured party any initial moral advantage; indeed, since the intention to retaliate is conscious where the original hurt was unintentional, it actually causes him to sink below the level of his injurer. Insofar as it admitted that vengeance is to be left to the Lord, the tradition had deprecated personal vengefulness; but Hawthorne puts in question the relevance of vengeance altogether.

As Hester pleads to Chillingworth, to end the vicious cycle of injury and vengeance, someone in the adulterous situation must make the effort to renounce his or her private interests in favor of the common weal. Yet even renunciation is not everything. All that renunciation could do, Anna Karenina for one certainly does. On her sickbed, after the birth of her and Vronsky's child, Anna professes remorse for her adultery and requires her husband and her lover to shake hands. Everyone weeps, the sickroom flows with Christian charity, and it seems that all will end well. Yet as Tolstroy documents without analyzing, as soon as Anna begins to mend, she is dismayed to find herself experiencing Aleksey Aleksandrovich as "insufferably irritating" (AK, p. 445) all over again; and ironically, her very repentance ends by spurring her to the act that, defiant, she had steadfastly refused to perform—deserting her son. It truly seems as if a "hostile demon"[12] (the words of Goethe's Ottilie) foils the adulteress and her companions in their best efforts at self-purification.

The guilt-stricken actors in the classic novel of adultery characteristically struggle to achieve ideal feelings, particularly the Christian feelings of penitence and forgiveness. Hester Prynne's lingering passion for Dimmesdale is something she typically "strove to cast ... from her" (TSL, p. 80), whereas her hatred for Chillingworth is something for which she "upbraided" herself (p. 176). Like these attempts of Hester's, however, all the conscientious efforts of classic literary adulterers to purify their feelings produce no fruit. While duly recording this phenomenon, The Scarlet Letter also suggests a more practical cause than the activity of demons. By the evidence of Hester and Chillingworth, the adulteress's and the cuckold's inability to cast off their ill feeling lies less in moral hardness than in mental confusion.

Mere humanity, The Scarlet Letter persuades, might sufficiently explain the adulteress's and the cuckold's incapacity to purely repent, purely forgive; for in the classic plot the grounds on which those acts are asked of them are arbitrary at best and at worst an outrage to their sense of personal justice. The bare Seventh Commandment hardly explains to the classic adulteress why she did not have the human right to do anything she could think of to pay back her husband for robbing her of, as she sees it, a woman's one chance for a happy life; yet as Hawthorne shows, the Seventh Commandment is all the classic adulteress is given as a reason to repent. The Sermon on the Mount is far from telling the cuckold why he is not justified in seeking vengeance for the outrage his wife has done his honor, pride, and affections; but again, it is the only incentive he is shown.

If the classic adulteress cannot achieve a sustained penitence, Hawthorne shows, the flaw need not be in her sincere will to do right. The instance of Hester shows that the adulteress may be as sincere as anyone could ask and still simply lack the practical reunderstanding of her situation that successful penitence requires. Like her sisters, Hester can and does try with all her heart to be sorry for having breached a commandment; but because she never intended her affair as a comment upon the decalogue, of course she fails. What the classic adulteress is asked to be sorry for simply does not correspond to what she is conscious of having done. The final reason the conventional religio-moral prescription for adultery is so ineffective, The Scarlet Letter shows, is that it leaves the basic emotional issues

untouched. It is their attempt to implement ideal solutions before they have identified their real problem that leads classic adulterers into their characteristic confusion. Describing Hester Prynne's attempts to repudiate her own enjoyment of
needlework, the narrator, far from applauding her, suggests that "This morbid
meddling of conscience with an immaterial matter betokened, it is to be feared, no
genuine and steady penitence, but something doubtful, something that might be
deeply wrong, beneath" (TSL, p. 84).

The novel of adultery had assumed that marital infidelity must be interpreted
in terms of injury. Yet *The Scarlet Letter* suggests that interpreting adultery thus can
only cause the husband and wife to paralyze themselves with brooding upon the
insoluble question of who injured whom first: whose, in Chillingworth's words, "was
the first wrong" (TSL, pp. 74–5). In the name of punishing the appearance of sin, the
society that criminalizes adultery may have the effect of creating the actuality. Nor
does Hawthorne indicate, nor the tradition bear out, that the Puritans were the
only culprits.

Hawthorne is leaving the tradition behind him when he allows Chillingworth
to achieve a glimpse of the impropriety of judging the participants within the
adulterous situation. Indeed, Hawthorne finally attributes to Hester's husband a
more forgiving final position on her adultery than he does to her lover. As the fruit
of seven years of contemplation, Chillingworth produces this insight: " 'Ye that have
wronged me are not sinful, save in a sort of typical illusion; nor am I fiendlike, who
have snatched a fiend's office from his hands' " (TSL, p. 175). Having become
acquainted with self-willed behavior in his own right, Chillingworth is now able to
see that they have been seeking the cause of their sufferings in the wrong place. The
germ of their trouble was never in the moral realm. As Chillingworth had already
unwittingly suggested by his words in the prison, the mistake was squarely in the
realm of nature, in the human world of love and marriage.

It was always clear in the tradition that the adulteress's warrant for her
behavior was a treacherous assumption that life owed every woman romantic
passion as a universal female birthright. But *The Scarlet Letter* goes on to illuminate
a point the tradition had left dark. The example of Chillingworth suggests that, in
Hawthorne's analysis, the traditional cuckold must have brought to matrimony a set
of overbeliefs of his own, through which he is as deeply implicated in their present
catastrophe as his wife.

For Chillingworth's recollections of married life betray that his warrant for
insisting on marriage to a girl who had announced she could not love him was his
own assumption that life owed every *man* a pleasant domestic arrangement. Indeed, he even imagines that he alone on earth had been invidiously denied this: " 'It
was not so wild a dream,—old as I was, and sombre as I was, and misshapen as I
was,—that the simple bliss, which is scattered far and wide, for all mankind to share,
might yet be mine' " (TSL, p. 74). Recalling his nuptial hopes to Hester, now, after
so many vicissitudes, Chillingworth still shows no greater awareness of the breath-
taking oversimplifications on which those hopes were based. Even if Chillingworth

were safe in supposing that wedded life were always "bliss"—even always "simple"—he still takes the risk of expecting Hester to be an instrument through which his male right to domesticity could be fulfilled. As for her, he vaguely expected that her happiness would follow from his. Now that it turns out that she, like Emma Bovary, had resented the very happiness she gave him, he, like Charles, is for the moment sincerely baffled.

Although Tolstoy also admits that Aleksey Aleksandrovich Karenin took his wife for granted, he betrays no suspicion that this might be a just ground for resentment on her part. Rather, it is made to seem one more variety of the unfortunate behavior, less harmful than Stiva's philandering, that wives must accept. But Hawthorne has Chillingworth himself admit culpability in his behavior. Though long before his feelings can have caught up to his rational words, he tells Hester in the prison:

> I ask not wherefore, nor how, thou has fallen into the pit, or say rather, ascended to the pedestal of infamy on which I found thee. The reason is not far to seek. It was my folly, and thy weakness . . . If sages were ever wise in their own behoof, I might have foreseen all this. I might have known that, as I came out of the vast and dismal forest, and entered this settlement of Christian men, the very first object to meet my eyes would be thyself, Hester Prynne, standing up, a statue of ignominy, before the people. Nay, from the moment when we came down the old church steps, a married pair, I might have beheld the bale-fire of the scarlet letter blazing at the end of our path! (TSL, p. 74)

By itself, of course, this self-punishing recognition is of limited use: If the cuckold-to-be could have thus known himself as such, he could have known to cancel his marriage. Penultimate as it is, however, the insight is more than the typical literary cuckold ever achieves.

And Hawthorne reserves to Chillingworth yet further light. Hester herself can only think to justify her adultery in terms of one particular personal passion, but Chillingworth achieves a larger view. In a powerful irony, it is Chillingworth, not Hester, who comes closest to articulating the antinomian conclusion which the plot of literary adultery had always implied: that a wife's adultery is a revelation not about a woman but about a marriage (and has nothing to do with romantic love). In *The Scarlet Letter*, the cuckolded husband provides the adulteress with the terms of her own vindication: " 'Hadst thou met earlier with a better love than mine,' " Roger Chillingworth sternly instructs Hester, " 'perhaps this evil had not been' " (TSL, p. 173).

Hawthorne does not deny that betrayal is, indeed, at the heart of the adultery plot. But he dissents from the traditional consensus that the most important betrayal is the sexual one. The cases of Chillingworth and Hester show that the husband and wife are victims of more than each other; a myth available on mother's lap, at father's knee, in the playhouse, or in the reading chair has victimized them both. By causing them to develop two mutually exclusive and equally impossible sets of expectations of marriage, their own culture has long since set up both the husband and wife for the injuries they come to do each other as individuals. So long as they insist on holding each other accountable for what was in fact a mutual disappointment, of course they will find no path out of their "dismal maze." And until they recognize the mutuality of their betrayal, the literary cuckold and adulteress cannot escape from the mutual recrimination that traditionally had served them for an effective fate.

The Scarlet Letter is at one with its generic tradition in admitting that marriages, being after all of human devising, can be better and worse made. But in implying that the worse made ones may fail, and that this is an event which it were kinder to provide for than to deny, the novel breaks fresh ground. Considered as a fact of social experience rather than one of transcendent morality or political symbolism, *The Scarlet Letter* suggests, adultery ceases to be an occasion of judgment and becomes an opportunity for charity. As the narrator finally pleads, "To all these shadowy figures,—as well Roger Chillingworth as his companions,—we would fain be merciful" (TSL, p. 260). For as Chillingworth admits, Hester's apparently absentminded breach of the commandment occurred in explicit relation to and was a direct by-product of their ill-conceived marriage.

The revisionistic implications of Hawthorne's interpretation are quickly seen. When the issue of blame is abandoned, the practical question of the adultery situation can finally emerge. Whether the husband and wife are willing to face it or not, the basic question is still, as Stiva puts it, " 'What can be done if a married couple finds that life is impossible for them together?' "

The traditional answer, which Hester Prynne uniquely passes beyond, is that someone or other must magically die. As long as everybody is still alive, however, the situation clearly remains as Stiva describes it: " 'You're wretched, he's wretched, and what good can come of it?' " As Tolstoy's own example of Levin and Kitty amply shows, the merely practical problems of marriage—sex, children, property, in-laws—are difficult enough. Added to them, adherence to a theory of marital indissolubility can only go on to render an honest mistake, like Karenin's or Chillingworth's, a gratuitous lifelong suffering. As thoroughly as Anna Karenina attempts to discredit the suggestion by the suggester, Stiva's own answer to his question arrives with all the force of logic. To insist that death is the only answer, he holds, his sister is simply being melodramatic and stubborn: " 'When divorce would solve everything' " (AK, p. 449).

Whether it fits anyone's theory or not, it is clear that although it is given to the literary adulteress and cuckold to pardon each other, their forgiveness will endure only if their sufferings are brought to an end. By the device of Anna's flight from Karenin's house after receiving his forgiveness, even Tolstoy tacitly acknowledges the impossibility of the classic adulteress and the classic cuckold's continuing to live together. The main reason Hester and Chillingworth move so far toward forgiveness as they do is clearly not that either of them is of superior moral fiber, but that

Hawthorne has arranged that forgiveness in their situation does not imply that they must resume living together.

In the Roman Catholic settings of the mainstream tradition—*The Princesse de Clèves, Red and Black, Madame Bovary, The Awakening*—historical social institutions prevented the novelist from giving his characters any practical option except to try, impossibly, to resume or continue living together; yet because the *donnée* of the plot is that this is what they cannot do, the classic ending of a novel of adultery became indeed, as Anna says, death. And because of the characters' real lack of choices, the central French tradition is authentically tragic. In a setting that permits divorce, however, if the characters end as sadly as their predecessors, it must be by someone's free choice. With *Elective Affinities*, the novel of adultery modulated from tragedy to irony. *The Scarlet Letter* is at the center of this development; *Anna Karenina* is a denial of it.

I V

It is not necessary to know that Tolstoy was a reader of Hawthorne (on at least one occasion sending a magazine the translation of a Hawthorne story)[13] to suspect that *Anna Karenina* is a retort to *The Scarlet Letter*. The likeness of the Karenins' married life to the Amsterdam days of Hester and Chillingworth seems too close for mere coincidence. And when Anna and Vronsky escape to Venice, they seem to be following Hester's plan for a flight to "pleasant Italy" (TSL, p. 197).

Whether an adulterous couple can by any means make a workable life for themselves and their children is a question *The Scarlet Letter* leaves open, but one that a major purpose of Tolstoy's seems to have been to close. By showing Vronsky and Anna, given every chance, yet failing to find happiness, Tolstoy appears to wish to clarify what was in *The Scarlet Letter*, to say the least, unclear: that adulterers always come to bad ends. As his epigraph proclaims, it is his purpose to demonstrate that, however sadly understandable, however painfully pitiable the situation of the individual adulterer, the relevant fact in the case—in Hawthorne, dangerously obscured—is finally only one: "Thou shalt not commit adultery," and the Old Testament God will repay. Distracted by Hester's charms, Hawthorne was clearly too sympathetic to what Edith Wharton would call "the dread argument of the individual case."[14] But although Tolstoy gives the devil her due, he nonetheless destroys her.

The problem with Tolstoy's position—and he is the most blatant novelist of adultery to invoke absolute standards of "right" and "wrong" (AK, p. 449)—is obvious. Although his morality requires the adulteress and cuckold to remain together, his art knows this is humanly impossible. Tolstoy explicitly urges the reader to pin his hopes on the successful marriage of Levin and Kitty. But it is not only glaringly obvious that just as Mme Homais is no Emma Bovary, Kitty is no Anna; the marriage itself is essentially different. Tolstoy establishes that Kitty and Levin are close in age, made their own choices of each other, and had all their romantic illusions over with before marriage. Such a fortunate marriage is perfectly possible, but it hardly helps with the problem of the less fortunate ones. If every marriage were like that of Levin and Kitty, the novel of adultery would never have developed in the first place.

Hester Prynne more than once considers killing herself and Pearl too. Dimmesdale tells her not to, and she ends, to her own surprise, living a long, healthy, and rather interesting international life—certainly a far more independent and original one than any she could have shared with either Roger Chillingworth or Arthur Dimmesdale. And in the end, not even the illegitimate Pearl suffers any lasting blight.

By insisting that Hester survives and that Pearl finds happiness, Hawthorne had unleashed the possibility that the grim fortune of the classic adulteress was just that: fortune, not fate. But if the adulteress's traditional death is not, after all, a consequence of her adultery, it must be a consequence of something else; if fate is not to blame, then something closer to home must be. By the time she commits suicide the classic adulteress is certainly insane, but what made her so? Was Emma, Emma (Hawthorne helps us ask) when she grasped the arsenic? Who really killed Madame Bovary?

If Hawthorne's comprehensive naturalism quietly undermines the somber tradition that disaster is simply the organic blossoming of the "black flower" (TSL, p. 174) of adultery, *Anna Karenina* appears calculated to reestablish it. Where Hester lives to theorize about the relation between the sexes and to counsel the women of Boston, Anna Karenina throws herself under a train. Where Hester and her companions achieve a sorrowful mutual forgiveness on the occasion of Dimmesdale's (nonsuicidal) death, Anna and Vronsky are finally as much estranged as Anna and Karenin; rather than fostering reconciliation, Anna's death causes Vronsky to seek his own death in battle in order to regain his self-respect. Where Pearl lives to find her happy ending, little Annie, left motherless, is snatched from her playboy father by her late mother's estranged husband for an unforeseeable future. At every point where Hawthorne seems to leave a loophole, Tolstoy steps in forcibly to close it.

If Tolstoy found *The Scarlet Letter's* naturalism threatening, he was not the first. "In Hawthorne's tale," the Reverend Arthur Cleveland Coxe had railed for a whole constituency in 1850, "the lady's frailty is philosophized into a natural and necessary result of the Scriptural law of marriage, which, by holding her irrevocably to her vows, as plighted to a dried-up old bookworm, in her silly girlhood, is viewed as making her heart a too-easy victim to the adulterer."[15] And indeed, in no consideration than that of his refusal to cast Hester into the blackness of darkness is Hawthorne further from the traditional novel of adultery.

Like Flaubert, Tolstoy progressively distances us from the character of the adulteress. He exaggerates Anna's jealousy, her ill temper, her coquetry, and suggests a positive viciousness in her lack of interest in her and Vronsky's child, her dependence on morphine, her smoking, and her use of birth control. Like Flaubert, adding insult to injury, he even stipulates that a woman under the influence of adultery grows fat.[16] In general, he simply heaps up Anna's mounting eccentricities until, although we can still pity her—as the Boston townspeople pity Hester, from comfortably far off—we no longer in the least identify with her. Anna safely dead, Tolstoy invites us to renew the hypothetical possibility (clearly too dangerous to raise while she was alive) that her actions might possibly have been justified. Pleasurable although it is, however, shedding tears over Anna's corpse hardly substitutes for doing justice to her position. His killing Anna finally confirms that Tolstoy has no rational account—or at least none he is willing to give—of adultery as a practical marital and social issue. Throwing Anna under the train, Tolstoy simply throws up that problem.

Tolstoy's cavalier commingling of symbolic mysteries with novelistic realism betrays the wishful fabulousness of his plot. Like Emma Bovary with her blind beggar, Anna is tormented by symbolic manifestations.[17] She and Vronsky are both terrified by dreams in which a hideous peasant mumbles unintelligible French (AK, pp. 375–6, 381). Given the slightest encouragement we would snicker, but Tolstoy is all too pious. That there was something inherently fatal in Anna's and Vronsky's connection from the beginning, *Anna Karenina* positively insists. Anna herself interprets the suicide that occurs at their first meeting in the train station as an "evil omen" (AK, p. 71)—and Tolstoy undertakes to bear her out.

Orthodox preference notwithstanding, Hawthorne allows no magic dreams and no symbolic beggars in *The Scarlet Letter*—not even so much as an ironic golden bowl. *Anna Karenina* upholds Anna's superstitions; but if Dimmesdale sees an A in the sky, or if certain Boston townspeople see A on his chest, that is strictly their business: "the reader may choose," and one of the choices is none of the above. If he were not merely to encourage readers to congratulate themselves on their own superior morality, the novelist of adultery, Hawthorne saw, had a particular need to eschew the kinds of fantastic effects that would seem to put the characters beyond what Hawthorne insists is a universal fellowship of "human frailty and sorrow" (TSL, p. 48).

The signal difference between Hawthorne and the authors of the mainstream tradition is that where the tendency of their storytelling is to perpetuate the same social institutions whose ill effects furnish them with their material, his is ultimately to put in question those institutions themselves. For where the perpetuation of their tragic tradition depends on the preservation of the unhappiness of the status quo, he makes it clear that he does not assume that tragedy is the only worthy dramatic form. As it is, he gives *The Scarlet Letter* the happiest ending he can; and he would clearly have given it a happier one if historical conditions—not only those of his setting but also of his literary audience—had permitted. If morality certainly consisted in the pretense of immediate, visible punishment for the breaking of cultural taboos, then Arthur Cleveland Coxe was right: *The Scarlet Letter* is an immoral book. But if morality had anything to do with justice to the individual, Hawthorne might have felt that his was the first novel of adultery to begin to be moral at all.

NOTES

[1] Q. D. Leavis, "Hawthorne as Poet," *Sewanee Review* 59 (Summer 1951): 426–58. For other comparisons of Hawthorne and Tolstoy, see William Dean Howells, *Heroines of Fiction,* excerpted in Kermit Vanderbilt, ed., *The Achievement of William Dean Howells* (Princeton, N.J.: Princeton University Press, 1968), p. 75; and Earl H. Rovit, "Ambiguity in Hawthorne's *Letter,*" in Arlin Turner, ed., *Merrill Studies in* The Scarlet Letter (Columbus, Ohio: Merrill, 1970), p. 121.

[2] By the "novel of adultery," I understand the tradition discussed by Tony Tanner in *Adultery in the Novel* (Baltimore: Johns Hopkins University Press, 1979) and Judith Armstrong in *The Novel of Adultery* (New York: Barnes and Noble, Import Division of Harper & Row, 1976) including such works as La Fayette's *Princesse de Clèves,* Rousseau's *Julie,* Goethe's *Elective Affinities,* Stendhal's *The Red and the Black,* Flaubert's *Madame Bovary,* and Kate Chopin's *The Awakening.* For Tanner, who proposes a tentative syllabus for the genre in a footnote (p. 12), the central texts in the tradition are *Madame Bovary, Elective Affinities,* and *Julie.* For Armstrong, *Madame Bovary, Anna Karenina,* and James's *Golden Bowl* are the indispensable works (p. 169). Without undertaking a discussion, Tanner identifies *The Scarlet Letter* as "Hawthorne's novel of adultery" (p. 357); Armstrong gives a brief reading (pp. 101–4) that essentially repeats the "love and death" interpretation of Leslie Fiedler.

[3] Quotations from *Anna Karenina* are taken from the Constance Garnett translation, rev. Leonard J. Kent and Nina Berberova (New York: Modern Library, 1965).

[4] Emma Bovary, for one, does this constantly, but especially in the episode with the clubfoot; see *Madame Bovary,* edited with a substantially new translation by Paul de Man (New York: Norton, 1965), p. 133.

[5] See, for instance, *Madame Bovary,* p. 122; cf. *Elective Affinities,* trans. Elizabeth Mayer and Louise Bogan (South Bend, Indiana: Gateway Editions, 1963), p. 261.

[6] See *Madame Bovary,* p. 133.

[7] *The Princesse de Clèves* spells out the fact that Mlle de Chartres's marriage is a political arrangement made by her mother; in addition, Mme de Lafayette makes clear that, as Mlle de Chartres admits, the bride "was not particularly attracted by [her husband's] person"; see *The Princesse de Clèves,* trans. Nancy Mitford (New York: Penguin Books, 1978), p. 47. And in *Red and Black,* Stendhal's narrator explains that Mme de Rênal is given in marriage to her older husband straight from the convent, without having any idea what love is; see *Red and Black,* trans. Robert M. Adams (New York: Norton, 1969), p. 35.

[8] See especially *The Princesse de Clèves,* pp. 130–40, 147–50, 166, 174–8.

[9] See *Madame Bovary,* p. 29, and passim.

[10] The Prince de Clèves sets the pattern of the cuckold whose unrestrained jealousy becomes, literally, the death of him; see *The Princesse de Clèves,* pp. 174–8.

[11] *Elective Affinities,* p. 267.

[12] Ibid., p. 288.

[13] *Tolstoy's Letters,* selected, edited, and translated by R. F. Christian, 2 vols. (New York: Scribner's, 1978), vol. 2, p. 464.

[14] Edith Wharton, *The Age of Innocence* (New York: Scribner's, 1968), p. 309.

[15] The *Scarlet Letter* section of Coxe's "The Writings of Hawthorne" (*Church Review,* vol. 3, January 1851) was reprinted by A. Mordell in *Notorious Literary Attacks* (New York, 1926). The present quotation is drawn from the Norton Critical *Scarlet Letter,* ed. Sculley Bradley, Richmond Croom Beatty, E. Hudson Long, and Seymour Gross, 2nd ed. (New York: Norton, 1978), p. 258.

[16] On Anna's jealousy, see, for instance, pp. 769, 772; on her ill temper, pp. 734–5; on her morphine addiction, pp. 668–9, 697; on her coquetry, pp. 659–60, 726–30, 733; on her lack of interest in her child, pp. 646–7, 696; on her smoking, p. 726; on her use of birth control, p. 666; and on her weight gain, p. 378. Cf. *Madame Bovary,* pp. 138, 140, and Chopin's *The Awakening* (Toms River, N.J.: Capricorn Books, 1964), p. 216. To judge from the literary tradition, adultery is illegal, immoral, *and* fattening.

[17] For Emma's beggar, see *Madame Bovary,* pp. 193, 219, 238. It almost seems that the mysterious beggar is an obligatory feature in a novel of adultery: cf. Goethe, *Elective Affinities,* pp. 55–6, 127. As Anna Karenina's death seems foreshadowed by the suicide in the train station at her meeting with Vronsky, so the drowning of Goethe's adulterers' infant son is foreshadowed by several drownings or near-drownings: see pp. 34, 99, 117–18, 241–4. There are a plethora of other supernatural or symbolic manifestations in *Elective Affinities* as well; see, for instance, pp. 75, 114.

James M. Mellard

PEARL AND HESTER:
A LACANIAN READING

Nathaniel Hawthorne's *The Scarlet Letter* is widely regarded not only as a masterpiece of moral, cultural, and religious, but also of prescient psychoanalytic insight. The classic Freudian psychoanalytic reading of the book is by Frederick C. Crews; there are non-Freudian readings as well, including several recent essays.[1] Because of its history of psychological interpretations, Hawthorne's romance is no longer merely one of any number of works of fiction that have elicited such readings; it has become almost a paradigm for the psychological interpretation of other fiction. Hawthorne's great work may do so in part because literature in general and fiction in particular appear to be our best model of the workings of the psyche. Such is in fact a major premise underlying psychoanalysis, whether initiated by Freud or reinterpreted by Jacques Lacan. Lacan makes the point for Freud and himself: "Indeed, how could we forget that to the end of his days Freud constantly maintained that ... a training [in literary analysis] was the prime requisite in the formation of analysts, and that he designated the eternal *universitas litterarum* as the ideal place for its institution."[2] But as Lacanian scholar Ellie Ragland-Sullivan points out, "Psychoanalytic meaning is not immanent in a text because it is the medical discourse of a symptom." Rather, "literature operates a magnetic pull on the reader because it is an allegory of the psyche's fundamental structure."[3] Viewed in the light of Lacanian theory, *The Scarlet Letter,* though perhaps not actually more privileged than other texts, does nonetheless provide a particularly insightful model for analysis, not least because its dominant symbol is precisely Lacan's: the letter.

I

In his essay called "The Agency of the Letter in the Unconscious or Reason since Freud," Lacan makes the claim upon which his theory of psychoanalysis is

From *Critical Essays on Hawthorne's* The Scarlet Letter, edited by David B. Kesterton (Boston: G. K. Hall, 1988), pp. 193–211.

based, namely, that "what the psychoanalytic experience discovers in the unconscious is the whole structure of language."[4] By this statement Lacan does not mean
to claim that the unconscious is a language, but only that it is structured like a
language and functions in similar ways. These ways are akin to the Freudian concepts of condensation and displacement, whose parallel linguistic concepts are
metaphor and metonymy. For Lacan, the letter is the "material support that concrete discourse borrows from language,"[5] the letter itself standing, metonymically
(part for whole), for the word or words upon which access to the unconscious
depends. As he writes elsewhere, Lacan drew from Freud the understanding that
"words . . . are the object through which one seeks for a way to handle the unconscious. Not even the meaning of words, but words in their flesh, in their
material aspect." Lacan's summation is very explicit: "words are the only material of
the unconscious."[6]

Regarding the unconscious as a linguistic object, Lacan also approaches it
through linguistic principles based on the concept of structure, or, more precisely,
on the structuralist principles of linguist Ferdinand de Saussure. Saussure revolu-
tionized the study of language by insisting upon the arbitrariness of the relationship
between words and things, words and their meanings. His primary formula, taken
over by Lacan, is the algorithm showing the relation of a signifier (a word or other
sign) to a signified (a thing or meaning). The algorithm looks like a fraction: S/s. It is
read, Lacan tells us, as "the signifier over the signified, 'over' corresponding to the
bar separating the two stages."[7] For Lacan, the bar represents a primordial barrier
separating signifier from signified and demonstrating the "arbitrariness of the sign."[8]
Lacan uses Saussure's algorithm largely because it suggests both the topographic
structure of the psyche and the functioning of the psychoanalytic subject. The
algorithm, that is, provides Lacan a topography of the psyche, because the linguistic
(really, the ontological) barrier between signifier and signified can be equated to the
barrier between the conscious and the unconscious topographic "regions" of men-
tality.

Lacan has formalized his conception of the structure of the psyche in a series
of schemas.[9] The most basic of these, in effect, merely turns the algorithm into a
square whose four corners are connected only through a mediating pattern that
forms a Z. Lacan calls his simplest one Schema L; it shows the fundamental topographical relation of conscious to unconscious processes, the fields of the two
"registers" (the Imaginary and the Symbolic) to each other, and the pattern of
mediation from I (self) to other (a mirror image) to *moi* (ideal self), and from Other
(law, father, ultimate authority) toward *moi* back toward other and I. Somewhat
modified, Schema L would look like this:

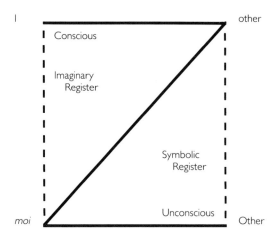

Although this schema in no way represents a "picture" of the psyche, it does represent the psyche's significant *topoi* of structure and functioning as Lacan envisions them. In the top triangular half of the square Lacan locates the field of consciousness and the Imaginary register; these are associated with the subject— the "I" who speaks or thinks—and with the projective or introjective relations of the subject consciousness to identificatory others and to the ideal self or ego-ideal reflected in images of the other or others. This triangle shows that the I and *moi* are mediated through the figures of the other, and, since they do not connect directly, that the I can reach no certainty about the *moi;* in this triangulation one begins to observe the unavoidable slippage, in Lacan's terms, that the structuralists posit in the relation between the signifier (here located on the line between the I and the other) and the signified (here located on the line between the *moi* and the Other). In the square's bottom triangular half, mirroring the top, Lacan locates the field of the unconscious and the register of the Symbolic; they are associated with the powerful cultural and linguistic domain into which the subject consciousness normally is absorbed and by which, beneath the threshold of awareness, it is ruled.

  Though Lacan has devised more complex versions of this schema, its two halves suggest clearly the splitting (or, in Freud, the *Spaltung*) of the primal neonate subject that comes with the formation of consciousness and an unconscious in the initiatory passage Lacan calls the mirror stage. The mirror stage (perhaps the most famous of Lacan's concepts) occurs in the life of the infant between about six months and eighteen months. In this developmental period the infant (cf. *infans,* from Latin *infari:* "not speaking") loses its intense symbiotic relation to the mother; the mother then becomes the primal identificatory other for the infant; simultaneously, the infant learns the power of abstract symbolization that informs the language of the culture into which, willy-nilly, in a second birth, it is now borne. Lacan calls this rite of passage the mirror stage because it is best represented in the phenomenon of mirroring or imprinting observed not only in the animal world, but also in the infant's imprinting on the mother. In a secondary imprinting that Lacan calls the mirror stage, the infant actually or symbolically recognizes its own image in a mirror. This mirror recognition initiates the infant's alienation from itself, for, individuated from the mother, it now gets caught up in the quest for identity in an object separate from itself, whether that object is its own specular image in the mirror or its now irremediably separate image of the mother.

To illustrate the separation from the mother and the accession to symbolization (in other words, to the domain of the symbolic represented in language), Lacan refers to a game—the *"Fort! Da!"* memorialized by Freud—in which the child finds a pleasure built on a loss.[10] In this game, the child discovers its ability to symbolize the departure and (hoped for) return of its mother in the willed disappearance and reappearance of a spool tossed away and retrieved by a thread tied to it. The German words, which stand for *there!* and *here!,* suggest the absence of the object (spool = mother) and then its reappearance. But for Lacan the real significance of the game is linguistic and lies in the ability of the contrasting vowel sounds (*oooh* and *aaah*) to suggest meanings in themselves apart from the actual object. The child discovers the principle of symbolization in the substitution of sounds for the object; as the spool had come to stand for mother and the abstract concepts of departure and return, absence and presence, so too will the "words" come to stand for them. On such structural differences, Lacan contends, are constructed not only the human capacity for language (as, say the structuralists, language itself is so constructed), but also the recognition of the mother's otherness and the otherness of the self, now (as a result of the mirror stage) invested in another person or even an object (for example, the child's image in the mirror).

In short, for Lacan the mirror stage and a child's game such as *"Fort! Da!"* represent the infant's identificatory absorption of an alienating self image, but at the same time they represent its recognition of the mediating authority of others and of objects, whether a specular image (as in the face of the mother or the child's reflection in a mirror), or a representative object (a spool, a Teddy Bear, or Linus's blanket), or a symbolic sound (*oooh* and *aaah,* or, more generally, the tones of a voice, or perhaps a nursery tune). Thus, all at once the child assumes an identity perceived in otherness and accedes to the law or principle of difference upon which language is predicated. In one moment, then, the infant is split into pieces, as it were. A previously unperceived unified being is suddenly separated into a subject and an object, and the lost and now desired unity becomes identified with the other, identity forever after to be sought in others or symbolic objects that Lacan calls *"objets petit a."*[11] The subject (thinking, speaking) self, now "split," shall be identified in the (triangular, topographical) register of the Imaginary, while the images of the evanescent objects over time shall be displaced by other images and shall slip into the register of the Symbolic, identified with the unconscious and found in the bottom topographical triangle of Lacan's schema.

Hawthorne's *The Scarlet Letter* is especially helpful in illustrating Lacanian principles because it focuses on four major characters whose experiences exemplify the major psychoanalytic issues as Lacan conceives them. The two I shall consider represent "normal"—as opposed to neurotic or psychotic—subjects. The child, Pearl, graphically illustrates the normal processes of the passage through the mirror stage, and her mother, Hester Prynne, equally well illustrates, in relation to the gaze, the dynamics of the registers of the Imaginary and the Symbolic in the adult subject. Though there is not space here to consider them, one should understand that the other two major characters represent pathological subjects. Arthur Dimmesdale illustrates Lacan's conceptions of neurosis, symptoms, and cure, and Roger Chillingworth illustrates psychosis even as he enfigures the analyst and the Lacanian Other. All four subjects illustrate the slippage of the signified beneath the signifier, as each of them at different moments takes different places in the schematized quadrature Lacan outlines as one inserts different characters in the place of the subject. A result of such analyses is that the four personalities, split into four agonistic parts whose mediations are effected by that most Lacanian agent, the letter A, seem finally to represent a total history of the subject.

II

Pearl's story, in Lacanian terms, is the most fundamental of those represented in the subject-consciousness of *The Scarlet Letter*. Pearl's development toward psychological maturity, in fact, is a paradigm case of the passage from infancy (meaning, in Lacan's terms, the *infans* stage of the child without speech) through the steps of the mirror stage. She is at the *infans* stage when she is first seen, on the scaffold of the pillory with Hester at the novel's beginning; there, her response is directed totally by visual and auditory stimuli. Then she is shown in the early chapters going through the first step of the mirror passage, where she finds images of identification and antagonism. Finally, in the last chapters, she is shown taking the climactic step of the mirror passage; this step takes her through recognition of the loss of the phallic symbol, through acceptance of symbolic castration, and at last through submission to the identity and authority of the father. Each of these moves clearly illustrates Lacanian principles, for Pearl experiences the world in relation to those dominant images of which Lacan so frequently speaks: the mother and images associated with her, objects symbolizing the other, and intimations of the symbolic presence of the Other to be found in the name of the father.

We might say that for Pearl, as in Lacan, the whole of the mirror passage is represented in the child's quest for a father to whose authority, vested in the name of the father, it might cede its life. An adumbration of this quest occurs in the earliest glimpse readers have of the infant Pearl. Even on the scaffold with Hester, the infant breaks her determined passivity in order to respond to the sound of Arthur Dimmesdale's voice. That voice, in retrospect, shall represent the intrusion of biological authority, just as it actually represents the voice of cultural authority speaking from the place of the father. As Lacan would have it, Pearl's response is not to words as such, but to the materiality of the sound itself. In this response she is little different from the crowd in the square. "The young pastor's voice was tremulously sweet, rich, deep, and broken," Hawthorne tells us, as Dimmesdale speaks over Hester's ignominious display on the scaffold. "The feeling that it so evidently manifested, rather than the direct purport of the words, caused it to vibrate within all hearts, and brought the listeners into one accord of sympathy. Even the poor baby, at Hester's bosom, was affected by the same influence: for it directed its hitherto vacant gaze towards Mr. Dimmesdale, and held up its little arms, with a half pleased, half plaintive murmur."[12] Pearl's gesture here foreshadows in every respect the aim and end of the infant's developmental relation to self, other, and the Otherness represented in the high place from which the minister speaks.

Although the goal (as *telos,* not as conscious aim) of the child's early life, in Lacanian terms, is to enter a proper relation with the authority of the father, the focus of the neonatal and postnatal infant inevitably is on the mother. Because Pearl is isolated not only from her father, but also from the larger community, her early development, besides serving Hawthorne's own aims as a storyteller, is especially representative of Lacanian principles. The first image on which the infant ordinarily fastens is the face of the mother, but, following the law of displacement, this image, by the process of metonymy, normally slides very quickly into other images. One image signifying the symbiosis of infant and mother is usually the maternal breast or bosom. What happens in Pearl's case, however, is that she quickly shifts the identity of the mother not to the image of the breast, but to the object located on Hester's breast—namely, the scarlet letter A. Though such metonymic displacements (according to Lacan) are not particularly unusual, Hawthorne makes an issue of Pearl's attachment to the emblem: "The very first thing which she had noticed, in her life," writes Hawthorne, "was—what?—not the mother's smile, responding to it, as other babies do, by that faint, embryo smile of the little mouth . . . By no means! But that first object of which Pearl seemed to become aware was—shall we say it?—the scarlet letter on Hester's bosom!" (96). The scarlet letter becomes Pearl's first "little object," the *objet petit a* that stands for the mother herself.

The object, at the outset, indeed stands for the mother. But as the child moves further along the path toward differentiation from the mother (in other words, toward the passage through the phases of the mirror stage), the child develops an ambivalent relation to her and, therefore, to the objects representing her. The ambivalence is illustrated very clearly in Pearl's behavior. Immediately after the revelation that Pearl's first significant object of Imaginary identification is the scarlet letter, Hawthorne also recounts Pearl's aggressive attack on it. "In the afternoon of a certain summer's day, after Pearl grew big enough to run about, she amused herself with gathering handfuls of wild-flowers, and flinging them, one by one, at her mother's bosom; dancing up and down, like a little elf, whenever she hit the scarlet letter" (97). Such ambivalence manifests the mirror process of psychic differentiation, for it acknowledges the child's awareness of the otherness of both self and mother in the other-directed aggressivity (as Lacan points out in an essay on that topic).[13] In Hawthorne's text, the ambivalence is also associated with the child's Oedipal awareness, its indebtedness for creation not to one, but to two (a recognition that Lacan, like Lévi-Strauss,[14] places at the center of human development). Pearl's attention here, Hawthorne shows us, is directed toward the question of paternity in the Real, not in the Symbolic. When Hester tells Pearl that the Heavenly Father had sent the child, Hawthorne writes that it is "with a hesitation that did not escape the acuteness of the child. Whether moved only by her ordinary freakishness, or because an evil spirit prompted her, she put up her small forefinger, and touched the scarlet letter" (98). With her finger on the symbol, Pearl tells her mother that the Heavenly is not her father, at least not her real father. The symbol under her finger suggests to Pearl that her real father lies elsewhere, indeed, lies somewhere behind the scarlet letter. Eventually, she will discover that both her Real and her Symbolic father are signified by the letter.

The other side of the ambivalent behavior that marks the Lacanian register of the Imaginary is Pearl's exaggerated veneration of the "little object." That veneration is evidence that Pearl has begun to identify herself with the letter, to see herself as much as her mother in the letter. Consequently, in certain moments typical of the ambivalence of the Imaginary identifications with the other or the objects representing the other, her aggressiveness is modulated toward what at root is a self-directed, narcissistic affection. In the chapter called "Hester and Pearl" (15), for example, Pearl injures a tiny bird as she flings pebbles at a flock; with its gray coloring and a brightly contrapuntal breast, the bird by metaphoric similarity, represents Pearl's mother, who dresses in gray, but wears the scarlet letter on her bosom. Thus, Pearl's aggressive rock-throwing is characteristic of the child's puzzling hostility toward Hester. But Hawthorne's text, by the further process of metonymy, clearly identifies the tiny birds with Pearl, too. First, we learn that she gave up her throwing "because it grieved her to have done harm to a little being that was as wild as the sea-breeze, or as wild as Pearl herself." Then, in a passage just further, Hawthorne notes that upon the child's hearing her mother's voice, she flits "along as lightly as one of the little sea-birds" (178). Thus, in the metonymic chain of metaphoric substitutions (bird for mother, and bird for child) the text's attention comes to rest on Pearl's imitation not of the bird, but of the scarlet letter. "As the last touch to her mermaid's garb," which Pearl had made for herself of sea-weed, "Pearl took some eel-grass, and imitated, as best she could, on her own bosom, the decoration with which she was so familiar on her mother's. A letter,—the letter A,—but freshly green, instead of scarlet!" (178). Finally, as if to assure readers of the connections among child, green letter, mother, and scarlet letter, Hawthorne recounts Pearl's pointing once again to the letter on Hester's bosom and inquiring of its signification. Once again, however, the end of this chain of displacements is none other than an invocation not of the maternal, but of the paternal signifier, as Pearl wonders if Hester wears the letter on her breast "for the same reason that the minister keeps his hand over his heart!" (179). Plainly, the letter A stands polysemously not only for mother, *l'autre* or other, but also for *L'Autre*—the law of the Other and the name of the father.

Hester will not answer the child's questions about the letter or the minister's hand over his heart, but it seems clear enough that Pearl's questions will stop only when (through the agency of the letter) she knows her real father and thus can recognize the authority of the Symbolic father and, along with it, the inevitability of the loss of phallic plentitude (associated with the mother and, here, with the scarlet letter) Lacan defines as castration. The scene in which this phase of the Lacanian mirror stage is depicted occurs most visibly in chapter 19, "The Child at the Brook-Side." This phase of the mirror passage is characterized by the overt emergence, in the consciousness of the subject, of the Oedipal triangle. That the Oedipal question has shadowed Pearl's life throughout is evident in her behavior, her almost mystical intimations regarding the identity of her father, and her inquiries regarding the metaphoric linkage between the letter on Hester's bosom and the hand over the minister's heart. The question, moreover, is central to each of the three scaffold scenes. It is broached in the first, nearly finds its answer in the second, where Arthur should have announced his true paternal relation to the child, and is finally answered in the third, which concludes Pearl's passage through the mirror. But the most dramatic evidence of the Oedipal structure (necessary, Lacan contends, if the child is to enter the Symbolic as a normally functioning subject) occurs earlier in the dark forest.

There, the brook that separates Pearl from Hester and Arthur serves as the mediating figure of the mirror. The brook, early on, is identified in the text both as mirror and as child. It is enfigured, for example, as an object that could "mirror its revelations on the smooth surface of a pool," but also as one whose babble is "kind, quiet, soothing, but melancholy, like the voice of a young child that was spending its infancy without playfulness" (186). Later, and most significantly, the brook forms the mirror in which, in remarkable Lacanian terms, Pearl herself is projected. On the one hand, as Lacan argues concerning the other in the mirror, this projection is idealized by the text, if not the subject: "it reflected a perfect image of her little figure, with all the brilliant picturesqueness of her beauty, in its adornment of flowers and wreathed foliage, but more refined and spiritualized than the reality" (208). On the other hand, the subject absorbs something of its own identity back from the mirror's reflection: "This image, so nearly identical with the living Pearl, seemed to communicate somewhat of its own shadowy and intangible quality to the child herself" (208). Most important of all, however, is the onset of alienation (but, Lacan would say, also of subjectivity and symbolization) that occurs in this reflection in the mirror. "In the brook beneath," Hawthorne writes, "stood another child,—another and the same." The alienation is observed by the mother as much as by the child. "Hester felt herself, in some indistinct and tantalizing manner, estranged from Pearl; as if the child, in her lonely ramble through the forest, had strayed out of the sphere in which she and her mother dwelt together, and was now vainly seeking to return to it" (208). Pearl—as Hester perceives—now belongs to a world of differences, of otherness even in the same, of identity found only in others or the other. Such is the fall from grace in Lacanian terms.

That which will prevent Pearl from returning to the sphere of union with the mother is the symbol of the other—that is, the father. "In the Oedipal complex phase," writes Eugen Bär, "the law imposes itself in the symbol of the father on the infant, separating the latter from the mother."[15] The contour of the Oedipal structure is plain in the forest scene, though Hawthorne ascribes Pearl's estrangement not to some inevitable passage of the child, but to an act of the mother. After the child has wandered from her mother's side there in the forest, "another inmate had been admitted within the circle of the mother's feelings, and so modified the aspect of them all, that Pearl, the returning wanderer, could not find her wonted place, and hardly knew where she was" (208). Her shock could not have been greater had she found Hester and Arthur copulating. The potent intruder, Hawthorne notes, points out "that this brook is the boundary between two worlds, and that thou canst never meet thy Pearl again" (208). But, for her part, Pearl does not yet know or acknowledge the minister as her father and certainly not as the signifier of paternity or authority awaiting her beyond the mirror. Instead, she directs her attention to the scarlet letter once more, for, again, the letter is the symbol of the child as a little thing that fulfills the desire of the mother, just as it is a symbol of the unity of being the child has identified with the body of her mother. Clearly, the letter has phallic significance for Pearl. When Hester, in a moment of abandon with Dimmesdale, takes the emblem from her breast and tosses it toward the brook, the gesture must represent her recognition of her own castration. Seeing the object symbolizing herself and her mother now separated from her mother, Pearl feels the panic of the child suddenly become aware of castration—its own and its mother's. Her demand, therefore, is for Hester to put it back on, Pearl (like the child in the *"Fort! Da!"* game) perhaps hoping its return will close the gap and restore the plentitude lost with the symbolic phallus. But now the letter will not and cannot fill or restore anything. Nor will the Oedipal kiss—proffered by Arthur— until it comes (in the third scaffold scene) with the acknowledgement (Pearl's *and* Arthur's) of actual fatherhood. Then, however, what the father's kiss will accomplish is not restoration of plentitude, but the impress of gender and the lesson of the law, the phallus, and castration.

The final step in Pearl's journey through the mirror, since it matches Dimmesdale's assumption of the Law of the Father, too, occurs in chapter 23, "The Revelation of the Scarlet Letter." The scene in the forest is, as it were, merely a reflection of the mirror stage: the appropriate Oedipal structure is present, but the immediate results are not conclusive for Pearl. By her imperious demands she forces Hester to don the letter again, and, by her hostility toward the minister, she drives him away from the mirroring, dividing brook. Thus, in the chapter leading up to the minister's revelation, Pearl displays the same intemperate, essentially lawless behavior that has always marked her. Not yet under the rule of law and the phallic authority, Pearl manifests pure, prepotent desire: "Whenever Pearl saw any thing to excite her ever active and wandering curiosity, she flew thitherward, and, as we might say, seized upon that man or thing as her own property, so far as she desired it; but without yielding the minutest degree of control over her emotions in requital" (244). So long as Pearl maintains such a relation to others and the world, she will remain caught in the illusory web of the Imaginary. For her psychic (and cultural) maturation to occur, she must move into the register of the Symbolic. The Imaginary gives any subject 1) a self and 2) an other, but the Symbolic gives a third, necessary agency: a concept of mediation, one represented in the father. "The child," writes Bär, "has to learn to receive his value, that is, what it desires to be, the phallus, from others, from the father, from the sociocultural system. In this process, he is divided into the roles, designed by others, which he has to assume, and the impulse of his own absolute desires, which he has to repress."[16] What Pearl gains when she is recognized publicly (and recognizes herself) as Dimmesdale's child is the obverse of what she loses: she gains identity under the law of the father, but she loses the absolute narcissistic freedom of her natural ("premirror") condition. She gains the phallus as a signifier in the register of the Symbolic, but she loses illusory plentitude in the register of the Imaginary. She loses her identity as a child, finally, but she gains the capability of mature womanhood. No description of the passage through the mirror stage could be better than Hawthorne's account of Pearl's acceptance of her father: "Pearl kissed his lips. A spell was broken. The great scene of grief, in which the wild infant bore a part, had developed all her sympathies; and as her tears fell upon her father's cheek, they were the pledge that she would grow up amid human joy and sorrow, nor for ever do battle with the world, but be a woman in it" (256).

III

The second of the two "normal" subjects of consciousness in *The Scarlet Letter* is Pearl's mother, Hester Prynne. The dynamics of Hester's first appearance manifest several Lacanian concepts, for the power of the cultural gaze to which she is subjected will activate the dialectic of the Imaginary and the Symbolic that develops in the mirror stage seen operating in Pearl. Forced to emerge from a dark jail into the bright noontime sun, then to stand exposed on the scaffold of the pillory of Boston, Hester is made to wear the letter in which her crime insists, but that is also the scopic object focusing her punishment under the communal gaze. Hester's crime—in Lacanian terms—is an expression of her psychic involvement in the Imaginary, her punishment an expression of the dominating authority of the cultural Symbolic. Thus, Hester's ambivalent relationship to the scarlet letter she wears becomes an expression of the general psychic ambivalence manifested in her apparent submission to communal law at the same time she finds a way to deny it. On the one hand, the letter is placed on her by the town fathers so that the gaze—being seen—is the only form of punishment to which she will be subjected;

on the other, she herself has transformed the stigma into such a compelling work of visual art that she and the letter she wears can hardly fail to attract the punitive gaze. The psychic split is evident in Hawthorne's first description of Hester's encounter with the audience for which her emblem is intended: "wisely judging that one token of her shame would but poorly serve to hide another, she took the baby on her arm, and, with a burning blush, and yet a haughty smile, and a glance that would not be ashamed, looked around at her townspeople and neighbours. On the breast of her gown, in fine red cloth, surrounded with an elaborate embroidery and fantastic flourishes of gold thread, appeared the letter A. It was so artistically done, and with so much fertility and gorgeous luxuriance of fancy, that it had all the effect of a last and fitting decoration to the apparel which she wore" (52–53). All Hester's problems as a subject caught between the Imaginary and the Symbolic are represented here, and it is these problems that Hester, accepting normality, will resolve by the narrative's end.

Hester is trapped at this initial moment—and will remain trapped for virtually the entire account—in the Imaginary. The Imaginary, according to Ragland-Sullivan, "is the domain of the *imago* and relationship interaction."[17] Whereas the register of the Symbolic operates "by a differential logic which names, codifies, and legalizes," the Imaginary operates by an "identificatory, fusional logic."[18] The crucial fact of the Imaginary, where Hester is concerned, is that without adequate recourse to the Symbolic she will be incapable of consistent self-reflection or self-awareness. Caught in the identifications of this register, she simply cannot understand or appreciate the drives operating on or within her. In effect, she must deny her unconscious. But, from an analytic perspective, it is clearly possible to make those unconscious drives or forces manifest. They will be evident in the images or figures of speech Hawthorne uses to represent her relation to others within her social environment. The most obvious others, of course, are Pearl, Dimmesdale, and Chillingworth. Hester's psychoanalytic profile can be drawn from her relations to these, for those relations will suggest the images that, within the topography of her psyche, fill the place of the other and provide glimpses of the personal *moi* and the cultural Other.

In the Imaginary, all identificatory others (persons, things, sensory impressions) become objects of desire in the field of the subject consciousness—that is, in the subject who relates through desire to those others. Hester—as desiring subject— relates to those identificatory others primarily through the function of sight—what Lacan calls the scopic field. Thus, for Hester, the Lacanian *objets petit a* (the objects that focus her identifications) will be visual, and, more than that, will be artistically shaped. The principal example of this scopic identification with an object representing desire is Hester's relation to the infant Pearl, on the one hand, and the scarlet letter, on the other. But under the gaze, these *objets petit a* are ambiguous. From the first moment of their appearance, the letter A and the infant are joined as tokens signifying Hester's phallic desire, but also her shame. Thus either may substitute, metaphorically, for her sexual desire and for her relation to the dominant, symbolic Other—the community and its punitive agent, the gaze. As signifiers, child and letter (as in the algorithm S/s) stand for the hidden signified that the community desires to see and that Hester determines to keep hidden: the name of the father. The index of Pearl's ambiguous objectivity to Hester as a subject lies in the contrapuntal aims of the two. It is the name of the father that Hester will not divulge; it is the father's name that Pearl shall demand. Similarly, the letter Hester wears denies the father's name, but at the same time it, metonymically (part for whole, A for Arthur), reveals it. In this respect, since the community and its gaze represent the Symbolic Other, Pearl and the letter as *objets petit a* mediate a relation for Hester to the unconscious. Thus, not only are Pearl and the letter A links to the name of the father; they also forge links between Hester's conscious and unconscious, Imaginary and Symbolic registers.

Pearl's identity, for Hester, is almost immediately absorbed into that *objet a* represented by the letter. Apparently unconsciously, Hester turns the child into a replica of the scarlet emblem, whereas at the outset the child and the letter were linked only by contiguity on Hester's bosom. It is the nature of identifications in the Imaginary that they function by similarity or contrast, sympathy or conflict. Both principles operate in the identificatory relation between Hester and Pearl. The contrast occurs in the drab attire of the mother compared to the bright finery of the child. The relation represented here in the difference is the same as that between the field (gray—or, as Hester's heraldic epitaph has it, sable) on which the letter stands and the letter (scarlet—or the heraldic gules) itself as opposed to the bright finery of Pearl and the field of drab Puritan fashion against which she stands. Of the relation between the exotically embroidered letter A and the communal standard, Hawthorne says that it "was a splendor in accordance with the taste of the age, but greatly beyond what was allowed by the sumptuary regulations of the colony" (53). Of the contrast between Hester's attire, generally, and Pearl's, Hawthorne writes: "Her own dress was of the coarsest materials and the most sombre hue; with only that one ornament,—the scarlet letter,—which it was her doom to wear. The child's attire, on the other hand, was distinguished by a fanciful, or, we might rather say, a fantastic ingenuity, which served, indeed, to heighten the airy charm that early began to develop itself in the little girl, but which appeared to have also a deeper meaning" (83).

The deeper meaning of Pearl as an identificatory other (or *objet a*) lies in Hester's use of her as a two-sided medium channeling her relation to the community. Pearl (like the scarlet letter) is one side of the artistic expression that Hester permits herself; the other is the "good work," "the exquisite productions of her needle" (83), that she performs for the Puritan community. In effect, Pearl becomes Hester's living letter to the Puritan world. Here the principle of similarity or affinity found in the Imaginary can be seen in operation. Hester mimics through Pearl the luxurious beauty of the scarlet letter so that there can be no doubt of the similarity (and, thus, symbolic identity) of the one object and the other, the child and the letter. Dressed by Hester all in crimson velvet tunics, "of a peculiar cut, abundantly embroidered with fantasies and flourishes of gold thread" (102), Pearl mirrors the

emblem on her mother's breast. The child's garb "irresistibly and inevitably reminded the beholder of the token which Hester Prynne was doomed to wear
upon her bosom. It was the scarlet letter in another form; the scarlet letter
endowed with life" (102). Thus, for Hester, Pearl is both "the object of her affection
and the emblem of her guilt and torture . . . [;] only in consequence of that identity
had Hester contrived so perfectly to represent the scarlet letter in her appearance"
(102).

   The identificatory association of Pearl and the letter, while representing the
contrasting values of affection and punishment, are no more ambivalently expressive of Hester's relation to the community than her other works—the "finer
productions of her handiwork" (82) that provide mother and child a livelihood. As
the child and the letter both focus and symbolize the punitive gaze of Hester's social
structure, so the works of her hands focus and symbolize the submissive relation
Hester exhibits to the representatives of authority there. Whereas Pearl and the
gorgeous emblem on Hester's bosom flout that authority, her other artisanal
creations unconsciously recognize its power. The market she discovers for her
products involves major domains of the social Symbolic: birth, death, and "public
ceremonies, such as ordinations, the installation of magistrates, and all that could
give majesty to the forms in which a new government manifested itself to the
people" (82). Although Hester, as a symbol of repressed female desire, is never
permitted "to embroider the white veil which was to cover the pure blushes of a
bride," she is given access through her good work to all the most potent symbols
of the law, up to and including the law of mortality: "Her needle-work was seen on
the ruff of the Governor; military men wore it on their scarfs, and the minister on
his band; it decked the baby's little cap; it was shut up, to be mildewed and moulder
away, in the coffins of the dead" (83). As Hawthorne points out, the exception
made of the bridal veil indicates "the ever relentless vigor with which society
frowned upon her sin" (83), but at the same time the various permissions give
evidence (in the symbolic difference) of the agency and the potency of the law.

   One of the impressions given by Hester's involvement in the plot of *The
Scarlet Letter* is that her psychic conflict as a subject is ended once she steps out
into the sunlight flooding the scaffold of the pillory. But awareness of the ambiguity
of her relation to Pearl and the letter, on one side, and to the authority of public
law, on the other, suggests that indeed there is a conflict that must be resolved. She
must finally accept the law, its symbols of authority, and through them the rule of
the register of the Symbolic. The signifiers of that register constantly appear in
aspects of what Lacan calls the gaze, along with the metonymical imagery associated
with it such as the eye, the look, and the stare. Together, these represent one of
the most important motifs in the narrative. The gaze, as Lacan might say, cuts in
many directions, as it links the subject to the object and by that linkage turns each
into the other whenever one reverses (by a shift in point of view) the scopic field.
For Hester, in her conscious life, the gaze dominates as a double for the
community—the public law to and under whose scrutiny (her "doom") she has

been sentenced. Thus, for her, the gaze is even more important as an image of the Imaginary other than her lover, Arthur Dimmesdale, who in the ordinary love story might normally be regarded as the dominant figure of her Imaginary register.[19] But the public's gaze and its symbols also connect Hester's unconscious with the more powerful source of law, authority, and the name(s) of the father in the Symbolic register. Says Lacan, "The gaze is presented to us only in the form of a strange contingency, symbolic of what we find on the horizon, as the thrust of our experience, namely, the lack that constitutes castration anxiety."[20] The gaze cuts like a knife, and what it excises—in the passage from the Imaginary to the Symbolic—is the phallus.

Dimmesdale—like most readers—assumes that Hester has escaped psychic torment simply because her sin has been made public. But the power of the gaze and the agency of the eye work their effects into Hester's life just as rigorously as the minister's self-scrutiny into his. The insistence of the law of the Other that must finally be observed comes to Hester in her punishment. The scarlet letter she wears, for example, is held "up to the public gaze" (55), and she feels the "heavy weight of a thousand unrelenting eyes" (57). Hester can escape the gaze, the eyes, of neither friends nor strangers, nor friends who are strangers, as in the case of Roger Chillingworth, who is really *Prynne* and Hester's husband, lost and presumed dead at the tale's start. Roger is "the stranger" in the opening scene who "had bent his eyes on Hester Prynne" (61), and it is he who looks into her eyes with "a gaze that made her heart shrink and shudder" (72). But actual strangers and familiar faces trouble her, too. "Another peculiar torture was felt in the gaze of a new eye" (85), we are told, yet the "accustomed stare," in its "cool ... familiarity" (86), is no pleasure for Hester either. Even Pearl—the one closest to Hester—is a constant reminder of the virtually absolute power of the gaze of the Other. "Weeks ... would sometimes elapse," we are told, "during which Pearl's gaze might never once be fixed" on Hester's emblem of sin, "but then ... it would come ... like the stroke of sudden death" (96–97). The only gaze not so painful is Arthur Dimmesdale's, but that is because Hester and Arthur share the same pain, as perhaps they wear the same letter on their breasts: "Here," in the forest tableau, "seen only by his eyes, the scarlet letter need not burn into the bosom of the fallen woman" (195–96). For her part, what Hester has endured for the seven long years has been, simply, "the world's ignominious stare" (251). That stare is nothing less than the Other of law, authority, and the place of the father Lacan associates with the register of the Symbolic.

Hester will move from the debilitating entrapment of the Imaginary into the ambivalent freedom of the Symbolic, but there is a suspenseful moment in the tale's plot that suggests she might fail. That moment, in which it appears that Hester will throw away not only the scarlet letter, but also seven years of development toward the Symbolic, occurs in the forest scene when she tries to persuade Arthur to escape Boston and the gaze of the Puritan law under which they both are condemned. The escape she plans would take them away from those eyes that seem always to penetrate her. Above all, the escape she plans would take the both of them away from Roger (Prynne) Chillingworth; "Thy heart," Hester tells Arthur, "must be no longer under his evil eye" (196). While there is never a doubt in the book that Roger is Hawthorne's agent of evil, the devil, the Black Man, he is also more importantly the ambiguous agent of the symbolic Other, the law of the father. Moreover, Roger's gaze is no less symbolic of the communal law under which they suffer and the more universal Oedipal law they had breached together. As Hester's husband under the law, he should have stood in the place of the father in relation to Hester's child. There is, as Hester discovers, no escaping Roger, just as there is no escaping the Black Man, who, we are assured, "hath a way of ordering matters so that the mark [of sin] shall be disclosed in open daylight to the eyes of all the world" (242). It is because Roger stands for the Other that Hester (with Pearl and Arthur) cannot give him the slip and depart on a ship bound for the "lawless" sea.

One cannot know for certain that Hester would have experienced the same sense of acceptance of the law of the Other had Roger not foiled her escape and Arthur not chosen to make his public revelation of his own share of her sin. But, psychologically, her acceptance—or capitulation—seems inevitable. Moreover, we do see one instance of that acceptance. Although it comes at a moment when she believes they all will indeed escape Roger together, "after sustaining the gaze of the multitude through seven miserable years as a necessity," Hawthorne writes, "she now ... encountered it freely and voluntarily" (227). But should one deny the importance of her acceptance here, one ought to consider her return to Boston later in life and to the very site of her public ignominy after she had for awhile sojourned in the Old World with the mature Pearl. Her return is precisely an acceptance of her life under the burden of the law, the rule of the Symbolic Other. That acceptance, finally, is most vividly symbolized in terms inevitably associated with the most potent reminder of our human submission to the Other. Death is the most emphatic expression of the human limitation represented in the Symbolic by the law of castration. In Hester's tale, the symbol of her final acceptance is the token, the tombstone, erected over her grave, bearing words authored by her and given authority by her submission to the Other: "On a field, sable, the letter A, gules" (264). That escutcheon is the ultimate expression of Hester's existence (*l'être*) under the letter and the law of the Lacanian *Autre*.

IV

As a way of concluding this discussion of Pearl and Hester in *The Scarlet Letter,* one might suggest the advantages that Lacanian analysis offers to literary criticism. There are two major ones. First, regardless of the close historical relation between the development of Freud's concepts and his literary examples, Lacanian analysis is immediately more "literary" than Freudian analysis, for Lacan insists upon the absolute primacy of language and tropes or figures of speech in psychoanalysis.

One does not need to search out traumatic events, actual happenings, in order to locate the psychological cruxes of character or personality. By focusing on language, on the mechanisms of language, Lacan brings his analysis immediately into the domain of literary analysis (or vice versa, Lacan might say), and whatever the consequences for psychoanalysis, that congruence between psycho- and literary analysis makes the work of the critic much more familiar and compatible to ordinary habits of work. The second major advantage of Lacanian over Freudian analysis is its ability to deal with the "normal" subject, and I have dealt with Hawthorne's Pearl and Hester in order to illustrate that feature. Although Freudian literary analysis is not limited to the neurotic and the psychotic, it appears that it is so limited in the critical praxis, despite the excellent analysis of the nonpathological that Freud himself performs in his essay on Jensen's *Gradiva*.[21] This limitation in the praxis, if not in the actual theory, can be observed in Frederick Crews's classic Freudian interpretation of *The Scarlet Letter*. Crews seems solely interested—perhaps only capable of interest—in one character: Arthur Dimmesdale. Crews occasionally refers to Hester and Chillingworth as potential subjects in his interpretation, but never to Pearl. Despite his insight that Chillingworth is "the psychoanalyst *manqué*,[22] virtually all his attention is devoted to Dimmesdale as the pathological subject in whom is manifest the combination of guilt and repression Crews's Freudianism must assess. While Crews's essay will remain a landmark in psychoanalytic interpretation of fiction, it may well remain as a representation of the blindness of Freudian analysis as well.[23] One may hope that the rereading of Freud found in Lacanian analysis, as well as the Lacanian reading of *The Scarlet Letter* through its two normal subjects, may illustrate the critical openness of the philosophy of psychoanalysis found in Jacques Lacan.

NOTES

[1] For Frederick C. Crews's Freudian analysis, see *The Sins of the Fathers: Hawthorne's Psychological Themes* (New York: Oxford University Press, 1966). See also Michael Vannoy Adams, "Pathography, Hawthorne, and the History of Psychological Ideas," *ESQ* 29 (1983):113–26; John Dolis, "Hawthorne's Letter," *Notebooks in Cultural Analysis* 1 (1984):103–23 and "Hawthorne's Morphology of Alienation: The Psychosomatic Phenomenon," *American Imago* 41 (Spring 1984):47–62; Thomas L. Hilgers, "The Psychology of Conflict Resolution in *The Scarlet Letter*: A Non-Freudian Approach," *American Transcendental Quarterly* 43 (Summer 1979):211–24; John Irwin, *American Hieroglyphics: The Symbol of the Egyptian Hieroglyphics in the American Renaissance* (New Haven: Yale University Press, 1980), 239–84; and Michael Ragussis, "Family Discourse and Fiction in *The Scarlet Letter*," *ELH* 49 (Winter 1982):863–88. For criticism considered structuralist, poststructuralist, or postmodernist, see also Millicent Bell, "The Obliquity of Signs in *The Scarlet Letter*," *Massachusetts Review* 23 (Spring 1982):9–26; *New Essays on* The Scarlet Letter, ed. Michael J. Colacurcio (Cambridge: Cambridge University Press, 1985); *Nathaniel Hawthorne: New Critical Essays*, ed. A. Robert Lee (Totowa, NJ: Barnes and Noble, 1982); John Carlos Rowe, "The Internal Conflict of Romantic Narrative: Hegel's *Phenomenology* and Hawthorne's *The Scarlet Letter*," *MLN* 95 (1980):1203–31; and Marianna Torgovnick, *Closure in the Novel* (Princeton: Princeton University Press, 1981), 80–100.
[2] *Écrits: A Selection*, trans. Alan Sheridan (New York: Norton, 1977), 147.
[3] "The Magnetism between Reader and Text: Prolegomena to a Lacanian Poetics," *Poetics* 13 (1984):381.
[4] Sheridan, *Écrits: A Selection*, 147.
[5] Ibid.

[6] "Of Structure as an Inmixing of an Otherness Prerequisite to Any Subject Whatever," in *The Language of Criticism and the Sciences of Man: The Structuralist Controversy*, ed. Richard Macksey and Eugenio Donato (Baltimore: Johns Hopkins University Press, 1970), 187.

[7] Sheridan, *Écrits: A Selection*, 149.

[8] Ibid.

[9] Lacan's different schemas L, R, and I appear in Sheridan, *Écrits: A Selection*, 193, 197, 212; Jacques-Alain Miller comments on them, 332–35.

[10] Freud's discussion of the *"Fort! Da!"* game occurs in *Beyond the Pleasure Principle*, in *The Standard Edition of the Complete Psychological Works of Sigmund Freud*, vol. 18 (New York: Macmillan, 1964–   ), 4–17. Lacan discusses the consequences of the *"Fort! Da!"* game in the formation of the register of the Symbolic in the essay in *Écrits* called "Function and Field of Speech and Language in Psychoanalysis," 30–113; esp. 103–4.

[11] Lacan's use of the term *objet a* (which sometimes appears as *objet petit a*, as *objet* only, or as *a* only) occurs throughout his work. In a "Translator's Note" to Lacan's *Four Fundamental Concepts of Psycho-Analysis* (New York: Norton, 1978), Alan Sheridan explains the *objet petit a* this way: "The *'a'* in question stands for *"autre"* (other), the concept having been developed out of the Freudian 'object' and Lacan's own exploitation of 'otherness.' The *'petit a'* (small 'a') differentiates the object from (while relating it to) the *'Autre'* or *'grand Autre'* (the capitalized 'Other'). Lacan refuses to comment on either term here, however, leaving the reader to develop an appreciation of the concepts in the course of their use. Furthermore, Lacan insists that *"objet petit a"* should remain untranslated, thus acquiring, as it were, the status of an algebraic sign" (282).

[12] Nathaniel Hawthorne, *The Scarlet Letter, The Centenary Edition of the Works of Nathaniel Hawthorne*, vol. 1 (Columbus: Ohio State University Press, 1962), 67. Further references to this text will be included parenthetically and without abbreviation within the text.

[13] See "Aggressivity in Psychoanalysis," in Sheridan, *Écrits: A Selection*, 8–29. It is very important to understand that the *imago* found in the mirror images may be both positive and negative for the subject, and thus treated quite ambivalently.

[14] Claude Lévi-Strauss exerted an important influence on Lacan, not only because the anthropologist was one of the fathers of Structuralism, but also because he shared Lacan's conviction regarding the centrality of language to human development, whether cultural or psychological. Like Lacan, Lévi-Strauss stressed the dominance of signs and the primacy in culture of Laws regarding incest; from the apparent universal human concern with incest comes the preponderance of myths (such as those Lévi-Strauss examines in *Mythologiques* I, II, III, *The Elementary Structures of Kinship*, and *The Savage Mind*, for example) regarding birth-from-one or birth-from-two. Lévi-Strauss also shares Lacan's emphasis (taken from Ferdinand de Saussure and Roman Jakobson) on metaphor and metonymy—that is, principles (or tropes) in language of substitution and displacement.

[15] Eugen Bär, "Understanding Lacan," in *Psychoanalysis and Contemporary Science*, vol. 3, ed. Leo Goldberger and Victor H. Rosen (New York: International Universities Press, 1974), 513.

[16] Ibid., 515.

[17] Ragland-Sullivan, *Jacques Lacan and the Philosophy of Psychoanalysis* (Urbana: University of Illinois Press, 1985), 130–31. This book has become the standard exposition and interpretation in English of Lacanian thought.

[18] Ragland-Sullivan, *Lacan*, 131.

[19] See Ernest Sandeen, "*The Scarlet Letter* as a Love Story," *PMLA* 77 (1962):425–35, for a discussion in which Hester and Arthur would, perforce, remain as objects to each other in Lacan's quadrant (in Schema L) of the "other."

[20] Lacan, *Four Fundamental Concepts of Psycho-Analysis*, 72–73.

[21] See Sigmund Freud, *The Standard Edition of the Complete Psychological Works of Sigmund Freud*, vol. 9, trans. James Strachey (London: The Hogarth Press, 1959), 7–95.

[22] Crews, *Sins of the Fathers*, 141.

[23] In fairness to Crews, one must point out that he later rejects Freudian literary analysis: see *Out of My System* (New York: Oxford University Press, 1975).

David S. Reynolds
TOWARD HESTER PRYNNE

Although Hawthorne is generally credited with having created the most intriguing heroines in pre–Civil War literature, little has been said about the relationship between these heroines and the women's culture of the day. The fact is that the rich variety of female character types in antebellum popular culture prepared the way for Hawthorne's complex heroines. Hawthorne's best fiction occupies an energetic middle space between the Conventional novel and the literature of women's wrongs. Skeptical of the Conventional and politically uncommitted, Hawthorne was in an ideal position to choose judiciously from the numerous female stereotypes and to assimilate them in literary texts. His career illustrates the success of an especially responsive author in gathering together disparate female types and recombining them artistically so that they became crucial elements of the rhetorical and artistic construct of his fiction.

As a creator of heroines, Hawthorne began as an unusually flexible but rather haphazard experimenter with various native and foreign character types. His earliest fiction, published between 1828 and 1837, can be distinguished from that of other American authors by the heterogeneity of its heroines. None of his early tales contains a heroine that can be called complex, but, taken as a whole, the tales are a remarkable testament to Hawthorne's ability to escape narrow, monolithic views of women. On the one hand, he proved himself capable of producing redemptive moral exemplars: in "Little Annie's Ramble" an angelic child revives and cheers an old man; "The Little Uncle" features a bright, sunshiny woman; in "The Vision of the Fountain" an angelic exemplar is the visionary creation of a narrator's fancy. On the other hand, he also gave graphic portrayals of female criminals, such as the wandering heroine who has cruelly abandoned her family in "The Hollow of Three Hills," and women victims, such as the persecuted Quaker woman in "The Gentle Boy" and the Puritan adulteress forced to wear a scarlet A in "Endicott and the Red Cross."

From *Beneath the American Renaissance: The Subversive Imagination in the Age of Emerson and Melville* (New York: Knopf, 1988), pp. 368–75.

His most complex early use of women characters occurs in "Young Goodman Brown," in which the affirmative values embodied in the allegorically named exemplar, Faith, are shattered by the protagonist's recognition of universal sinfulness, represented by the gathering of saints and sinners in the forest. In previous chapters we have seen that "Young Goodman Brown" was in many senses a representative 1830s piece whose ambiguities owed much to dark popular writings of the decade. It also drew on the ironic perception of the underlying similarity of respectable and fallen women that was being discussed in reform writings. When Hawthorne describes "chaste dames and dewy virgins" consorting with "women of spotted fame" and when he mentions outwardly good women who kill their babies or husbands, he is tapping ironies that surrounded fallen women and women criminals in several popular works of the 1830s.[1] When he has the angelic Faith appear at this demonic gathering, he dramatically undercuts the power of the moral exemplar. For the first time in his fiction, real density of meaning surrounds his heroines because he boldly brings together under one fictional roof moral exemplars, fallen women, and women criminals, a combination that produces an explosion of ironic meaning. The explosion is all the more powerful because Hawthorne uses a Puritan setting, so that the contemporary ironies take on a universality and a resonance because they are treated with Calvinistic seriousness. It must be emphasized, however, that there Hawthorne creates a *combination* of character types but not a real *fusion*, as he would in more interesting later heroines. His portrayal of various kinds of women in a single tale is significant but is finally subordinated to his main purpose of studying the disillusionment of Young Goodman Brown himself.

In short, his early tales reveal his remarkable openness to various character types, his occasional success in bringing together different types in a single tale, but his minimization of gender-specific themes. It was only in the early 1840s that his fiction revealed his growing awareness of both women's wrongs and women's rights. It was during this period, we should recall, that he spent time at Brook Farm among progressive thinkers, including the period's leading feminist theorist, Margaret Fuller. His exposure to feminist ideas during a time of economic depression and widespread exploitation of working women had a strong impact upon his fiction. Unlike Catharine Sedgwick, he did not blithely dismiss the sufferings of American working women. He succinctly but powerfully registered the sufferings of seamstresses in "The Procession of Life" (1843), which contains the following alarmed description: "But what is this crowd of pale-cheeked, slender girls, who disturb the ear with the multiplicity of their short, dry coughs? They are seamstresses, who have plied the daily and nightly needle in the service of master-tailors and close-fisted contractors, until now it is almost time for each to hem the borders of her own shroud."[2] In "The Christmas Banquet" (1844), a dark tale about an imagined gathering of the most wretched people on earth, Hawthorne shows that his sympathy extends not only to seamstresses but to all women victimized by overwhelming wrongs against their sex. Among the guests at the sad Christmas banquet are two women: "one, a half-starved, consumptive seamstress, the representative of thousands just as wretched; the other, a woman of unemployed energy, who found herself in the world with nothing to achieve, nothing to enjoy, and nothing even to suffer. She had, therefore, driven herself to the verge of madness by dark broodings over the wrongs of her sex, and its exclusion from a proper field of action."[3]

While these tales reveal his new sensitivity to women's wrongs, other tales of the period demonstrate his simultaneous recognition of women's rights. Among the reformers who appear in "Earth's Holocuast" (1844) are a number of women who propose to fling into the bonfire their petticoats and gowns, "and assume the garb, together with the manners, duties, offices, and responsibilities of the opposite sex."[4] Although here Hawthorne gently satirizes public agitation for women's rights, in "The New Adam and Eve" (1843) he endorses a kind of moral exemplar feminism when, imagining the wholesome Eve sitting in an American legislative hall, he writes: "Man's intellect, moderated by Woman's tenderness and moral sense! Were such the legislation of the world, there would be no need of State Houses, Capitols, Halls of Parliament."[5] A new political consciousness, therefore, characterized his fictional treatment of women in the early 1840s.

By 1844 Hawthorne was in a unique position among American authors dealing with women's issues. No other American writer had approached him in producing so large a variety of fictional heroines, from his heterogeneous characters of the 1830s to his more topical, socially representative heroines of the early 1840s. He was now ready to produce a heroine who fused opposite qualities and thus assumed stature as a truly complex, memorable literary character. All his earlier tales had achieved *combinations* of different types of heroines but not *fusions* of different qualities in one person. In Beatrice, the poisonous angel of "Rappaccini's Daughter" (1844), he created such a complex heroine.

Beatrice Rappaccini is both the angelic moral exemplar and the feminist criminal, both the pitiable woman victim and the deadly avenger of women's wrongs. She even has the magnetic voluptuousness of the sensual woman. On the one hand, she is the ultimate disenfranchised woman, totally removed from meaningful employment despite her reputation as a learned woman capable of being a university professor. True, her scientist father has endowed her with fatal power that he believes will enable her to redress wrongs against her sex—in his words, to "be able to quell the mightiest with a breath" and to avoid "the condition of a weak woman, exposed to all evil and capable of none."[6] But the very thing that gives her power over the mightiest prevents her from having a normal human relationship. To her lover Giovanni she seems by turns a heavenly angel and a terrible monster. Torn between love and horror, worship and loathing, Giovanni suffers an emotional conflict summed up in Hawthorne's exclamatory comment: "Blessed are all the simple emotions, be they dark or bright! It is the lurid intermixture of the two that produces the illuminating blaze of the infernal regions." Giovanni's confusion seems to have mirrored a confusion in Hawthorne's own mind. According to his son Julian, when Hawthorne was writing "Rappaccini's Daughter" he read from the unfinished manuscript to his wife, who interrupted him with the question: "But how is it to end? . . . is Beatrice to be a demon or an angel?" Julian records his father's baffled confession: " 'I have no idea!' was Hawthorne's reply, spoken with some emotion."[7]

The tale itself provides no clear answer, for even though Beatrice is said to be headed toward heaven as she dies, she has proved poisonous to everything she touched. Given the inscrutability of his heroine, Hawthorne might, perhaps, be charged with equivocation or artistic confusion. But instead of criticizing "Rappaccini's Daughter," we should recognize it as a transitional tale in which contradictory female stereotypes are fused in a single heroine. And it must be noted that the process of creative fusion creates a character who, despite residual similarities to popular heroines, has a symbolic density that makes her altogether different from these heroines. She is like the plants in her father's garden—a strange hybrid of different strains forced together by the crafty experimenter. The "Eden of poisonous flowers" in which she lives is the beautiful but (from a conventional standpoint) deadly garden of Hawthorne's art. What makes this artistic garden so intriguing is the lurid intermixture of qualities that make Beatrice Rappaccini at once the victim and the aggressor, the exemplar and the criminal.

Although interesting as an exercise in fused women stereotypes, Beatrice Rappaccini lacked the topicality and the Americanness of Hawthorne's next major heroine, Hester Prynne. The five years between the publication of "Rappaccini's Daughter" and the writing of The Scarlet Letter were, it should be recalled, important ones for literary treatments of American women. In popular sensational literature, the most important phenomenon was the devaluation of male authority figures and the intensification of iconoclastic female character types such as the sympathetic fallen woman, the feminist criminal, and the sensual woman. In popular Conventional literature, a defensive reaction against the sensationalists led to a valorization of the actively virtuous moral exemplar, leading toward the mythic exemplars in the famous domestic best-sellers of Maria Cummins and Susan Warner. Certain popular authors of the 1840s attempted crude but intriguing fusions of women character types. For instance, Lippard's The Quaker City traces the self-destruction of a moral exemplar, Mary Arlington, as a result of her deluded faith in the Conventional; it also includes the complicated Dora Livingstone, the intellectual, voluptuous, scheming confidence woman who sleeps around and even plots her husband's murder in order to get ahead. On the level of political activism, the late 1840s was the watershed moment when the Seneca Falls feminists initiated heated public agitation for women's rights.

Witnessing these swirling images of women in his contemporary culture, the observant Hawthorne brought them together in the figure of Hester Prynne. Given the cultural conditions and Hawthorne's personal experiences, it is understandable that he made a complex woman the center of his most famous novel. The widespread attacks on male authority figures in popular novels was paralleled in Hawthorne's experience at the Salem custom house, where his untimely firing by Whig merchants and officeholders gave him the bitter resolve to produce a poisonous novel that he said would act as "a pervasive and penetrating mischief" against his enemies.[8] At the same time, his suddenly tight financial straits made him wish to write a novel that would be popular and broadly representative. The novel he produced was indeed representative, since it featured both a secretly corrupt man and a strong, majestic woman. By 1849 the devalued male and the powerful female had become a commonly featured pair in both Subversive and Conventional novels, but in each case this pair had different significations. In the Subversive novel, devalued males such as the reverend rake or the churchgoing mogul were contrasted to a variety of women (the feminist criminal, the fallen woman, or the working woman) who were often strong and sympathetically portrayed but did not serve as moral replacements for the males. In the Conventional novel, the central figure of the female exemplar did function as potent alternative to weakened male authority.

In *The Scarlet Letter* Hawthorne retains the devalued male figure but takes the wholly original step of fashioning a heroine *who embodies all the dark female roles of the Subversive novel and who at the same time serves the redemptive function of the Conventional moral exemplar.* No character in antebellum fiction is so rich a compound of popular stereotypes as Hester Prynne. She is the sympathetically portrayed fallen woman whose honest sinfulness is found preferable to the furtive corruption of the reverend rake. She is the struggling working woman who plies her needle as a seamstress. She is the feminist criminal bound in an "iron link of mutual crime" with a man whose feebleness through most of the novel is contrasted with her indomitable firmness.[9] She is the sensual woman who has, in Hawthorne's words, "a rich, voluptuous, Oriental characteristic" and who is bold enough to whisper to her lover, "What we did had a consecration of its own." She is the feminist exemplar who privately broods over women's wrongs and dreams of a revolution in relations between the sexes. She is all of these iconoclastic things—but she is also a moral exemplar, in both the angelic and the practical sense. She elicits from the Puritans "the reverence due to an angel," and one of the meanings associated with her letter is "Angel." Along with her angelic quality goes a practical ability to help others as a charity worker and an adviser.

She is, in short, the quintessential American heroine, reflecting virtually every facet of the antebellum woman's experience. As was true with Beatrice Rappaccini, the innovative fusion of contrasting stereotypes creates a wholly new kind of heroine who bears little resemblance to any individual popular character. The fusion serves specific rhetorical functions for Hawthorne. The gathering together of different female types in Hester Prynne is an assertion of unity in the face of a fragmentation of women's roles that Hawthorne perceived in his contemporary culture. It was precisely this fragmentation of roles that would produce an indirect, elliptical style among some American women writers of the 1850s and 1860s. Through a majestic act of artistry, Hawthorne temporarily fends off the potential confusion inherent in shifting women's roles by creating a heroine who is magically able to act out several of these roles simultaneously.

What makes possible this complex heroine is Hawthorne's adept use of the

Puritan past. Just as Puritanism added moral depth to sensational themes that had degenerated in popular literature into flat prurience, so it offered historical materials conducive to a serious, rounded treatment of women's issues that had become sensationalized in popular Subversive fiction and circumvented in Conventional fiction. In *The Scarlet Letter* Hawthorne not only adopts but also *transforms* popular female stereotypes, and the chief transforming agent is Puritanism. The sympathetic fallen woman, who in radical-democrat novels had led to a gleeful inversion of moral values, here is treated with high seriousness. We sympathize with Hester but, because of the enormity of her punishment (a punishment reflecting the moral severity of Puritan New England), we are impressed with the momentousness of her sin. That is to say, she is not the fallen woman of the antebellum sensational novel who becomes callously amoral or vindictively murderous. Similarly, she is not the typical working woman, one who either gives way to suicidal despair, or becomes a prostitute, or contemplates armed revolution. Hawthorne knew well the plight of American seamstresses, and in the novel he points out that needlework was "then, as now, almost the only one within a woman's grasp."[10] But instead of emphasizing the degradation accompanying woman's work, he transforms this work into a triumphant assertion of woman's artistic power, as evidenced by the intricate, superb patterns Hester produces. The sensual woman, who in pamphlet novels of the 1840s was an insatiable nymphomaniac demanding many sexual partners, is here changed into a passionate but restrained woman who worships the sexual act with just one partner and whose dream of escaping with her lover is carefully squelched by Hawthorne.

The feminist exemplar is another popular stereotype Hawthorne transforms. At key points in the novel we are told that Hester broods over women's wrongs and dreams of a total change in male-female relations. But she never agitates publicly for women's rights, and it is clear by the end of the novel that Hawthorne has in mind not a militant, angry feminism but rather a gradualist moral exemplar feminism with utopian overtones. As a counselor of troubled women, the aged Hester assures them that "at some brighter period, when the world shall have grown ripe for it, in Heaven's own time, a new truth would be revealed, in order to establish the whole relation between man and woman on a surer ground of mutual happiness." Not only is the feminist revolution delayed to a vague, ideal future, but also Hester discounts her own capacities as a feminist exemplar by stressing that "the angel and apostle of the coming revelation must be a woman, indeed, but lofty, pure, and beautiful" and wise "not through dusky grief, but the ethereal medium of joy."

Hawthorne, therefore, attempts in *The Scarlet Letter* to absorb his culture's darkest, most disturbing female stereotypes and to rescue them from prurience or noisy politics by reinterpreting them in terms of bygone Puritanism and by fusing them with the moral exemplar. Evidently, his attempted brightening of dark stereotypes through the character of Hester was not altogether successful for either Hawthorne or his wife. Hawthorne lamented what he described as the unrelieved gloom of *The Scarlet Letter,* which he hoped would be published in a volume that would also contain more cheerful tales. As for his wife, after reading the novel she reportedly went to bed with a throbbing headache. He had created a magnificent fusion of different character types in Hester but had in the process sacrificed clear meaning. If he and Sophia were puzzled whether Beatrice Rappaccini was an angel or a demon, they had reason to be even more puzzled over Hester. To this day, critics still argue over the degree to which Hawthorne sympathizes with his most famous heroine. Actually, as was true with Beatrice, no absolute meaning or distinct authorial attitude can be gleaned from the complicated Hester. He recognized the disparate female types in his contemporary culture and created in Hester Prynne a multifaceted heroine in whom these types were artistically fused.

NOTES

[1] "Young Goodman Brown," *Mosses from an Old Manse* (1846), Centenary Edition (Ohio State University Press, 1974), p. 85.
[2] "The Procession of Life," *Mosses,* pp. 209–10.
[3] "The Christmas Banquet," *Mosses,* p. 303.
[4] "Earth's Holocaust," *Mosses,* p. 389.
[5] "The New Adam and Eve," *Mosses,* p. 253.
[6] "Rappaccini's Daughter," *Mosses,* p. 127. The next quotation in this paragraph is on p. 105.
[7] Julian Hawthorne, *Hawthorne and His Wife: A Biography* (1885; rpt., Boston: Houghton Mifflin, 1892), I, 360.
[8] June 1849 letter to H. W. Longfellow, *The Letters,* ed. Thomas Woodson, L. Neal Smith, Norman Holmes Pearson, 2 vols., Centenary Edition (Ohio State University Press, 1984 [Vol. XV], 1985 [Vol. XVI]), XVI, 270.
[9] *The Scarlet Letter* (1850), Centenary Edition (Ohio State University Press, 1962), p. 160. The subsequent quotations in this paragraph are on pp. 83, 195, 32.
[10] Ibid., p. 81. The quotations in the next paragraph are on p. 263.

CONTRIBUTORS

HAROLD BLOOM is Sterling Professor of the Humanities at Yale University and Henry W. and Albert A. Berg Professor of English at the New York University Graduate School. He is a 1985 MacArthur Foundation Award recipient, served as the Charles Eliot Norton Professor of Poetry at Harvard University (1987–88), and is the author of eighteen books, the most recent being *Poetics of Influence: New and Selected Criticism* (1988). Currently he is editing the Chelsea House series Modern Critical Views and The Critical Cosmos, and other Chelsea House series in literary criticism.

D. H. LAWRENCE was one of England's greatest modern novelists and poets. His novels include *Sons and Lovers* (1913), *The Rainbow* (1915), and *Women in Love* (1920). *Studies in Classic American Literature* (1923) was his principal work of literary criticism, although other critical essays are found in the posthumous collections *Phoenix* (1936) and *Phoenix II* (1968).

LESLIE A. FIEDLER teaches English and American literature at the University of Montana. His *Love and Death in the American Novel* (1960) now stands as a classic work in American literary criticism. Among his more recent works of criticism are *The Inadvertent Epic* (1979) and *What Was Literature? Class Culture and Mass Society* (1982). Fiedler has also written several novels.

AUSTIN WARREN taught English at the University of Michigan. He is the author of many essays on English and American literature, some gathered in *Connections* (1970). With René Wellek he wrote the influential *Theory of Literature* (1949).

MICHAEL DAVITT BELL is Professor of English at Williams College. He is the author of *Hawthorne and the Historical Romance of New England* (1971) and *The Development of American Romance* (1980).

ROBERT PENN WARREN is regarded as one of America's foremost poets. He is the author of the Pulitzer Prize-winning novel *All the King's Men* (1946). His *Selected Essays* appeared in 1958 and his *New Selected Poems 1923–1985* in 1985.

JUDITH FRYER is Professor of English at the University of Massachusetts. She is the author of *The Faces of Eve: Women in the Nineteenth Century American Novel* (1976) and *Felicitous Space: The Imaginative Structures of Edith Wharton and Willa Cather* (1986).

KRISTIN HERZOG teaches English at Duke University. She has written *Women, Ethnics, and Exotics: Images of Power in Mid-Nineteenth-Century American Fiction* (1983).

EVAN CARTON is Professor of English at the University of Texas—Austin. He is the author of *The Rhetoric of American Romance: Dialectic and Identity in Emerson, Dickinson, Poe, and Hawthorne* (1985).

CAROL BENSICK teaches English at the University of Denver. She has written *La Nouvelle Beatrice: Renaissance and Romance in "Rappaccini's Daughter"* (1985).

JAMES M. MELLARD is Professor of English at Northern Illinois University. His books include *The Exploded Form: The Modernist Novel in America* (1980) and *Doing Tropology: Analysis of Narrative Discourse* (1987).

DAVID S. REYNOLDS teaches English at Rutgers University. Among his works are *Faith in Fiction: The Emergence of Religious Literature in America* (1981), *George Lippard* (1982), and *Beneath the American Renaissance: The Subversive Imagination in the Age of Emerson and Melville* (1988).

BIBLIOGRAPHY

Abel, Darrel. "Hawthorne's Hester." *College English* 13 (1951–52): 303–9.

Axelsson, Arne. *The Links in the Chain: Isolation and Interdependence in Nathaniel Hawthorne's Fictional Characters.* Stockholm: Almqvist & Wiksell, 1974.

Baym, Nina. *The Shape of Hawthorne's Career.* Ithaca: Cornell University Press, 1976.

Becker, John E. *Hawthorne's Historical Allegory: An Examination of the American Conscience.* Port Washington, NY: Kennikat Press, 1971.

Bell, Millicent. "The Obliquity of Signs: *The Scarlet Letter.*" *Massachusetts Review* 23 (1982): 9–26.

Branch, Watson. "From Allegory to Romance: Hawthorne's Transformation of *The Scarlet Letter.*" *Modern Philology* 80 (1982): 145–60.

Broadhead, Richard H. *The School of Hawthorne.* New York: Oxford University Press, 1986.

Browning, Preston M., Jr. "Hester Prynne as a Secular Saint." *Midwest Quarterly* 13 (1972): 351–62.

Cantwell, Robert. *Nathaniel Hawthorne: The American Years.* New York: Rinehart, 1948.

Carlson, Patricia Ann. *Hawthorne's Functional Settings: A Study of Artistic Method.* Amsterdam: Rodopi, 1977.

Cottom, Daniel. "Hawthorne versus Hester: The Ghostly Dialectic of Romance in *The Scarlet Letter.*" *Texas Studies in Literature and Language* 24 (1982): 47–67.

Cuddy, Lois A. "Mother-Daughter Identification in *The Scarlet Letter.*" *Mosaic* 19, No. 2 (Spring 1986): 101–15.

Darnell, Donald. "*The Scarlet Letter:* Hawthorne's Emblem Book." *Studies in American Fiction* 7 (1979): 153–62.

Dauber, Kenneth. *Rediscovering Hawthorne.* Princeton: Princeton University Press, 1977.

Davis, Sarah I. "Another View of Hester and the Antinomian." *Studies in American Fiction* 12 (1984): 189–98.

Deamer, Robert Glen. "Hawthorne's Dream in the Forest." *Western American Literature* 13 (1978–79): 327–39.

DeSalvo, Louise. *Nathaniel Hawthorne.* Atlantic Highlands, NJ: Humanities Press, 1987.

Donohue, Agnes McNeill. *Hawthorne: Calvin's Ironic Stepchild.* Kent, OH: Kent State University Press, 1985.

Doubleday, Neal Frank. "Hawthorne's Hester and Feminism." *PMLA* 54 (1939): 825–28.

Dunne, Michael F. "Hawthorne, the Reader, and Hester Prynne." *Interpretations* 10 (1978): 34–40.

Elder, Marjorie J. *Nathaniel Hawthorne, Transcendental Symbolist.* Athens: Ohio University Press, 1969.

Erlich, Gloria C. *Family Themes and Hawthorne's Fiction: The Tenacious Web.* New Brunswick, NJ: Rutgers University Press, 1984.

Fogle, Richard Harter. *Hawthorne's Fiction: The Light and the Dark.* Rev. ed. Norman: University of Oklahoma Press, 1964.

Foster, Dennis. "The Embroidered Sin: Confessional Evasion in *The Scarlet Letter.*" *Criticism* 25 (1983): 141–63.

Gerber, John C., ed. *Twentieth Century Interpretations of* The Scarlet Letter. Englewood Cliffs, NJ: Prentice-Hall, 1968.

Greiner, Donald J. *Adultery in the American Novel: Updike, James, and Hawthorne.* Columbia: University of South Carolina Press, 1985.

Gross, Seymour Lee, ed. *A* Scarlet Letter *Handbook.* San Francisco: Wadsworth, 1960.

Hansen, Elaine Tuttle. "Ambiguity and the Narrator in *The Scarlet Letter.*" *Journal of Narrative Technique* 5 (1975): 147–63.

Harris, Kenneth Marc. *Hypocrisy and Self-Deception in Hawthorne's Fiction.* Charlottesville: University Press of Virginia, 1988.

Hoeltje, Hubert H. *Inward Sky: The Mind and Heart of Nathaniel Hawthorne.* Durham, NC: Duke University Press, 1962.

Holmes, Edward M. "Requiem for a Scarlet Nun." *Costerus* 5 (1972): 35–49.

Houston, Neal Bryan. "Hester Prynne as Eternal Feminine." *Discourse* 9 (1966): 230–44.

Hunt, Lester H. "*The Scarlet Letter:* Hawthorne's Theory of Moral Sentiments." *Philosophy and Literature* 8 (1984): 75–88.

James, Henry. *Hawthorne.* New York: Harper & Brothers, 1879.

Jenkins, R. B. "A New Look at an Old Tombstone." *New England Quarterly* 45 (1972): 417–21.

Katz, Seymour. " 'Character,' 'Nature,' and Allegory in *The Scarlet Letter.*" *Nineteenth-Century Fiction* 23 (1968–69): 3–17.

Kaul, A. N. "Character and Motive in *The Scarlet Letter.*" *Critical Quarterly* 10 (1968): 373–84.

Lane, Lauriat, Jr. "Allegory and Character in *The Scarlet Letter.*" *Emerson Society Quarterly* 26 (1961): 13–16.

Lee, A. Robert, ed. *Nathaniel Hawthorne: New Critical Essays.* Totowa, NJ: Barnes & Noble, 1982.

Leverenz, David. "Mrs. Hawthorne's Headache: Reading *The Scarlet Letter.*" *Nineteenth-Century Fiction* 37 (1982–83): 552–75.

Lloyd-Smith, Allan Gardner. *Eve Tempted: Writing and Sexuality in Hawthorne's Fiction.* Totowa, NJ: Barnes & Noble, 1983.

McAleer, J. J. "Hester Prynne's Grave." *Descant* 5 (Winter 1961): 29–33.

McWilliams, John P., Jr. *Hawthorne, Melville, and the American Character: A Looking-Glass Business.* Cambridge: Cambridge University Press, 1984.

Male, Roy R. *Hawthorne's Tragic Vision.* Austin: University of Texas Press, 1957.

Martin, Terence. *Nathaniel Hawthorne.* Rev. ed. Boston: Twayne, 1983.

Mayhoak, J. Jeffrey. "Bearings Unknown to Heraldry in *The Scarlet Letter.*" *Nathaniel Hawthorne Journal,* 1977, pp. 173–214.

Mellow, James R. *Nathaniel Hawthorne in His Times.* Boston: Houghton Mifflin, 1980.

Michaud, Régis. "How Nathaniel Hawthorne Exorcised Hester Prynne." In *The American Novel Today: A Social and Psychological Study.* Boston: Little, Brown, 1928, pp. 25–46.

Newberry, Frederick. "A Red-Hot 'A' and a Lusting Divine: Sources for *The Scarlet Letter.*" *New England Quarterly* 60 (1987): 256–64.

Person, Leland S., Jr. *Aesthetic Headaches: Women and a Masculine Poetics in Poe, Melville, and Hawthorne.* Athens: University of Georgia Press, 1988.

Ragussis, Michael. "Family Discourse and Fiction in *The Scarlet Letter.*" *ELH* 49 (1982): 863–88.

Reid, Alfred S. *The Yellow Ruff and* The Scarlet Letter: *A Source of Hawthorne's Novel.* Gainesville: University of Florida Press, 1955.

Reynolds, Larry J. "*The Scarlet Letter* and Revolutions Abroad." *American Literature* 57 (1985): 44–67.

Rosa, Alfred. *Salem, Transcendentalism, and Hawthorne.* Rutherford, NJ: Fairleigh Dickinson University Press, 1980.

Rozakis, Laurie N. "Another Possible Source of Hawthorne's Hester Prynne." *American Transcendental Quarterly* 59 (1986): 63–71.

Sarracino, Carmine. "*The Scarlet Letter* and a New Ethic." *College Literature* 10 (1983): 50–59.

Shear, Walter. "Characterization in *The Scarlet Letter.*" *Midwest Quarterly* 12 (1971): 437–54.

Stone, Albert Edward. "The Antique Gentility of Hester Prynne." *Philological Quarterly* 36 (1957): 90–96.

Stone, Edward. "The 'Many Morals' of *The Scarlet Letter.*" *Nathaniel Hawthorne Journal,* 1977, pp. 215–38.

Stubbs, John Caldwell. *The Pursuit of Form: A Study of Hawthorne and the Romance.* Urbana: University of Illinois Press, 1970.

Thickstun, Margaret Olofson. *Fictions of the Feminine: Puritan Doctrine and the Representation of Women.* Ithaca: Cornell University Press, 1988.

Todd, Robert E. "The Magna Mater Archetype in *The Scarlet Letter.*" *New England Quarterly* 45 (1972): 421–29.

Turner, Arlin. *Nathaniel Hawthorne: A Biography.* New York: Oxford University Press, 1980.

————, ed. *The Merrill Studies in* The Scarlet Letter. Columbus, OH: Merrill, 1970.

Wagenknecht, Edward. *Nathaniel Hawthorne: Man and Writer.* New York: Oxford University Press, 1961.

————. *Nathaniel Hawthorne: The Man, His Tales, and Romances.* New York: Ungar, 1989.

Waggoner, Hyatt H. *Hawthorne: A Critical Study.* Cambridge, MA: Harvard University Press, 1955.

————. *The Presence of Hawthorne.* Baton Rouge: Louisiana State University Press, 1979.

ACKNOWLEDGMENTS

"The House of Pride" by Newton Arvin from *Hawthorne* by Newton Arvin, © 1929 by Newton Arvin. Reprinted by permission of Little, Brown & Co., Inc.

"The Scarlet Letter" by Mark Van Doren from *Nathaniel Hawthorne* by Mark Van Doren, © 1949 by William Sloane Associates. Reprinted by permission of William Morris Agency.

"The Return into Time: Hawthorne" by R. W. B. Lewis from *The American Adam: Innocence, Tragedy and Tradition in the Nineteenth Century* by R. W. B. Lewis, © 1955 by The University of Chicago Press. Reprinted by permission.

"The Skeleton in the Closet" by Harry Levin from *The Power of Blackness: Hawthorne, Poe, Melville* by Harry Levin, © 1958 by Harry Levin. Reprinted by permission of Alfred A. Knopf, Inc., and the author.

"Psychological Romance" and "The Ruined Wall" by Frederick C. Crews from *The Sins of the Fathers: Hawthorne's Psychological Themes* by Frederick C. Crews, © 1966 by Oxford University Press. Reprinted by permission.

"The Woman as Hero" by Carolyn G. Heilbrun from *Toward a Recognition of Androgyny* by Carolyn G. Heilbrun, © 1973 by Alfred A. Knopf. Reprinted by permission of Curtis Brown Ltd.

"The Scarlet Letter" by Richard H. Brodhead from *Hawthorne, Melville, and the Novel* by Richard H. Brodhead, © 1976 by The University of Chicago. Reprinted by permission.

"The Myth of America" by Sacvan Bercovitch from *The Puritan Origins of the American Self* by Sacvan Bercovitch, © 1975 by Yale University Press. Reprinted by permission.

"Who? The Characters" by Nina Baym from The Scarlet Letter: *A Reading* by Nina Baym, © 1986 by Twayne Publishers, a division of G. K. Hall & Co. Reprinted by permission.

"Nathaniel Hawthorne and *The Scarlet Letter*" by D. H. Lawrence from *Studies in Classic American Literature* by D. H. Lawrence, © 1961 by The Estate of Mrs. Frieda Lawrence. Reprinted by permission of Viking Penguin, Inc.

"Accommodation and Transcendence" by Leslie A. Fiedler from *Love and Death in the American Novel* by Leslie A. Fiedler, © 1960 by Criterion Books, Inc. Reprinted by permission of Stein & Day.

"The Scarlet Letter" by Austin Warren from *Connections* by Austin Warren, © 1970 by The University of Michigan Press. Reprinted by permission.

"Another View of Hester" (originally titled "Fathers and Daughters") by Michael Davitt Bell from *Hawthorne and the Historical Romance of New England* by Michael Davitt Bell, © 1971 by Princeton University Press. Reprinted by permission.

"Hawthorne Revisited: Some Remarks on Hellfiredness" by Robert Penn Warren from *Sewanee Review* 81, No. 1 (January–March 1973), © 1973 by Robert Penn Warren. Reprinted by permission of the Estate of Robert Penn Warren.

"Hester Prynne: The Dark Lady as 'Deviant' " by Judith Fryer from *The Faces of Eve: Women in the Nineteenth Century American Novel* by Judith Fryer, © 1976 by Oxford University Press. Reprinted by permission.

"The Scarlet A: Aboriginal and Awesome" by Kristin Herzog from *Women, Ethnics, and Exotics: Images of Power in Mid-Nineteenth-Century American Fiction* by Kristin Herzog, © 1983 by The University of Tennessee Press. Reprinted by permission.

"The Prison Door" by Evan Carton from *The Rhetoric of American Romance: Dialectic and Identity in Emerson, Dickinson, Poe, and Hawthorne* by Evan Carton, © 1985 by The Johns Hopkins University Press. Reprinted by permission.

"Demystified Adultery in *The Scarlet Letter*" (originally titled "His Folly, Her Weakness: Demystified Adultery in *The Scarlet Letter*") by Carol Bensick, from *New Essays on* The Scarlet Letter, edited by Michael J. Colacurcio, © 1985 by Cambridge University Press. Reprinted by permission.

"Pearl and Hester: A Lacanian Reading" by James M. Mellard from *Critical Essays on Hawthorne's* The Scarlet Letter, edited by David B. Kesterton, © 1988 by Twayne Publishers, a division of G. K. Hall & Co. Reprinted by permission.

"Toward Hester Prynne" by David S. Reynolds (originally titled "Hawthorne's Heroines") from *Beneath the American Renaissance: The Subversive Imagination in the Age of Emerson and Melville* by David S. Reynolds, © 1988 by David S. Reynolds. Reprinted by permission of Alfred A. Knopf, Inc.

INDEX